for KENNETH REXROTH

ACKNOWLEDGMENTS

For permission to reprint these essays, thanks
are due to the authors, publishers, and journals
where many first appeared.

Harry Stiehl, "At the Edge [a review]," San Francisco Bay
Window, October 29, 1958.

Jerome Mazzero, "Antoninus: Trihedral Poet," Fresco,
winter 1958.

"The Beat Friar," Time Magazine, May 25, 1959. Copy-
right © Time Inc. 1959.

Thomas P. McDonnell, "The Poetry of Brother Antoninus,"
Spirit, May 1961.

A. V. Krebs, "Poet of Insurgence," Way: Catholic View-
points, January-February 1963.

Brendon Cavanaugh, Alfred Camillus Murphy, and Albert
Doshner, "Brother Antoninus: A Symposium," Domini-
cana: A Quarterly of Popular Theology, spring 1963.

Thomas P. McDonnell, "Poet from the West," The Common-
weal, March 29, 1963.

Ralph J. Mills, Jr. , "Brother Antoninus," in his Contem-
porary American Poetry, New York: Random House,
1965.

Robert Duncan, "Single Source: An Introduction," in William
Everson's Single Source, Berkeley, Calif. : Oyez, 1966.

William E. Stafford, "Brother Antoninus: The World As
Metaphor," The Achievement of Brother Antoninus,
Glenview, Ill. : Scott, Foresman and Co. , 1967.

Kenneth Rexroth, "The Residual Years: An Introduction,"
in William Everson's The Residual Years, New York:
New Directions, 1968.

Ronald F. Webster, "The Rebel's Metaphysic of Existence,"

a chapter of his Mimesis of the Absolute: The Revolt of Brother Antoninus, unpublished master's thesis, Gonzaga University, 1969.

Harry Cargas, "The Love Poet," Marriage, February 1969. Reprinted (slightly revised) by permission of Marriage and Family Living magazine.

Samuel Charters, "In the Fictive Wish," in his Some Poems/ Poets: Studies in American Underground Poetry Since 1945, Berkeley, Calif. : Oyez, 1971.

Allan Campo, "The Woman of Prey," a chapter of his Soul and the Search: Mysticism and Its Approach in the Poetry of Brother Antoninus, unpublished thesis, Loyola University of Los Angeles, 1966.

Paul A. Lacey, "The Inner War," in his The Inner War: Forms and Themes in Recent American Poetry, Philadelphia: Fortress Press, 1972.

Linnea Gentry, "On William Everson As Printer," Fine Print, July 1975.

Joseph Blumenthal, The Printed Book in America, Boston: David R. Godine, 1977.

Lee Bartlett, "Birth of a Poet: A Foreword," in William Everson's Birth of a Poet, forthcoming from Black Sparrow Press.

Albert Gelpi, "Everson/Antoninus: Contending with the Shadow," Sequoia, Winter 1977.

Vicky Schrieber Dill, "The Books of William Everson," in Books at Iowa, 1978.

David Carpenter, "Taproot of Instinct," in Bill Hotchkiss and his William Everson: Poet from the San Joaquin, Rocklin, Calif. : Blue Oak Press, 1978.

Bill Hotchkiss, "The Roots of Recovery," in Bill Hotchkiss and David Carpenter's William Everson: Poet from the San Joaquin, Rocklin, Calif. : Blue Oak Press, 1978.

CONTENTS

vii

viii Contents

INTRODUCTION

This volume collects what might be called the bench-
mark pieces tracing the poetic emergence of William Ever-
son. From the radical California poet of early promise
who converted to Roman Catholicism and surfaced with the
San Francisco Renaissance as Brother Antoninus, Dominican
monk, to the mature artist Albert Gelpi calls "the most im-
portant religious poet of the second half of the century,"
these articles chart his progressive emergence in its larger
outline. Singular enough in its details to be strikingly un-
orthodox, at a deeper level Everson's journey is the arche-
typal quest of the American Bard.

Charles Olson used to tell his Black Mountain stu-
dents that the poet "was always on time," a statement which
implied both the prophetic powers of the artist and the time-
gap between creation and recognition. In this sense, William
Everson has certainly been "on time"; he has written over
twenty-five books in thirty years, yet because of his region-
alist sympathies and his anti-Modernist, Dionysian aesthetics,
Everson's work, like that of Whitman, Jeffers, and Henry
Miller, has had a difficult time gaining critical acceptance.
Still, as these essays show, some perceptive critics have
been hot on his trail for the past twenty years.

This collection is not, strictly speaking, a "casebook."
It does not even collect the poet's major reviews. However,
it does approximate one dimension of the casebook approach,
as it offers the more considerable articles written since
1958 to acquaint the reading public with Everson's achieve-
ment. While not of equal merit or importance, being drawn
from popular as well as scholarly sources (there are a few
blazes between the benchmarks), all are distinct signs. In
their chronological sequence, these pieces throw light on what
constitutes an artist's emergence in the American milieu.
Hence this book stands as much a study of the poet in Amer-
ica as a handbook to William Everson's life and work.

Behind all these essays stands a singular pronounce-
ment, Kenneth Rexroth's nuclear "San Francisco Letter" in
the now famous issue of Evergreen Review (summer 1957),
the document which introduced the West Coast movement to
the world. It was Rexroth's essay which focused attention
on the California poets in general (Robert Duncan, Philip
Lamantia, James Broughton, et al.), and on the figure of
Everson (as Brother Antoninus) as central to the group.
Everson himself attributes to Rexroth's essay the precipita-
tion of his critical recognition, and it is very probable that
without it many of the papers included here would never have
been written. Although Thomas P. McDonnell quotes Rex-
roth briefly in his essay "The Poetry of Brother Antoninus, "
the statement is so central to an understanding of Everson's
emergence that I include it here in full. "There are few
organized systems of social attitudes and values, " wrote Rex-
roth,

> "which stand outside, really outside, the all cor-
> rupting influences of our predatory civilization.
> In America, at least, there is only one which
> functions on any large scale and with any effec-
> tiveness. This of course is Roman Catholicism.
> Not the stultifying monkey see monkey do Ameri-
> canism of the slothful urban backwoods middle-
> class parish so beautifully satirized by the Cath-
> olic writer James Powers, but the Church of
> saints and philosophers--of the worker priest
> movement and the French Personalists. So it is
> only to be expected that, of those who reject the
> Social Lie, many today would turn towards Cathol-
> icism. If you have to 'belong to something bigger
> than yourself' it is one of the few possibilities and,
> with a little mental gymnastics, can be made quite
> bearable. Even I sometimes feel that the only con-
> stant, consistent, and uncompromising critics of
> the World Ill were the French Dominicans.
>
> So, William Everson, who is probably the most
> profoundly moving and durable of the poets of the
> San Francisco Renaissance, is a Dominican Terti-
> ary and oblate--which means a lay brother in a
> friary under renewable vows ... he doesn't have
> to stay if he doesn't want to. It has been a long
> journey to this point. Prior to the Second War he
> was a farmer in the San Joaquin Valley. Here he
> wrote his first book of poems, San Joaquin. Like
> so many young poets he was naively accessible to

influences his maturity would find dubious. In his case this was Jeffers, but he was, even then, able to transform Jeffers' noisy rhetoric into genuinely impassioned utterance, his absurd self-dramatization into real struggle in the depths of the self. Everson is still wrestling with his angel, still given to the long oratorical line with vague echoes of classical quantitative meters, but there is no apparent resemblance left to Jeffers. During the War he was in a Conscientious Objectors' camp in Oregon, where he was instrumental in setting up an off time Arts Program out of which have come many still active people, projects and forces which help give San Francisco culture its intensely libertarian character. Here he printed several short books of verse, all later gathered in the New Directions volume, The Residual Years. Since then he has printed two books, Triptych for the Living and A Privacy of Speech. In the tradition of Eric Gill and Victor Hammer, they are amongst the most beautiful printing I have ever seen. Since then--since entering the Order, he has published mostly in the Catholic Worker. In my opinion he has become the finest Catholic poet writing today, the best since R. E. F. Larsson. His work has a gnarled, even tortured, honesty, a rugged unliterary diction, a relentless probing and searching, which are not just engaging, but almost overwhelming. Partly of course this is due to the scarcity of these characteristics today, anything less like the verse of the fashionable quarterlies would be hard to imagine. "

Rexroth works ingeniously not only to render Roman Catholicism amenable to the values of the Beat Generation, but to discount Everson's derivation from Robinson Jeffers, then at a low point in literary reputation. By such stratagems literary revolutions are effected; and in the literary cold war of the fifties, stratagems were the order of the day.

The insularity of the American public to poetry and poets makes it almost inevitable that writers band together in groups for survival; yet American poets, who tend to be rather cranky and individualistic, often resist this. W. H. Auden pointed out that while the British poet naturally thinks of himself as a member of a "clerkly caste" regardless of the number of his readers, the American poet can think of himself only as constituting an "aristocracy of one." This means that he instinctively steers clear of arbitrary groupings, although it seems to do him little good. The public understands him in terms of "schools" and "movements," and insists on bracketing him among them as a way of bringing his work into comprehension.

Everson's career attests to this tendency. His first three books, published privately, went virtually unnoticed. During the Second World War, however, when as a conscientious objector Everson was interned at Camp Angel, at Waldport, Oregon, the situation changed; critics and the reading public could get a fix on the poet by grouping him with other pacifist and anti-war writers and artists. So too with the emergence of the Beat Generation. Kerouac and Ginsberg invented the movement (a birth gracefully recorded in John Tytell's recent study, The Fallen Angels), but it was Rexroth who presided over the unveiling, and it was he who singled out Everson for attention. Everson believes the camera portraits in the Evergreen Review endowed them all with a common mood, the product of the photographer's point of view, an identity they did not actually possess. Whatever it was, however, it took, and again Everson's work could be subsumed by critics into a popular movement.

Likewise, it was his identity as a Dominican monk which gave Everson, as Brother Antoninus, his widest audience and his deepest impact. Beginning with the Catholic Crooked Lines of God, which was nominated for a Pulitzer Prize, William Everson's books were more widely reviewed in the general press, yet this did not yield any studies of the poet's overall achievement by secular critics until William Stafford's essay in 1966. Everson's impact on the Catholic literary community, however, was instantaneous. Following Mazzaro's essay in 1958, written before Crooked Lines and directly attributable to the Evergreen Review appearance, almost every year witnessed some effort by Catholic critics to get the poet in focus. As Albert Gelpi was to write later, "It is the very history of religious, especially Christian, poetry in the twentieth century, with its fixation on human fallibility and its consequent insistence on necessarily prescribed forms, that makes Everson's poetry seem radical, original, transformative."

Not all reviewers agreed with Gelpi, however, and the poet's road from farm to monastery, from Everson to Antoninus, was not traveled without peril. Reviewing Antoninus, the poet James Dickey wrote, "I feel somewhat as if I were reviewing God. " He argued that while Everson's early poetry was some of the first verse he "ever truthfully liked, " Crooked Lines contained "enough solemn, dead metaphors to fill the stuffed owl's mouth for generations to come. " Too, in many reviews Catholic formalists fiercely resisted Everson, corresponding to the hostility of academic critics at large to the Beat Generation. These writers took particular exception to Everson's attempt to restore a sort of erotic mysticism (born of the poet's own excursions into Jungian depth psychology) to Catholic faith.

On December 7, 1969, Antoninus read his sequence "Tendril in the Mesh" publicly for the first time. At the conclusion of the reading, he stripped off his religious habit of eighteen years and returned to public life as William Everson: "And the monk, gone crazy, / Flies his cell, / Forsakes his holy vows. " He has married, and has worked for the past eight years as poet-in-residence at the University of California, Santa Cruz, and as master printer for the Lime Kiln Press. As I write this, Black Sparrow Press, easily the most important and influential independent publisher of poetry on the West Coast, has just published Everson's collected Catholic poetry, the massive Veritable Years; it will be followed by the poet's seminal prose work, Birth of a Poet: The Santa Cruz Meditations. Oyez Press has collected Everson's essays and interviews for publication in the spring of 1979. In addition, the poet's masterwork of handpress printing, Jeffers' Granite & Cypress, has recently been accorded by Joseph Blumenthal a position at the apex of American printing. These successes are important, for they demonstrate that critics and the reading public may be ready to allow Everson's work to stand on its own, without recourse to some larger movement of mind.

Thus the studies collected here are valuable because they represent the first attempts to see the poet whole, and they pave the way for his reception into the larger community of letters. That he was able to make this transition and emerge before the world with the approval of both the religious and the secular wings attests to the centrality of Everson's achievement. Taking the cultural cleavage at full stretch, he has transcended the gap between the sacred and the profane in the unifying vision of his art.

Lee Bartlett   Davis, California

CHRONOLOGY

1912   William Oliver Everson born September 10 in Sacra-
        mento, California.

1931   Graduates from Selma Union High School, Selma,
        California. Briefly enrolls in Fresno State College.

1933   Enters Civilian Conservation Corps.

1934   Returns to Fresno State College where he discovers
        the work of Robinson Jeffers, confirming his own
        vocation as poet.

1935   Leaves Fresno State College to return to the land.
        These Are the Ravens published by Greater West
        Publishing Company.

1938   Marries Edwa Poulson, May 30. Settles on a farm
        near Selma.

1939   San Joaquin published by Ward Ritchie Press.

1940   Selective Service Act. Registers as conscientious
        objector. Death of mother.

1942   The Masculine Dead: Poems 1938-1940 published by
        James A. Decker.

1943   Drafted January 17.   Sent to Camp Angel, Ore-
        gon. Co-founds the Untide Press. X War Elegies
        published by the Untide Press. Director of Arts
        Program.

1944   Waldport Poems and War Elegies published by the
        Untide Press.

1945   The Residual Years: Poems 1940-1941 and Poems
        MCMXLII published by Untide Press. Death of fath-
        er; separated from Edwa in the summer.

1946   January 1, transfers from Waldport to Cascade Locks, Oregon, where he remains until late June. Released from Weaverville, California, and moves to "Treesbank," Sebastapol, California. Meets poet/artist Mary Fabilli; in November, they move to Berkeley.

1947   Takes job as janitor at the University of California, Berkeley. In spring, transfers to campus printing plant. In fall, establishes the Equinox Press.

1948   The Residual Years: Poems 1934-1946 published by New Directions. Marries Mary Fabilli in Reno, Nevada, June 12. Christmas Eve, experiences intense religious awakening.

1949   Receives Guggenheim Fellowship. Takes instruction in Catholic faith at St. Augustine's Church. Separated from Mary Fabilli in May. Baptized July 23. Equinox Press publishes A Privacy of Speech: Ten Poems in Sequence. William Andrews Clark Library, UCLA, acquires Everson's manuscripts up to this point.

1950   Enters Catholic Worker House, Oakland, California.

1951   June, enters Dominican Order at St. Albert's College, Oakland, as a donatus and is given the name Brother Antoninus. Triptych for the Living published by the Seraphim Press. In autumn, begins work on printing the Novum Psalterium Pii XII.

1954   Spring, completes 72 pages of the Psalter, then closes his press to take up studies for the priesthood. In September enters clerical novitiate in Kentfield, California; returns to St. Albert's the following spring.

1957   The "San Francisco Issue" of the Evergreen Review.

1958   At the Edge published by Albertus Magnus Press. Antoninus' first reading tour to Los Angeles.

1959   The Crooked Lines of God: Poems 1954-1959 published by the University of Detroit Press. First Midwest reading tour: Detroit and Chicago.

1960   Meets Rose Tunnland.   There Will Be Harvest, Al-
        bion Press.   First East Coast tour: Troy, Boston,
        Cambridge.

1961   The Year's Declension published by Albion Press.

1962   The Hazards of Holiness: Poems 1957-1960 published
        by Doubleday.   Reads The Poet Is Dead at the San
        Francisco Arts Festival.

1963   Transfers to Novitiate House, Kentfield.

1964   Takes first vows as lay brother.   The Poet Is Dead
        published by Auerhahn Press.

1965   Meets Sue Rickson.

1966   Educational television program, "American Poets, "
        with Michael McClure.   Single Source: The Early
        Poems of William Everson published by Oyez.

1967   Everson takes second vows.   The Rose of Solitude
        published by Doubleday.   In the Fictive Wish pub-
        lished by Oyez.

1968   The Residual Years: Poems 1934-1948 published by
        New Directions.   Robinson Jeffers: Fragments of
        an Older Fury published by Oyez.   A Canticle to the
        Waterbirds published by Eizo.   The Springing of the
        Blade published by the Black Rock Press.   Everson
        returns to St. Albert's.   "The Savagery of Love"
        Caedmon recording.   Awarded Commonwealth Club's
        Silver Medal for The Rose of Solitude.

1969   Tour of Europe--readings in Dublin, London, Ham-
        burg, Berlin, Munich, Rome, and Paris.   The Last
        Crusade published by Oyez.   December 7 at the Uni-
        versity of California, Davis, Brother Antoninus con-
        cluded poetry reading by taking off his monk's habit
        and returning to lay life.   December 13, marries
        Sue Rickson; they settle at Stinson Beach, California.

1971   Becomes poet-in-residence at the University of Cali-
        fornia, Santa Cruz, and master printer at the Lime
        Kiln Press.   Everson, Sue, and son Jude move to
        Kingfisher Flat in Swanton area near Davenport,
        California.

1972   Who Is She That Looketh Forth as the Morning published by Capricorn Press. Everson's Lime Kiln Press project completes portfolio, West to the Water.

1973   Tendril in the Mesh published by Cayucos Books. Black Hills published by Didymus Press. Everson's Lime Kiln Press project completes Jeffers' Tragedy Has Obligations.

1974   Man-Fate: The Swan Song of Brother Antoninus published by New Directions. Bancroft Library, University of California, Berkeley, acquires Everson manuscripts from monastic period.

1975   Jeffers' Granite & Cypress completed by the Lime Kiln Press.

1976   River-Root: A Suzygy for the Bicentennial of These States and Archetype West published by Oyez.

1977   The Mate-Flight of Eagles published by Blue Oak Press. Granite & Cypress chosen by Joseph Blumenthal in his exhibition "The Printed Book in America" as one of the seventy best-printed books in American history. William Everson: A Descriptive Bibliography published by Scarecrow Press.

"AT THE EDGE" [a review]

Harry Stiehl. 1958

I begin this collection with Harry Stiehl's brief review of
Everson's early broadside, "At the Edge," because it speci-
fies, as a seed or capsule, almost everything for which the
poet would be recognized later. Stiehl, a close friend of
Everson, also pinpoints the thawing of the writing block the
poet complains of in the preface to Crooked Lines Of God.
This was in the San Francisco Bay Window, October 29, 1958.

> Buttressed by moral theology and
> by depth psychology, Everson's
> massive investigation of the Ec-
> stasy and the Anguish of the life
> wholly given to God is of incalcu-
> lable value to our age ...

Written a few years back but only recently issued as
an elegantly framed broadside, At the Edge (Albertus Magnus
Press, 6172 Chabot Road; Oakland, California; $7.50) is an
arresting new work by Brother Antoninus, O.P. The mag-
nificence of the printing--the letters, black and sharp as
coffins, biting acridly into the rich paper made, in some
halcyon pre-war period, to conform to the demanding standards
of William Morris--is consonant with the high reputation of
the Albertus Magnus Press. The long, sea-haunted lines of
the text itself demonstrate the major qualities of Brother An-
toninus, who is generally conceded to be the finest poet of our
famed "San Francisco Renaissance."

This Dominican lay brother has intrigued atheists--
and alarmed some of his more conservative fellow Catholics
--by his vigorous exploration of the dark problems of the

modern psyche. Perhaps no other modern Catholic writer has more profitably used the depth psychology of Jung to drag into the light the hidden and recurring terrors of men. He probes (with what surpassing pity!) the soul's terrible wounds.

His life is well known. A Californian of Norwegian descent, he was born William Oliver Everson in Sacramento in 1912, grew up in the San Joaquin Valley, gradually established himself as a poet during the Thirties and early Forties, refused to conform to the demands of the State during World War Two, and turned in the post-war period from a deeply beautiful relationship of love to a way of renunciation that led him to the Church of Rome.

There are many roads to Rome, but that of Everson has been especially strange. As a young man, a farmer-writer in the San Joaquin Valley, he was a disciple of Lawrence and Jeffers and the exponent of a kind of pastoral pantheism. His almost mystical view of the integrity of unspoliated Nature he was to see, in the retrospect of the war years, as an essentially religious view. But during the War, when he stood forth courageously to say Non serviam!, he did not yet adhere to any specifically formulated religion: his was the non-doctrinal devotion of a basically religious temperament as ready to respond to Berdyaev or Kierkegaard as to St. Thomas Aquinas. In a never-published manuscript of poems written during 1947 and 1948 (the New Directions volume, The Residual Years, selects from the earliest work through 1946), Everson made an anguished assessment of his past life, a sort of poetic "examination of conscience" which made possible his conversion to Catholicism during 1949. He entered the Dominican Order in 1951, assuming the name by which he is now widely known as a Catholic poet: Brother Antoninus, O. P.

Like the poems of his great predecessor, Raymond Larsson, the poems of Everson challenge the claims of the prevailing climate of critical opinion. The excessively formalist reviewers, disturbed at their naked power, have been quick to label these poems "Dionysian," and even "formless." Yet they have a quality which can conquer the recalcitrant reader. Buttressed by moral theology and by depth psychology, Everson's massive investigation of the Ecstasy and the Anguish of the life wholly given to God is of incalculable value to our age and to Catholic culture everywhere. Like Whitman and like Jeffers (two masters he would acknowledge and honor), he is most impressive in a sustained passage in which the interlaced long and short lines crash and subside with the intolerable power of the sea.

The sea is everywhere in this new work, symbolically present as a "Sea of Death, " rhythmically present in the tidal lines. At the death of the body, the sin-heavy soul is seen as a coffin sea-buried: "And like a coffin at sea, weighted, and the weights are its sins, it swings outward, tips down, drops, / And sinks fast down into the body of the Sea of Death, which is the Hell;/ And the weights of the coffin take it rapidly down to that scrupulous mark/ Where the drag of the sin, and the buoyant life of the mercy of God hang in exquisite balance--" Sin and Hell: those unfashionable concepts are back in fashion again, and it is the great gift of Brother Antoninus to limn them with the ancient power.

From the quiet opening--"There is a mark, made on the soul in its first wrongdoing"--down to that awesome last line describing "the terrible contentment of the damned, " this is a poem which illumines what Graham Greene has called "the appalling strangeness of the Mercy of God. " For the Divine Justice, too, is everywhere in this poem: "Over the Ocean of Death shines the great ambient light of the Lord. "

It is an impressive work, which the Universities should certainly acquire. And how marvelous it is to see Brother Antoninus back at his truest vocation: the making of poems. In August he wrote a strange and compelling poem on the Crucifixion, "What Birds Were There"; a week ago he completed a long symbolic poem on "Jacob and the Angel. " The springs of his art are flowing again, the fountain is fresh in the desert.

ANTONINUS: TRIHEDRAL POET

Jerome Mazzaro. 1958

This first academic attempt to appraise the background of William Everson, appearing in <u>Fresco</u> in the winter of 1958, shows the quickening effect of his few magazine appearances on Catholic literary intelligence even before the publication of <u>The Crooked Lines of God</u>.

> The last poem of the "Chronicle"
> sinks everything--guilt, doubts,
> fears, frustrations--into the giant
> womb image of the sea. It seems
> that in it Everson has realized
> not only the fruitlessness of his
> views on nature but also his in-
> ability to solve them in anything
> less than their total annihilation.

It is always interesting to note the growth of a poet from his beginnings to his most recent work; but, when the poet is Brother Antoninus, the notation becomes doubly interesting, not only because the growth of Bill Everson into Brother Antoninus involves the disintegration and replacement of an earlier and rather complete metaphysical system, but also because the growth results in some of the finest poetry published in recent years. The Bill Everson who begins the metaphysical sprouting with an alliance of a man and nature becomes increasingly important as a poet when viewed from the later Everson who resolves the growth first by the realization that nature is responsible to a larger force and then by the realization that this force is God.

Bill Everson begins his probings for a higher law

4

simply enough with the publication of his <u>These Are the Ra-</u>
<u>vens</u> (Greater West Publishing Co. , 1935) in which he out-
lines the ties of man and nature. The title poem, for in-
stance, compares the yearnings of man's soul to ravens:

> These are the ravens of my soul,
> Sloping above the lonely fields
> And cawing, cawing.

The effect is similar in kind to Dylan Thomas' later drives
which permeate both man and nature in such poems as "The
Force That Through the Green Fuse. " "Winter Plowings,"
the second poem of Everson's book, sees a continuation of
this concept as both plowman and blackbird are united in
contentment, each in his way subsisting on the products of
the same land. By extension of the metaphorical tie, man
becomes "natural" as the fugitive of "To an Indian-Hunting
Posse":

> Ride him into the earth and break him ...
> But neither your walls nor the wind of your revenge
> Can keep for your own the sky-yearning fierceness of
>   his heart!

Here man has become the animal, charged with the same
wild spirit of nature. In a poem like "Who Lives Here Har-
bors Sorrow," he can also extend this spirit to become bo-
tanical in nature: "These folk breed children strong as
mountain weeds. "

    But nature is more than just the animal or vegetable
spirit of all living objects. It is permanence. It is con-
nector of past and present, the great organizer of purpose
in man. Nature is, additionally, the means for the contin-
uance of tradition as blood, as shown in "I Know It as the
Sorrow. " Here Everson's Viking blood is associated with
natural phenomena:

> I know it now as the grief of long-gone women
> Shivering in the cliff-wind
> While the lean boats dipped in the fjord ...

and finally objectified in children weeping "in the gloom of
the Norway pines. "

    In "Tor House," nature becomes the means of the
common experience uniting the experiences of the past with

those of the present. So long as the permanence of the countryside remains, so does the possibility of tradition: "Now that I have seen Tor House/ And crouched among the sea-gnawed granite under the wind's throat,/ Gazing against the roll of the western rim," becomes the means by which Everson begins to understand the character of Robinson Jeffers.

Man, however, is not always the receptor of the gifts of this drive. "Do Not Brood For Long" suggests that in return man owes the drive of his will to persist:

It is for us to mourn, indeed,
But mourn dry-eyed, along these lanes,
Heeding the herons' cry,
And knowing the noisy wind too well to weep.

Thus, mourning "dry-eyed," man achieves a better understanding of nature and his purpose in the larger scheme of it.

"Muscat Pruning" shows nature as offering diversion to man's daily work. The poem, set among pruners in the field, describes the effect of a flicker swooping overhead:

After his call the silence holds the drip-sound of trees,
Muffling the hushed beat under the mist.
Over the field the noise of other pruners
Moves me to work.
I have a hundred vines to cut before the dusk.

The sum of these concepts adds to a total view of nature--drive and phenomena--which has sufficed many a less talented writer. Briefly, for Everson nature seems to offer man a feeling of permanence which offers a faith in the present. Man has to be close to nature to appreciate its importance. "Martin's Homestead" suggests that man try farming toward this end: "Father and son, and father and son/ Have given their sweat to the plow/ And the torn earth leaving the shore." The suggestion is not surprising for Everson, especially as he had just spent ten months in the Civilian Conservation Corps during a year when the big American dream was clouded by a depression and the persistance of man was closely allied with his ability to live off the land.

Conspicuously lacking, however, in this first volume

is a love poem, or even the mention of physical love. Everson seems not to be able to fit such an emotion into the general scheme of his concept of nature. By 1938 he had published a poem, "The Phoenix," which moves toward this end. It tries by description to approximate the sensual and succeeds primarily in being over-written. By the process, Everson does manage to make the movements of procreation the movements of nature, so that the individuals and nature are merged in the action into the same lockstep of being. Sex, consequently, has taken its place, so to speak, in the Everson order of things.

But just when it seems Everson has fitted enough of his views of the permanence of nature to his poetic needs, both emotions and concepts of permanence are disturbed by the outbreak of World War II. He realizes that in war nature is in upheaval and far from the permanent structure necessary to give order to past and present. The fear fills his mind that war would permanently disrupt nature, forbidding man to have any assurance of either past or present. Two books of disillusionment follow: War Elegies (Untide Press, 1944) and Poems: mcmxlii (Untide Press, 1945). War Elegies, written while Everson was in a camp for conscientious objectors, deals with the disintegration of his ideas of nature.

The first of these elegies, War Elegy I, is the raison d'être of his conscientious objection to war. For him war not only takes life wantonly, but it is the battler of tradition and the disintegrator of man's ties with the past. He compares its effects to the natural upheavals of flood and winter, and concludes that only a pacifist can maintain the necessary tie with nature and ultimately with understanding.

War Elegies II and III continue this theme with respect to destruction:

> We would wait in these rooms
> And watch them go down,
> The raiders hawking the low sky,
> And see all about us the forms we have loved
> Blasted and burned, nor rise against it.

and the necessity of a past:

> But let him rather, turning to the past
> Seek out that iron rib of conviction

Bearing beneath the steep thought of all times,
The unbending belief of men holding to truth ...

Elegy IV, based on a London address of Winston
Churchill, denies the rightness of any war, indicating that
there is something beyond courage, strength, and speech, a
morality deeper than national claims which man must adhere
to. It is related to the larger concept of the past which
gives meaning to the actions of the present. It is also allied
with nature. Elegy V is Everson's restatement of the neces-
sity of nature and natural phenomena, especially in those
aspects which affected his own growth.

Elegy VIII has nature destroying the objects of war
as a squadron of planes from an aircraft carrier return to
the home ship only to find it gone and fall ineffectually into
the waters of the ocean. Thus, nature retaliates in part for
the general destruction done it during the battle. The re-
taliation, however, is not complete. Elegy X reveals, in a
description of a soldier who has lost his life's continuity,
the past destroyed completely by war. "After the War ...
after the War--" but the soldier finds only the image of a
"Soldier and girl,/ In their surd tussle,/ Sprawled in a
jeweller's door" disrupting his attempt to order such exis-
tence.

Poems: mcmxlii continues this process of the dis-
integration of nature. The poems, biographical rather than
autobiographical in tone, oppose almost point for point the
avowals of nature expressed in These Are the Ravens. "The
outlaw" portrays the dilemma of a man unable to set up the
close association with nature suggested by "Martin's Home-
stead. "

Blind in their past,
The past betrayed them.

In "the lovers" nature again expands as it had earlier
in the Phoenix poem to include sex, but now, far from be-
coming a lockstep of being, sex is portrayed as coarse and
brutal, because the lovers of the poem have lost all ties
with nature and are motivated by a sense of their own self-
importance.

"Invocation" reposes the dilemma: "Only as I have
encountered the past, can I measure the margins of what I
am. " It becomes a search for those associations which one

can relate to a sense of the past and which a few years pre-
viously had been openly natural. "The revolutionist," "the
citadel," "the brothers," and "the answer" outline the failure
to find these associations with respect to causes, work, mar-
riage, and flesh.

Everson returns to some empty successes with "the
friends": "Having fashioned the present out of the past/ The
past and its promise achieved fulfillment." The past here
is recapitulation, not nature. Likewise in "the divers" the
past becomes recollection. Finally, the last poem in the
volume, "the stranger," speaks of the disruption of nature
and sex through the sheer caprice of the appearance of a
man from Omaha. The man reflects in part Everson's own
disillusionment at the caprice of something as disrupting and
unpredictable as war on his total concept of being.

The Residual Years (New Directions, 1948) carries
this disintegration further. Section I, "Chronicle of Division,"
is a new addition to what amounts to a volume of his collected
verse. The opening poem of the "Chronicle" reiterates not
only the loss of the past, but also suggests the possible trend
which Everson will be taking. Describing the religious con-
scientious objectors, Everson writes:

> For most, there is prayer.
> No food passes lip without mute blessing,
> And the black book carried against the heart
> Assures, assures.

He is among others who lack the assurance and who must
conclude that they "have learned in this that all achievement/
Is only attained by the thick sequence of forced beginnings."

The second poem of the "Chronicle" shows the pri-
soners living devoid of everything but the expectation of the
bits and sentiments of letters. They are men trying through
this means to grasp reality. It is followed by two poems
which deal with the release of these conscientious objectors.
The world has changed. Nature has changed. They have
changed. And yet in their being there is a hint of continuity
inexplicable and unprobed.

The last poem of the "Chronicle" sinks everything--
guilt, doubts, fears, frustrations--into the giant womb image
of the sea. It seems that in it Everson has realized not
only the fruitlessness of his views on nature but also his in-
ability to solve them in anything less than their total annihila-
tion.

Recent poems, appearing under the name of Brother Antoninus, O. P. , the name Everson took on entering the brotherhood, reveal the eventual solution Everson found to his outgrowings. God is permanence. He is connector of past and present, the Great Organizer of purpose in man. Nature persists through His permanence. Thus, in "The South Coast" (Evergreen Review, II:2) nature is portrayed not as autonomous, but as the creation of God:

> Whose hand stacks rock, cairn-posted,
> Churched to the folded sole of this hill,
> And Whose mind conceives?

Man is still closely allied to this concept of nature, but it is no longer imperative as a concept that he demand a feeling for the past. In fact, Antoninus asks in "A Penitential Psalm" that he might be expunged, eradicated from time. Because time is under the new Great Organizer, this has little if any meaning.

Sex in "Annul in Me My Manhood" becomes spiritual union, rather than nature:

> Annul in me my manhood, Lord, and make
> Me woman-sexed and weak
> If by that total transformation
> I might know Thee more.

Antoninus seeks this union, but it is now God and not woman with whom he is seeking to unite.

"Out of the Ash" portrays Christ as immortal and persistent in a manner nature could never be. "A Siege of Silence" (Chicago Review, XII:3) restates more vividly Antoninus' new belief that God controls both nature and the nature of man:

> God? God? what storms of the dredged deep
> Your absence lets, the rock-croppage mind,
> Kelp-girthed, sunken under swell;
> All seas of the unislanded soul
> Typhooned, hurricaned to hell!

Finally "The Encounter" suggests that Antoninus' long philosophical search for meaning and belonging has been resolved.

THE BEAT FRIAR

The Editors of Time Magazine. 1959

In 1959 the Beat Generation, introduced in the Evergreen Re-
view two years before, was beginning to stir the popular
imagination. That spring, Everson (as Antoninus) made his
first tour into the Midwest, reading in both Detroit and Chi-
cago. His radio and television appearances in those cities
attracted the attention of Time magazine, and on May 25 it
introduced the poet in its Religion column.

> "Someone has said American po-
> etry is divided into Smoothies
> and Shaggies. I'm a Shaggy."
> So says a poet who has been a
> Christian Scientist, agnostic,
> anarchist and conscientious ob-
> jector. Yet today he wears the
> white tunic and black scapular
> of a Roman Catholic Dominican
> lay brother.

"I am a man of God." said the tall, black-clad man
as he smiled shyly at his audience. "I'm beat to the square,
and square to the beat, and that's my vocation." The
Prior of his Dominican monastery would probably express
the vocation differently, but he gladly permits Brother An-
toninus to give readings of his own poems, as he is doing
this week in Los Angeles for the Commonweal Club. His
poetry and his whole career may be way out, but his purpose
is to move men way in to Christ.

Moment of Faith. Brother Antoninus, 46, came to
his vocation through labyrinthine ways. Born William Ever-

11

son in Sacramento, Calif. , to a Norwegian-born bandmaster turned printer, he put in some time at Fresno State College, married his high school sweetheart ("A square thing, but it happens to be the truth"), and was overwhelmed by the poetry of Robinson Jeffers. His other literary landmarks: D. H. Lawrence's Lady Chatterley's Lover and Henry Miller's Tropic of Cancer. "They were the crystallizing books of my pre-Catholic formation," says Brother Antoninus. "They have a kind of terrible vitality that enabled me to strip the merely conventional away and expose my soul so that when the moment of faith actually came, I was free within myself to make the act of faith. "

Bill Everson learned about religious anarchy at a camp for conscientious objectors during the war. When that was over, his marriage on the rocks, he joined the group of creative and not-so-creative bums around Poet Kenneth Rexroth that began the "San Francisco renaissance," before Beatniks Jack Kerouac and Allen Ginsberg came out from Manhattan and put the movement in the news. "I'm pre-beat," says Brother Antoninus.

He moved in with a divorcee who was a painter, writer and Trotskyite trying to find her way back to the Roman Catholic Church. "She was going to Mass when I met her, so I went along because I couldn't stand being deserted. I hated the religion. Catholicism intruded a ritual between God and man. As an anarchist, I couldn't stand the idea of an institution between God and man. "

But on Christmas Eve in 1948, he became a Catholic. Since he and his girl could not be married (the church ruled both of their previous marriages valid), they split up. After a year writing poetry on a Guggenheim fellowship, Everson joined the Catholic Worker movement in Oakland. Fourteen months later he became Dominican Brother Antoninus at Oakland's St. Albert's College. Except for an unsuccessful attempt to study for the priesthood ("I couldn't see it through for psychological reasons") and a three-week protest walkout (he objected to the installation of a TV set in the priory), Everson has served faithfully, washing dishes, scrubbing floors, making beds and working in the print shop. He explains: "I live, under obedience, the life of a vowed brother. But I am not vowed. I could leave any time, or they could send me away. "

No Route Back. For his poetry readings Brother An-

toninus takes off his white tunic, black scapular and hood, to
dress his 6-ft. 4-in. frame in clerical street garb--a plain black
suit, black tie. Says he: "Society has two structures, the
institutional and the visionary. There has to be a synthesis.
I feel that I have found that religion in which the institutional
and the visionary are reconcilable.... The beat have repu-
diated the institutional. They have no route back theologically. "

"The beat is different from the other generations of
revolt. Other generations have wanted to set up a counter-
institutional world; even we anarchists wanted to do that.
But the beat sees all these movements as being entrapped
in the world of the square. The word square means four-
cornered, or lacking flexibility. Of course, we all have
some element of squareness in us. But the point is that the
beat refuses to have any real dialogue with the world of the
square, and this to me is fatal. "

Brother Antoninus' dialogue is in his poetry, which
he prefers to have spoken rather than set in type. Sample:

Now the lance-riddled man on that pronged tree
    stretched in the death dance there
opens his executing eye and gibbets me.

THE POETRY OF BROTHER ANTONINUS

Thomas P. McDonnell. 1961

With the publication of An Age Insurgent and The Crooked
Lines of God, Everson's reputation as one of America's
most powerful post-modern religious poets was achieved, and
a first overall appraisal of his work could be attempted.
This essay, tracing Everson's poetry from farm to monas-
tery, appeared in Spirit, May 1961.

> There are times in the poetry of
> Brother Antoninus, and these re-
> curring more frequently than to
> be merely coincidental, when the
> principle of inscape would seem
> to obtain to an even greater in-
> tensity than it does in the poetry
> of Hopkins. It is, poetically
> speaking, as if Brother Antoninus
> were recognizing the "immanence"
> and "transcendence" of God in
> one simultaneous flash of poetic
> intuition.

There is a certain disadvantage in beginning a piece
of criticism with frank and open praise of its subject--at
least this would seem to be the case when you consider the
almost deliberately inhibited restraint which has become the
all too accepted canon of modern literary criticism. Under
such conditions, if you state an opinion in the most candid
terms, you are taken to be completely naive and unworthy
of serious consideration. And even if you happen to be taken
seriously, you are then expected to defend your conclusions
in the manner of a Pavlovian scientist and in the language

of a Government attorney. But in speaking of the poetry of Brother Antoninus, I shall gladly forego the pleasures of these two rather precious indulgences, and state immediately that I believe it to be some of the finest yet written by a Catholic poet in the United States.

· Brother Antoninus, before his conversion and affiliation with the Dominican Order, was, in the world, William Everson. I must confess that I do not know much about the pre-conversion period of his life. But Kenneth Rexroth has given us the following valuable information from the second issue of Evergreen Review:

"... Prior to the Second War he was a farmer in the San Joaquin Valley. Here he wrote his first book of poems, San Joaquin. Like so many young poets he was naively accessible to influences his maturity would find dubious. In his case this was Jeffers, but he was, even then, able to transform Jeffers' noisy rhetoric into genuinely impassioned utterance, his absurd self-dramatization into real struggles in the depths of the self. Everson is still wrestling with his angel, still given to the long oratorical line with vague echoes of classical quantitative meters, but there is no apparent resemblance left to Jeffers. During the War he was in a Conscientious Objectors' camp in Oregon, where he was instrumental in setting up an off time Arts Program out of which have come many still active people, projects and forces which help give San Francisco culture its intensely libertarian character. Here he printed several short books of verse, all later gathered in the New Direction volume, The Residual Years. Since then he has printed two books, Triptych for the Living and A Privacy of Speech. In the tradition of Eric Gill and Victor Hammer, they are amongst the most beautiful printing I have ever seen. Since then--since entering the Order, he has published mostly in the Catholic Worker. "

This information, brief as it may be, is submitted in the belief, contrary to the exclusive poem-on-the-page isolation of the New Criticism, that the kind of man matters very much to the kind of poem--presupposing, of course, the authenticity of the poem itself. I do not, as I have said,

know much about the man who was William Everson. But
the catharsis of conversion, despite the facile accounts of it
in autobiographies by the dozen, is still a complex, and even
mysterious, process of the psychic and spiritual nature of
the individual. What is apparent in the poetry of Brother
Antoninus, however, is that the grace of conversion somehow
released those full poetic resources which had lain more or
less dormant within him: "God makes. On earth, in us,
most instantly,/ On the very now,/ His own means con-
ceives./ How many strengths break out unchoked/ Where
He, Whom all declares,/ Delights to make be!" It is this
sense of urgency and declaration that seems to me to be the
meaningful quality in Brother Antoninus's poetry; but it is
more than this, I think, more than the ritual celebration of
even the most enraptured psalmist. Brother Antoninus him-
self has best described the character of his work in the word
insurgence:

> "I think the insurgence will be apparent to al-
> most anyone. The age that is insurgent began
> with Christ and will continue to the end of time.
> Christianity is always insurgent, and when it
> loses its insurgent character it loses its soul-
> force, the life disappears from the husk of its
> material observances, ceases to inspire. When
> I woke up one day and discovered that Chris-
> tianity is not dead and cannot be killed, then I
> became a true insurgent, a Christian, who had
> theretofore been only a rebel." (From a short
> preface to An Age Insurgent, Blackfriars Pub-
> lications, 1959.)

It is obvious that this kind of credo is not likely to
produce the comfort-and-consolation verse of poets of the
easy pieties. For much is demanded of a poetry which at-
tempts to engage Christianity at the source of its personal
and historical nature--in other words, in its insurgent char-
acter. Further, it demands a creative tension arising from
the need of the artist, not an acquired one constructed for
the sake of art. The creativity of tension in the poetry of
Brother Antoninus is, of course, inherent in the nature of
form--not that vagueness of form usually reserved to de-
scribe poems which are at last impenetrable--but a move-
ment of meaning that can actually be observed to work itself
out in the most fully realized of his poems.

Consider, for example, "In the Dream's Recess,"

whose opening section declares our identity with created being: "Let from no earth-engendered thing your friendship be forsworn." This at first (despite the formality of inversion) may seem a simple enough statement, but it is not a sentimental one when followed to its consequences. A romantic pantheist recently described the mutual colloidal substance in all creatures as establishing the bond of empathy between them. But the Christian poet asks if some exception is not to be made in our affiliation with the lower forms of nature:

Not from the Scorpion, that arcs its poison-shafted barb?
Not from the Spider, nor the quick claw-handed Crab?

And then answers his own questions:

There is a place where all snake-natured things obtain,
Where squats the Toad: see there between his eyes
The carbuncular gleam break forth! The Sow-bug
        breeds there,
And the Sphynx-moth takes her vague compelling flight.

Incidentally, although this capital "T" Toad may seem at first the Platonic idealization of all toadal nature, it is the very real one of Marianne Moore--yet not to be found in any of her imaginary gardens, but in the real one, again, of fallen nature itself. The movement of meaning turns on the pivotal line, "These are the dangerous kingdom's least inhabitants." But there is another and more dangerous kingdom:

For deep in the groin of darkness, in the dream's recess,
Far back in the self's forbidden apertures,
Where clangs the door, comes forth the One.
Great prince, most baleful lord,
Clad in the adjuncts of his powerful craft;
The brimstone blazes on that unrelenting brow.

That last magnificent line leaves no doubt in the mind as to who may be the adversary in that other kingdom, but the point is that the Satanic presence can become effective only in the deliberately perverted realms of our human nature:

There lies a world of willfulness beyond one's best intent.
How may one reconcile it? There lies a universe of darkness.
Far past the reaches of the wish. How may one
Civilize the obdurate realm?

This, of course, is the unconscious--and it is now
that we come to see the revealed ambivalence of the poem--
the darkness of nature and the nature of darkness, where
the creatures of the fallen garden assume a symbolic identity
with the gropings of the unconscious, which is itself the fallen
grace of the intellect:

> ... Deep down
> The Scorpion lurks, the Salamander
> Twists his chilly flesh. Deep down
> The Horned Toad and the Crab consort,
> All evil copulates, each loathly thing
> Peoples the dark with its sloth-gotten spawn.

What, then, is left? The soul at the nadir of its ex-
istence must necessarily cry out to the "Great God," to be
scoured "out with brightness! Make me be clean!" And
yet this is not an easy answer--as many critics have accused
Hopkins of easy solutions in his terminal invocations to the
so-called nature poems. For still, to post-Freudian man,

> The sullied presence crouches in my side
> And all is fearful where I dare not wake or dream!

This tension of the creative process also works itself
out in another fine poem, "Past Solstice." In this poem
the time is past solstice, "not yet the length of a month
past;/ And now to leave, to go forth from the house,/ Aware
of a first lack in the light/ Where nothing but light sprouted."
And then the nostalgic realization: "So. That autumn edges?
days go short?/ Is it not of God's hand, all?" Following
the poignancy of these questions on the ephemeral nature of
life, the poet recalls the summer at its fullness, the shore-
line strewn with "Many wonderful things of the drift." And
yet all this, at the next tide, "As solemnly gone, quite taken;
that glittering beach,/ Even the gulls/ Gone." But the
spirit, like nature, abhors a vacuum; and the poem in its
seeking turns again toward the motion of meaning:

> And yet the sea was the same,
> The sea was the source in which all tides are manifest.
> It was the sea we went to.

"So God in His seasons," the changeless and the chang-
ing, "And the God-seeker, the man God-loving," will not
worship even the best of what the seasons in all their glory
have to offer, "But will look rather to that eternity within

the flux/ Where the source of all seasons holds them back
at His mighty Heart,/ And breathes on them in their order. "

It cannot be said of a poem like this, without being
something less than superficial, that it is, after all, only
another nature poem. Of course that sounds condescending
to begin with--"only another nature poem"--since poets like
Horace, Wordsworth, and Robert Frost have all added their
vitality to the tradition of poetry from the natural order.
But Brother Antoninus is more than a nature poet; he is a
supra-natural poet, because he sees things in the proper per-
spective and hierarchy of being:

> For the seasons seen are only the things of time,
> And time seen is only the order of things,
> And all things will fail.
> But the Source of all things will never fail.
> For the nature of things lies in their being apart,
> They may suffer reduction.
> But the Source of things is not fashioned of parts,
> And may not be reduced.

But this implies neither a divorce from created na-
ture nor a mystical abandonment of our sensuous human na-
ture. On the contrary, "we, being things, love things, and
the sequence of things. " Yet the Christian poet cannot stop
short of ultimates--he is not only willing to go beyond the
point at which the nature-poet stops--he is compelled to do
so, for "what we seek of the thing/ Is that greaterness with-
in the thing/ Which keeps it in being. " This, of course, is
the inscape of Hopkins. But there are times in the poetry
of Brother Antoninus, and these recurring more frequently
than to be merely coincidental, when the principle of inscape
would seem to obtain to an even greater intensity than it
does in the poetry of Hopkins. It is, poetically speaking,
as if Brother Antoninus were recognizing the immanence and
the transcendence of God in one simultaneous flash of poetic
intuition. It is this intuition which finally resolves the op-
posites of tension established earlier in the poem:

> Therefore praise Autumn, praise opulent Autumn;
> And breathe the white breath of Winter;
> And revel with Spring.
>
> But love what Autumn will never succeed,
> Nor Winter curb, nor Spring survive,
> What even Summer, the tall triumphant Summer,
> Will never surpass.
>
> Love Him.

Significantly, though, the "Love Him" is not a merely perfunctory signature, a final admonition tacked onto the poem; it is the answer to the existentialist nadir arrived at midway in the poem with the word, "Gone." For the Christian poet, as true existentialist, will always perceive that identity of being within (and beyond) the change and movement of created nature--and that is what makes him something more than a pastoral poet, on the one hand, or an apocalyptic one on the other. That is why Brother Antoninus is not inhibited, as so many modern nature-poets are, to praise and celebrate man's encounter with created being. We are told nowadays that it is the direction of the "new nature poetry" to represent the "mindlessness of nature, its nonhuman otherness." But this seems as much a reaction from the error of anthropomorphism in the "old nature poetry" as it is a drift into the new error of isolating man from creatures and creation. It also contains the associate fallacy of attempting to write a so-called "pure poetry" in contradistinction to, and separation from, the poet-observer himself. Our age has abandoned that awareness of relationships which in itself we once considered a kind of penultimate wisdom.

It is just this sense of the relationship of things that makes the "Canticle to the Waterbirds" one of the truly joyful poems in contemporary poetry. After a profuse litany in recognition of all kinds and species of coastal waterbirds, Brother Antoninus declares, "You leave a silence. And this for you suffices, who are not of the/ ceremonials of man....

Yours is of another order of being, and wholly it compels.
But may you, birds, utterly seized in God's supremacy,
Austerely living under His austere eye--
Yet may you teach a man a necessary thing to know
Which has to do of the strict conformity that creature-
    hood entails,
And constitutes the prime commitment all things share.
For God has given you the imponderable grace to be
    His verification,
Outside the mulled incertitude of our forensic choices;
That you, our lessers in the rich hegemony of being,
May serve as testament to what a creature is,
And what creation owes.

Kenneth Rexroth has accurately described the verbal texture of Brother Antoninus's poetry as having "a gnarled, even tortured, honesty, a rugged unliterary diction, a relentless probing and searching, which are not just engaging,

but almost overwhelming." It is not the kind of poetry you
are likely to find in the quarterlies. But it would be wrong
to conclude from this that Brother Antoninus is incapable of
artfully metered English, or that he has never written, so
to speak, in the formal mode. For example, one has only
to read "A Canticle to the Christ in the Holy Eucharist," a
marvelously organized poem, in order to realize the consid-
erable powers of Brother Antoninus in the direction of formal
poetry. It is written in anapestic, or rising rhythm, and
while this is a particularly exhausting meter when poorly or
too frequently used, its organic pertinence to the "Canticle"
is entirely credible and tastefully performed. The poem,
after all, is a canticle and implies the rhythm of a psalmic
chant: "In my heart you were might. And thy word was
the running of rain/ That rinses October. And the sweet-
water spring in the rock. And the brook in the crevice."
It is not easy to be done with quoting good poetry; but I
should like, finally, to offer this particular stanza, even in
its chronological displacement from the lines already quoted:

> There is nothing known like this wound, this knowledge
>   of love.
> In what love? In which wounds, such words? In what
>   touch? In whose coming?
> You gazed. Like the voice of the quail. Like the buck
>   that stamps in the thicket.
> You gave. You found the gulf, the goal. On my tongue
>   you were meek.

In all respects, therefore, I believe this to be poetry
of a very high order. In fact, I do not think it excessive to
say that the complete "Canticle" is probably the finest "mys-
tical" poem written in the United States. (Quotes around
mystical, because a poem has its own autonomy of being be-
fore it has any classification.) It is a poem, moreover,
which may be favorably compared with the poems of St. John
of the Cross. But in the more typical poems of Brother An-
toninus--typical, that is, in their qualities of insurgence and
hard-wrought strength--a self-revealing identity stands clearly
forth, not only in contemporary terms, but in the light of a
vision which is timeless. His quarrel with the world is not
that of the whining anti-materialist, but of a man who knows
something of our human alienation in a world resplendent
with beauty and terror.

THE POET OF INSURGENCE

A. V. Krebs, Jr. 1963

An attempt to set the record straight in the wake of Everson's growing popularity, this paper (published in Way: Catholic Viewpoints, January-February 1963) places its emphasis on the poet's life and bibliography, rather than on an examination of his verse.

> Time magazine dubbed him "the beat friar" and there were other magazines and newspapers that featured both his poetry and his personal life in what at best can be called a highly sensational manner. The tall, gaunt 45-year-old Dominican tertiary thus became another sacrificial lamb offered up on the altar of creative journalism.

The Hazards of Holiness, a new book of poems by Brother Antoninus, has called attention once again to one of the 20th century's most talked-about religious poets. If past performance be indicative, one might safely guess that in certain circles the book will be savagely attacked while in others it will be acclaimed as an important development in the work of a poet of great significance. Some, mistaking the term "religious poetry" for saccharine rhymes, and turning to this latest volume, will be shocked by the powerfully sensual nature of its contents. For many, however, the poet will remain a name, a name surrounded in their minds with contradictory statements gleaned from the press and idle conversation. For these, certain questions must stand out:

22

Who is Brother Antoninus?

What is the significance of his work?

Why is he so often identified with the so-called "beat generation"?

Born in Sacramento, California, the first son and second child of Louis Waldemar Everson and Francelia Marie Herber, William Everson grew up in the small San Joaquin Valley town of Selma, California. In 1934, at Fresno State College he was introduced to the poetry of Robinson Jeffers. It was through Jeffers' work that he came to see the "religiousness of Nature." In 1939, Ward Ritchie of Los Angeles published a series of William Everson's poems titled San Joaquin. It was from this pamphlet publication that he received his first review, a favorable one, from Poetry.

"I was still insecure at this time," he recalls, "very vulnerable and I couldn't stand the critical gaff that I would have to take to get out into the literary politics of the time which was dominated by a kind of fight between the 'new critics' who were trying to get a foothold and the proletariat who dominated the scene. I knew I would run afoul of both because they had written savage attacks against Jeffers, and I was a Jeffers man."

Later when World War II began, the hostility that grew through childhood toward the paternal image conjoined with the fear of destroying nature which represented to him the maternal image, so William Everson declared himself a conscientious objector and was sent to Camp Angel at Waldport, Oregon. Placed in charge of the Fine Arts Group at the camp, he achieved his first real success with an "in-group" audience through the mimeographed publication of his 1941 pacifist poems, titled Ten War Elegies.

In 1946 William Everson returned to California and went through what was later described by one commentator as his "pre-beat" period, a period of time when the young writers, artists and poets were attempting to resolve the problems posed by Hiroshima through their art. His participation in this movement, however, was more of an emotional identification than an actual participation. Psychologically he had already been involved in so many intense, consequential and concrete issues--both in his decision to be a conscientious objector and in the daily life at Camp Angel--that the theoretical, quasi-religious, quasi-cultural, quasi-political discussions being held by the young rebels of the immediate post-war era were a bore.

"Most of the criticism or objections you can level at the ordinary beat discussion now, I felt then. Essentially it was not constructive enough."

In 1948, through the urging of critic Kenneth Rexroth, New Directions published The Residual Years, a cumulative edition of many of William Everson's pre-1946 poems. Rexroth, who had met Everson on a furlough during the war, was deeply impressed by the young poet from Selma. "When the book came out," Rexroth commented later, "James Laughlin (publisher of New Directions) and I hoped that we were launching a new leader for a badly needed poetic revolution. His work has a ruggedly honest unliterary quality that is engaging. It has the ultimate, agonized sincerity that makes for a great, truly personal style."

The Residual Years was a controversial book. Most of the controversy did not involve William Everson directly, however, but was concerned with Rexroth's biting denunciation of contemporary academic circles which appeared on the dust jackets of the book: "This kind of poetry may outrage academic circles where an emasculated and hallucinated imitation of John Donne is still considered chic; but others, who have been waiting for modern poetry to stop clearing its throat and stammering, should be delighted."

In the spring of 1949, while working as a janitor at the University of California Press, Everson created a mild sensation in the literary world by being the recipient of a Guggenheim Fellowship in poetry. Later that same year, he entered the Catholic Church. For more than a year he labored in the Catholic Worker's Peter Maurin House in Oakland, California, and then was accepted as a Dominican oblate at St. Albert's College, the Dominican House of Studies for the Province of the West, in that same city.

At the beginning of the 1950's as America cautiously passed mid-20th century, a bleak, dry wind was sweeping across the creative arts frontier. The cries of futility echoing from Korea had begun to subside as the decade aged, and the nation emerged from an "age of suspicion" to an "age of apathy." Disillusioned youth began to swell the ranks of the inhabitants of Greenwich Village and North Beach. New sounds, new voices began to be heard.

What Rexroth, Everson and others had earlier dubbed the "San Francisco Renaissance" had grown to such proportions that it could no longer be ignored. The popular press turned its writers loose and the public was introduced to the cultural and social phenomena which--for purposes of easy digestion by its readers--it labeled "the beat generation," lumping all the writers, poets, artists and hangers-on into one category: "beatniks." New names like Lawrence Ferlinghetti, Allen Ginsberg, Gregory Corso, Phillip Whalen and Jack Kerouac began to appear in the slick magazines of the day. Many were called but few were chosen.

When the Evergreen Review chose to publish four of Brother Antoninus' religious poems, it did so in its Fall, 1957 issue, an edition of the review giving the first public presentation of "The San Francisco Scene," the literary bellwether of the "beat generation." Criticism from all sides was leveled at not only the "beat" movement, but also at any writers and artists identified with it. Time magazine dubbed Brother Antoninus "the beat friar" and there were other magazines and newspapers that featured both his poetry and his personal life in what at best can be called a highly sensational manner. The tall, gaunt, 45-year-old Dominican tertiary thus became another sacrificial lamb offered up on the altar of creative journalism.

Not that Antoninus has turned his back upon his past. For him and the other writers and artists early involved in the Renaissance, the 1957 emergence was simply a public statement of "an age insurgent." Antoninus enunciated this idea in a preface to a collection of his early religious poems (An Age Insurgent, Blackfriars Publications, 1959) when he stated: "the form one's insurgence is to take becomes the mystery of vocation, for in the divine plan one finds oneself sometimes in what are apparently the least insurgent of circumstances. But then the circumstances must somehow be made insurgent, or at least, made to serve the insurgent."

The spotlight of national publicity having fallen upon him in 1957, requests for readings of his poetry began to pour into St. Albert's and in the following months and years his "Poetry and the Life of the Spirit," readings were heard from Seattle, Washington, to Boston, Massachusetts. At St. Albert's Brother Antoninus set up his hand press in the loft of the college and there, in 1959, printed The Crooked Lines of God, published in conjunction with the University of Detroit Press Contemporary Poet Series. This volume, con-

taining the poetry of his conversion, his integration into the
Church and his early religious life, was greeted with a host
of favorable reviews, ranging from the New York Times
Book Review to The Critic. One critic, at this time, lev-
eled an often heard objection to his poetry in an observation
of the book: "What goes wrong is the reliance on the shock
itself of conjoining sexual and religious figures.... The in-
sistence on intensity (as opposed to the creation of it) leads
naturally to ... Hollywood touches...."

Brother Antoninus answered this type of criticism in
an interview printed in the American Benedictine Review un-
der the title "The Artist and the Religious Life." There
the poet pointed out that "the tendency of the religious artist
is to shy away from the most imaginative demand because
of the fear of the power of the imagination and the danger
of falling into sin. This is what I mean by the inner censor,
[and is] the artist's first problem. I call it a pseudo-prob-
lem because the Thomistic principle is clear: 'Now the de-
lectation of the thought itself results from the inclination of
the appetite to the thought. But the thought itself is not in
itself a mortal sin. Sometimes, indeed, it is only a venial
sin, as when a man thinks of such a thing for no purpose;
and sometimes it is no sin at all, as when a man has a pur-
pose in thinking of it; for instance he may wish to preach or
dispute it' (ST, II-II, q 179). Or, I might add, he may, if
he is a religious artist, seek to transform it in the univer-
sality of the life of man in God, purged of its decadent soft-
ness, and epitomized in the extremes of moral consequence
through the projected truths of the aesthetic vision."

Such a statement is given strong underlining when seen
in the light of the man who uttered it. For Brother Anto-
ninus continues to work out the "mystery of vocation" through
his art. "Each of us," he comments, "is obliged to re-in-
terpret the meaning of life, but we cannot afford to lose
sight of the center of reference. Art is man's medium of
interpreting life, but without that center all his accomplish-
ments are fruitless."

Anyone reading the poetry of William Everson and
Brother Antoninus will immediately see that the search for
that "center of reference" has been the hallmark of the poet's
life. Now as a Dominican oblate he is still deeply committed
to the struggle of re-interpreting life and working to solidify
the link between the visionary and the institutional.

Reflecting on the sensational publicity given the "beat

generation," Brother Antoninus says, "the fact that the Beat
Generation, in spite of its dangerous recklessness, has pro-
duced valid art testifies at least to its essential seriousness,
its preoccupation with the real, rather than the pseudo. For
by the very fact of delivering itself over in a kind of trust,
to the deepest forces of the psyche, it has, in some instances,
succeeded in liberating art from the preoccupation with sur-
faces which has dominated it since the Renaissance. In so
doing it has, be it ever so blindly, exposed the essential
seriousness of the disordered human soul. Those who are
saddened rather than ostracized to see young men and women
damage themselves in an effort to achieve authenticity must
understand the need of youth for self-immolation will mani-
fest itself, if not in good ways then in bad ones; that the
world of 'civilization-as-usual' (of reasonable men) is no
longer capable of stemming the uprush of ecstatic forces
from the repressed instinctual and spiritual life of man. The
beat generation has in its favor the repudiation of all philis-
tine values, a salutary contempt for the attitudes of 'this
world' to a degree that puts many a Christian to shame, an
earnest quest for actual existential engagement. "

Recently a prominent national magazine took a birch-
twig in hand and began thrashing at the latest work of James
Jones and Jack Kerouac, commenting: "America's once
promising crop of young post-war writers has so far shown
no knack at all of growing old greatfully. Critics, casting
about for the causes of failed promise, justly note a complex
of external factors ... but much of the trouble is internal.
So few younger writers age well these days because so many
of them have difficulty in growing up at all. "

Such commentators and reviewers prefer to lightly
pass off these "complex of external factors" precisely be-
cause such commentators and reviewers--through their ex-
ploitation and sensationalism--have been one of the greatest
external factors in hindering artistic growth. Yet, Brother
Antoninus is himself a poet who has "aged well," not only
"growing old great-fully" but gracefully.

His early promise has matured so that few would deny
his place as one of the twentieth century's most significant
religious poets. Once, in a retrospective mood, he said:
"My poems have been an attempt to serve my insurgent age.
In them I sought the insurgent instance beneath the death of
all phenomenal fact. And if the death of fact wins out over
them, over me, I inveigh the reader to profit by the explicit
defeat, burnish the soul of his spirit, clean its living edge,
and to the last gasp of his being, serve the truth. "

BROTHER ANTONINUS: A SYMPOSIUM

Brendon Cavanaugh, O. P. , Alfred Camillus Murphy, O. P. , &
Albert Dosher, O. P. 1963

This symposium may be considered Everson's vindication in
his Order and among his co-religionists. The sensational
nature of his work and public stance had been deplored by
many of the more conservative members of his brotherhood.
With this symposium written in the spring of 1963 by three
religious, Everson's name, in effect, was cleared.

> The poet has not just thrown off
> before an audience some psychic
> material of his, but has trans-
> formed his inner conflicts in com-
> manding, tough, and vibrating
> language. . . .

Who Am I?   Where Did I Come From?

It is as though the ivy-hung East Coast looked across
the Atlantic at the war-made skeletons scattered about Europe
and shuddered; and a wave of introspection swelled and moved
across the nation, gathering height as it went, until it crested
in the foam line of the San Francisco Renaissance. Its gen-
eral causes were multiple. Probably it began with the mass
brutality of the Second World War inflicted in the name of a
myth about race supremacy or the cataclysmic effects of
nuclear warheads dropped on Japan. Then there seems to
have been other things to keep it going: trainloads of men
and women slaughtered during the Indian national apportion-
ment or Africans shot on sight in Apartheid reprisals. It
doesn't really matter which particular one of these mass
atrocities was seen and experienced by young Americans;
each was nauseating.

28

Against this horror of mass warfare, philosophers, theologians and poets have violently reacted by reasserting the worth of the individual man. They are asking the same questions Gaugin wrote in the corner of his painting; where do we come from?, what are we?, where are we going? But they are not looking at the picture.

Kierkegaard, Camus, Sartre of the existentialist world; Kerouac, Salinger and now Golding of the introverted heroes are all insistent on the part that the individual must play in life. His responsibility is not to be discounted. He has obligations and rights and the duty to assert them.

These, as others, are speakers for the people, in a broad sense. They both reflect and develop the 'common mind,' feeding it and feeding on it in turn. Step by step presentation, clarity, reasoned procedure is part of their mode of communication.

Besides these and different from them, there are the intuitive voices of the nation's poets such as the late Robert Frost of the East and Brother Antoninus of the West. For these men, communication is as dependent upon rapport as words. Words may be the tools of their careful craft, but the intangible form and spirit is just as essential to the completed work, perhaps even its dominant part. In like manner, generally speaking, sophistication is usually accompanied by a greater dependence upon form or spirit than upon concrete, material things.

A poet is said to be one to whom the gods speak. Certainly there have been those to whom God has spoken. The Old Testament poets stagger at times under the weight of God's message. Our modern poets have a message for us. They must be heard even if we must go to the desert to listen, or, as it is in this case, to the hidden valleys of the West Coast echoing with the sharply struck verses of Brother Antoninus.

For many reasons Antoninus is a pebble in society's sandal, a true scruple. To a society educated to believe that the chief virtue of morality is public chastity, Antoninus speaks in vivid sexual imagery. To a pleasure loving people, he preaches a sermon of pain and sorrow. In a secular modern world he wears the thirteenth century black and white habit of a Dominican friar. Where sophistication is a cultivated art, he affronts with simplicity and honesty.

Some knowledge of Antoninus' background is necessary in order to understand the man and his poetry. Following this discussion, a second part will investigate the theological implications of his poetry and a third will attempt to analyze the complex relationship between the two.

The Man

William Everson is a Californian. Born in Sacramento fifty-one years ago, he spent his youth in Selma. Slighting his formal education, he married and began to support his wife and himself by working as a laborer and a farmer. It was during these early years that he was drawn to poetry. In those years the names he knew were Lawrence and Robinson Jeffers. They sang a humanistic theme that lacked a certain solidarity.

If the historical theory of action and reaction is correct, it might explain this humanism which found its expression in philosophy, education and poetry. Maybe it was a reaction to the overpowering sense of inhumanity and evil that men practiced upon each other. Before, mass atrocities had been what counted. Now it was the individual experience of natural beauty which was important. As an answer to the paradox of God and the existence of evil in the world, a pantheism was cultivated which sought out the gods of nature in the quiet valleys and solitary splendor of the West Coast mountains.

William Everson became something of a disciple of Robinson Jeffers, taking up his theme of pastoral humanism in his own early attempts at poetry. A series of slight volumes was printed, not so much because they were good, because they weren't; not so much because they had something to say to the world, because they didn't; but mostly because he wanted to be able to hold his past between his fingers and weigh it in his hand. Then he could go on, knowing that the past need not be repeated. In fact he could use it as a tangible foundation for his future.

The war came and young men went. But how was this man nursed on pastoral idylls and humanistic good will to kill and maim and wound. He could not; he would not; so he was interned as a conscientious objector in a camp with those who would not pick the bitter fruit of man's pride.

After his release from camp he hung around the San

Francisco Bay area. Something of an anarchist by this time,
he became interested in pacifist groups. He came in contact
with Kenneth Rexroth who considerably influenced his poetry.
Since 1933 he had been doing more writing. By 1948 he had
quite a collection of poems and, what is more important, an
inkling of direction. In this year New Directions published
The Residual Years, a collection of the last fifteen years'
work. Outside of the fact that it served as a sort of marker
in his life, it didn't have a great deal of significance--not,
at least, in the light of his latest poems.

During the next year he received a Guggenheim Fel-
lowship and married a second time. The woman he married
was a remarkable woman who experienced the finding of her
once lost Faith. He saw her kneel and pray; he wondered
just what this was all about. Questions and answers. He
thought about it. More questions, some answers.

The Christmas of 1948 brought with it an experience
which changed his whole life. He had gone to Christmas
Mass with his wife. Sitting beside her as she knelt, his
eyes rose to the red turban she had wound around her hair,
then across the heads and shoulders of the people slowly as-
sembling for Mass until it reached the Christmas crib and
rested upon a statue of a shepherd.

A shepherd meant something to him. And here this
shepherd had a place in the Catholic Faith. Watching his
Catholic wife regain her own peace of soul he gradually for-
mulated the fact that Faith was what he most desperately
needed--a man's religion. There was a book, there was a
church, there was himself.

Nature for him had been tantamount to God. The
dread of renouncing this world tormented him. But in this
faith, he realized, Christ would not exact the dreaded renun-
ciation of his natural world ... after all, it was His.

But here was a statue of a shepherd set on the same
straw bed as the figure of the infant God. He had known
shepherds in the bleak hills of the West. A shepherd was
"most low ... half-crazed, it is thought with solitude, and
hence impenetrably ignorant, unfit for any more noble em-
ployment and in consequence depraved, he had become in
the obscene humor of the smoking room, a kind of minor
rural god of the vice of sodomy." This was the creature
whose statue was in this holy place. This extreme outcast of
society was one of those admitted to the sanctuary of the stable.

His mind reeled at the thought of that "terrible universal enmity, set against the isolate human heart ... the loneliness of man trapped in a universe he cannot subdue." And then it focused on "the Sacrifice of Man, where God stoops and proffers, stoops and proffers, descends, rises, is nailed to the sky; 'restoration' driven through the chaos of the world."

He rose and walked up to the crib to kneel in half-dazed wonder at the scene. "A man's touched. His pride-stiff soul crumbles before an ineffable grace and he comprehends ... Christ pours out the running wave of his grace." And a moment of self knowledge gleams within him; "Adam-like you prefer your wretched fig-leaves to prime spiritual nakedness." This was "the unspeakable Lover who draws the loved as out of the web of afflictions, remakes him as His own...." And at the crib he knelt "to make his assent such as it was--one more poor wretch, who had nothing to bring but his iniquities."

As he knelt there behind him was a "rising of people, a sound coming up out of the hush that held it ... gathering in waves from here and there, as section after section, in the gathering awareness, rose to the feet ... a kind of inner spontaneous coming-up as a flock of birds of the fields, out of some instinctual thing, rises. They knelt and it was the spread of the sound as the whole of Christendom bending into the Confiteor." Mass began. William Everson was converted to Catholicism.

He then worked for a time in an Oakland hospitality house. In addition to this he had learned to print in order to be able to print his own poetry. Working a hand press, he turned out excellent work, collector's items.

After this there was a short stint with the Catholic Worker Movement. Then in 1951 he and his wife separated and he gave himself as a donatus or gift-of-self to the Dominican Community at St. Albert's College, San Francisco. Clothed with the white tunic, black scapular and capuce, the rosary belted to his side, he was given the new name of Brother Antoninus.

In 1957 he re-emerged with the San Francisco Renaissance and has become one of the most talented and commanding personalities of that entire group. For the last few years he has given public readings at major university cam-

puses throughout the country, especially in the East. In 1959
The Crooked Lines of God was published and then in 1962
The Hazards of Holiness.

There are two aspects of Brother Antoninus which
should be discussed at least in broad phrases: Antoninus the
Friar and Antoninus the Poet. Both of these are necessary
to an understanding of the man Antoninus and his relation to
the rest of men, as he wants it to be and as it is.

The Friar

As a friar, Antoninus is not confined to one place.
In the words of a satirist 'a friar is a monk whose cell is
the world and whose cloister is the ocean.' As a tertiarius
donatus he is bound to the Dominican Order by ties of mu-
tual acceptance and agreement but by no vows. His external
life conforms to that of a laybrother. He has simple house
duties; he works as a Master Printer on Albertus Magnus
Press; and of course, he has the special work of writing and
reading his poetry.

Within the fold of the Order he has a place that is at
once part and not part of it. Dominicans are professional
students, yet Antoninus writes of himself, "I, a laybrother,
contingent to that study but not engaged in it." However he
does study the 'high flung cross' which, after all, was the
major textbook of St. Thomas Aquinas. Yet every textbook
in the end is doomed to scant the vision of a transcendental
God etched on the heart of man.

He sees Dominicans as having chained themselves to
their desks of necessity to maintain their innocence. And
he judges that finally, it is true, they will die exhausted,
expunged of the ineluctable burden of truth. They have en-
gaged in a contemplative, unceasing commitment, and will
die on that line where the violence of the individual and the
violence of God engaged each other, to be transformed by
that violence into the last tranquillity of heaven.

And he, as a friar musing in his cloister, who had
only to move through the life of secular learning to find it
not whole, has turned in here to a deeper integration.

He has brought a vivid past into the cloister and out-
bursts are not rare. But the monastic life has witnessed
many an outburst such as Antoninus', yet has made no judge-

ment, knowing its slow silence will heal all in time. For
him the monastery is not so much a place as a condition.
It is a type of spiritual perspective, an attitude, a transcen-
dent motive. Men bring to it their individual conformation
and are transformed into Christ.

When he sneers at his own "fake medieval attitudiniz-
ing in a modern cloister" it is not the friar thumbing his
nose at the cloister, it is the man belittling the friar.

Transformation is a long, painful process. It is a
rebirth not now rendered painless by the yet dormant senses
of the infant, but acutely painful to the fully developed senses
of a grown man, who must suffer the contradictions and
pressures and the blinding light of self knowledge as he strug-
gles to be born again from darkness into the life of Christ.
It is not a process easily undergone. No wonder he admits
his poetry is not much more than the agonized cry of his
pain. His poetry is the cry of a friar badly burnt by the
love he has dared to embrace; he can no more help it than
he can direct it. Full control should not yet be expected,
for he is not yet delivered, not yet fully weaned. Perhaps
above all it is this materialization of his interior pain that
gives his friarhood its authenticity.

The Poet

Antoninus the poet is another aspect, related to the
first, yet distinct from it. The office of poet is like the
office of priest in that it is for others. Not every friar is
a poet, yet the fact that this poet is a friar elevates his po-
etry from the level of nature to the realm of the supernatural.
For a friar-poet speaks of a love beyond the wildest hopes
of mere natural man. The poet of nature is demanding out
of poverty; "They seek splendor: who would touch them must
stun them; a nerve that is dying needs thunder to rouse it."
The man of supernature is demanding out of love; "Violence
touches man, he reacts ... in his heart's own torment the
world's anguish is taken up." Antoninus would have turned
under the grass and flowers of the monastery garden and
made it into a desert adorned only by the long spiked cactus
"to evoke Passion and Death ... that we might be called
hourly to our own passion." But who would willingly suffer,
were it not for love of Him who so suffered for us.

Would Antoninus be the rigorist in the monastery as

well as the stark and dramatic figure strutting across a
stage in the glareheat of spotlights were it not for his par-
ticular and present status? It takes much suffering to make
a man.

The explanation lies perhaps in the Spanish concept
of mystical marriage. The language of the Spanish mystics
in mystical flights was the language of eroticism and quasi-
erotic experience. This is admittedly one of the things which
has attracted Antoninus to the religious life among Domini-
cans. His poetry filled with the violent images of erotic
pleasure and experience can hardly be held to be reflections
of the natural order, and it would not seem that he would
want them to be. They are mystical flights and should be
taken as such (even though it may be that they are more the
product of desire and hope than fact and experience.)

The effect of such a concept of marriage would neces-
sarily end in a desire to act as a means by which others
might attain this Infinite Lover. And this in fact is the in-
tention of Antoninus--to act as a bridge. A bridge between
what and what? The square and the hip; the humanist and
the realist; perhaps the Lover and loved.

Intensity is an outstanding characteristic of Antoninus
the man as well as Antoninus the poet and friar. The why
and where of intensity is not clear; perhaps it is in the
mind's realization that this good thing, whatever it be, is so
good for it that all else pales beside it, an intensity of con-
centration that spills over into the body and its expressions.
However, it is a fearful trait, one that sets a man off from
his fellows. One doesn't know whether such a man could be
all that serious, not realizing that even this is but the sur-
face of it, the spilling over.

He describes the clerical students coming down the
stairs to chant the hour of Matins--"the hood over the head,
and the white scapular dancing before and behind, floating
out from the movement of the feet, which gives the light and
buoyant tread that somehow catches up the indefinable blithe-
ness, the gaiety of the Order"--and couples it immediately
with the thought of death--"and as they descend they intone
between them the De Profundis. " It is only a man who sees
beyond the gray mist of life to the stark finalities who dares
couple blitheness and death so easily and so closely.

The fact that he is a bridge between extremes of society cannot be doubted in the face of breathless audiences made up of these extremes who look upon him as a mean between them. Intensity is a mark of a lover; a lover is the shortest way to be loved.

Brother Antoninus is a Friar Preacher, an intense lover, and a strong bridge. His consequent relation to other men is obvious in these offices; it is now left to consider his relation to God. --Brendan Cavanaugh, O. P.

****

Advent and Divine Presence in Antoninian Verse

> Invitavi te, Domine, ad convivium variis instructum
> hymnis.
> Vinum nostra desiderat mensa, laudum tuarum,
> scientiam;
> Qui vocatur ad nuptias hydrias mero optimo
> implevisti,
> Reple, precor, os meum laude.
> --Saint Ephraem the Syrian

"I have invited Thee, O Lord, to a banquet of songs," runs the above introduction of Saint Ephraem to his "Fourteenth Sermon upon the Faith, against the Disputers." This is the Saint Ephraem to whom Brother Antoninus has been compared. Nor was the comparison lacking in rather complimentary tone, for this Ephraem, the Deacon, besides being both Father and Doctor of the Church, was also considered the greatest of the Syrian poets. This prolific fourth-century writer was called "the Lyre of the Holy Spirit."

The above quatrain has something more in common with Brother Antoninus than the mere extrinsic denomination of author to author. The four lines speak of a depletion of the poet's wine of praise and a supplication for a duplication of the miracle of Cana within the festivities of his religious hymns. Brother Antoninus mentions a similar diminution of image-flow in the preface of his latest collection of verse, Hazards of Holiness. The latter describes the outpouring that followed his conversion and the quasi-aridity that came after. Perhaps it represents the passage from a consideration of the Omnipotence of God in creation that blares forth in the whirling, careening wings and piercing shrieks Antoninus captures in his "A Canticle to the Waterbirds" to the "immutable silence" and the restrained waiting etched in his subdued, restive prayer for contemplative fullness, "I am long weaned."

If one may be permitted to generalize on the basis of the continual religious theme of Brother Antoninus' last two collections of poems, namely, The Crooked Lines of God, and The Hazards of Holiness, there would appear to be two aspects of God therein that correspond to the movement of the author's thought. One representation is that of God as the One Who is coming, the Advent of the Omnipotent. The other is concerned with the Divine Presence within the soul, the Divine Indwelling and the sanctifying effect of the Holy Spirit. The one poses nature to Divinity, confusion versus order, but understanding over ignorance. The shock of this contrast could hardly be more evident than in the ode to his conversion, "The Screed of the Flesh":

I cried out to the Lord
    That the Lord might open the wall of my heart
And show me the thing I am....
     . . . . .
Lord, Lord, I sang, but I had not understanding.
Lord, Lord, I sang, but the mouth of my soul was shut.
     . . . . .
He showed me my soul.

The other general aspect deals with God's presence in the soul that is constituted in supernatural life by sanctifying grace and is seeking spiritual perfection. This latter note is obvious from the title of the last collection.

That this coming of God to man, to the soul, to be emphasized in the first collection appears even upon a casual glance at the poems. "Triptych for the Living" opens with the message to the shepherds, continues through the Nativity, and closes with the manifestation to the Magi. "My Lord came to me in the deep of night" and "Come Christ ... be born, be born" are lines from "The Encounter" and the final item "Out of the Ash," sustaining the advent theme.

Hazards might at first seem more in the vein of pre-Christian outlook upon God. The work opens with the figures of Jacob and the Angel; we are later brought into the tent of Holofernes as Judith prepares for his decapitation; and the Semitic flavor of the Canticle of Canticles rises to a strong point in "The Songs the Body Dreamed in the Spirit's Mad Behest. " The recurrent note of struggle and violence and the author's grouping of one series of poems under the heading, "The Dark Face of God," seem to indicate a distant Deity, hidden and obscured. Does not the author's association of darkness and death with his reflections upon God place this mood in Old Testament currents? The way of conversion is often oppositely thought of, as one of a passing from darkness to light and from light to more light. In addition, the yoke of the Lord is sweet, yet here the path is rough and thorny with inner strife. Is this the way of holiness that is embodied within the verse, or has the bard's inventive imagination succumbed to the hazards?

Whatever may be conjectured concerning the author's deeper meaning, the words are open to a more felicitous interpretation. When, therefore, in "A Savagery of Love" the figure of the dying Redeemer is followed by "the grappling of the soul in its God" and "there could be no death you had not already died ... the day ... the Cross tore a hole in the sky," it is apparent that the author's imagery of struggle is Christian. Although he will indicate later that Christ is the Light and opposed to the dark of sin, nevertheless, by comparison of lights one may be as night to the other. So in the "Conversion of Saint Paul" there occurs "A brilliance so bright the noon blanked black. " It is the journey in Christian Faith, radiance beyond the sun in comparison to lower things but interstellar night in comparison to the Divine Light Itself.

God, as source of light, purification, and redemption shines forth in the Crooked Lines. It is a veiled Being on the other hand that guides the way of the spiritual traveler in Hazards. How explain this difference? In the earlier work the author shares his experiences of conversion, and something of a broadening knowledge of Our Lord, the Saints, and the Church. Still, however, the Jeremiads and laments of Job and penitential vigils recur.

An insight into the underlying basis for the poet's self-repudiation first seems to be traced in "A Penitential Psalm. " The following indicate a new awareness:

> Crime of my corruption!
> When will it find a cease?
>
>   . . . . .
> I suffer a day of dread in what I am!
> I beg the cleanly thing I could become!

The agitated soul depicted in these heaven-storming supplications seeks more than a minimal satisfaction of duties. This searcher yearns for perfection in union with God: "I Will Know God." This transforming desire is sharply spelled in the poem, "Annul Me in My Manhood." Brother Antoninus draws from Saint John of the Cross' descriptions of the Divine Light in comparison to which the soul is darkness and impurity. In this Light it is blinded. The soul's vision, however, is more distinct to see its own defects and "acknowledges its own unworthiness before God and all creatures." The Revealer of hidden thoughts shows him his soul. The spiritual heights beckon almost tauntingly in view of the weak and faltering human apparatus that stumbles with every step and wheezes with every breath of the rarefied atmosphere.

In the new view of the all holiness and infinite purity of God human imperfections disturb the soul's composure. God is looked to as a divine "cautery," a purifier, a deliverer. This deliverance from self by the transforming effect of God's grace is presented in clever biologic format in the poem "In the Breach." "God! The I-killer, the me-death, rip me out! ... Caul-freed I cry!" The veil of self (the caul or amnion covering) is removed; the birth-cry is heard of the new-born in spiritual life. The answer to Nicodemus is thereby developed in full-length metaphor.

The author makes no claim to have reached great heights of perfection for himself. He beseeches God's healing grace. It is to the Omniscient Reader of souls that he pleads the choral refrain: "I too, O God, as you very well know, am guilty...." These words, from the poet's last selection in Hazards do not appear in context to be concerned with the simple relief obtained by freedom from the guilty "sorrows of the wicked" (Ps. 31:10). This clinging sadness that threads through many of Brother Antoninus' poems seems rather to be born out of the acute realization that the Christian soul, yearning for full union with God in heaven, for dissolution in Christ, must patiently bear the burden of the years that separate from this full consummation. Even within man's mortal span, however, a more perfect union is impeded by the treacherous imperfections within the human composite, the heritage of original sin. Hence the woe expressed in these lines:

> Let me forgive myself of my terrible sins
> That I may have peace ...
> Let me forgive myself
> That thought to be a saint
> And am proved to be a monster....

The groanings of the "Miserere" can be heard in the dim
background: "my sin is before me always" (Ps. 50:5). The
need for patient attendance upon the work of the Holy Spirit
within the soul is admittedly opposed by the aggressive dy-
namism of the natural forces which are still disordered in
their drives:

> What uselessness is housled in my loins,
> To drive, drive, the rampant pride of life,
> When what is needful is a hushed quiescence?
> . . . . .
> Draws off the needer from his never-ending need, diverts
> The seeker from the Sought.

The work of sanctification proceeds in God's chosen time.
The driving, active, male human attitude is impatient with
delay. It would cut and burn all imperfections now.* Thus,
guilt-laden inaccessible depths of the unconscious id and the
unshakeable memory of uncharted nerve plexi disturb our
interior ease with roiled up spectres of past defections:
"Which is a terrible thing, to know how wrong you have been,
and remains the strictest part of the torture" ("The Massacre
of the Holy Innocents," Crooked Lines, p. 53).

The author's last poems in Hazards propose the
searcher's return to the "city of man" and to the "ways of
man." This return however is not a rejection of the drive
for perfection. It is rather a new course that is proposed.
Perhaps it is something of a reconsideration of an earlier
theme in "Hospice of the Word":

> For in the crucible of revulsion
> Love is made whole. St. Francis
> Ran on gooseflesh towards the leper's sore:
> He saw his God.

This would seem to be consistent with a desire for the love
of God that concretizes itself in the effective love of neighbor.
It is the radiation of the love we should have for God, to
use a phrase of Father Garrigou-Lagrange.

Frequently these poems of Brother Antoninus have re-

---

*It is, however, only when the human combatant places his
strategy under divine regulation that ascetical practices and
great works offer hope of true victory in the demeaning war-
fare between higher and lower orders operating within man.

course to erotic allusions when describing the spiritual states of the soul. The final poem of Hazards seems to be marked by an almost total absence of fleshy metaphor. It is as though the "return to the ways of man" is the result of a "new insight into divine things." A section from The Three Ages of the Interior Life where Father Garrigou-Lagrange treats of the phenomenon of second conversion appears to recount a state that parallels the elevated tone and new direction of these terminal verses. His account of the second conversion that attends a fervent contrition is characterized by the coming of a greater grace to the soul. This greater grace may bring the soul to "a higher region of the spiritual life. The soul then receives a new insight into divine things and an impulse which it did not know before" (vol. II, p. 32).

As the reader finishes the lines of Brother Antoninus it would appear that he is reading a rendering of a new impulse, a new search. It is a search for good works to do in the "city of man"; to convert the sinner, to suffer humiliation, to show pity, to forgive wrongs, and out of self-giving to find true peace. The litany of resolutions favors Saint Teresa's description of the fraternal charity evidenced in the perfect, which flows from their total love of God. The perfect "love others far more, with a truer, more generous, and intense affection.... These souls are more ready to give than to receive ..." (Way of Perfection, c. vi).

Saint Ephraem, as mentioned above, was called "The Lyre of the Holy Spirit." The term would not seem to suit the cadence and mode of many of these poems of Brother Antoninus. A lyre, being composed of strings and intended to be played as a harp, implies something of a flowing, melodic stream of song. The Antoninian themes of violence and post-violence brooding in many lines seem to be located in the more percussive section of the religious orchestra. Sometimes his figures burst upon us with the clash of cymbals; for example, when he has a great mule-deer or elk crash leaping out of a forest into the fatal cataract. At times, confused, smoldering guilt feelings reverberate as though to the muffled echo of kettledrums. Frequently it is a plaintive woodwind that rises in lament or mournful psalm. In the final poem, on the other hand, something of the lyricism of rhapsodic dedication purifies and elevates the verse.

It is interesting to wonder what melodies will issue when Brother Antoninus writes for full orchestra. Will his imagery follow the direction of his thought from earth-based figures stuffed with aggressive, forceful motion to symbols

that soar with grace-transformed reality? Some expressions
of the author in depicting the relation of the soul to God
seem unusual and, indeed, too biologic to suit the supreme
excellence of divine things. This fact is explained by the
author himself in his poem, "Annul Me in My Manhood,"
wherein he writes:

And in that wrenched inversion caught
Draws off the needer from his never-ending need, diverts
The seeker from the Sought.

Mood and figure thus at times reflect the state of soul de-
scribed. Where disorder prevails some disturbance of har-
mony may well be expected. The state of soul herein de-
scribed is not that of the poet but that of the protagonist
portrayed in the poetic simile.

Beyond the image there would also be the question of
the theme for future works seemingly promised in the final
poem. The resolutions touching upon dedicated Christian
striving for spiritual perfection, for the service of others in
so far as they participate the image of God. One would ex-
pect perhaps the employment of more sublime metaphor to
convey the historic presence of the God of Revelation in the
world of human events. How translate divine charity, super-
natural humility, and all the panoply of Christ-like activities
to the modern fall-out conscious audience in these quasi-
apocalyptic days? Future out-pourings will prove whether
the quest for finer wine at the banquet of celestial song will
be fulfilled.   --Alfred Camillus Murphy, O. P.

****

Love's Uplifted Stroke

My two colleagues have discerningly discussed the psychology
and theology of Brother Antoninus. Man was examined; God
was contemplated. Now it seems that a connecting link,
however weak, must be forged between Antoninus the psychol-
ogist and Antoninus the theologian, for he is not content to
make a scientific study of Homo sapiens, nor does he pretend
to speculate about the attributes of God.

All I mean to say is that the poems of Antoninus are
the outpourings of his essential understanding and existential
expression of the living relationship between God and man.
This understanding and expression are not abstract and im-
personal; they are concrete and very personal.

Antoninus is a poet. As a poet, he is not fascinated by "a hypostatized aesthetic object," for his poems are representations of himself. His poems are flags of victory, monumental witnesses of his battle, veils which bear the imprint of the Savior's face. Reproductions that they are of his inner experiences, the poems are nevertheless integral, but only to the extent that the mysterious soul-workings of the poet are truly registered.

Man, in the working-out of his salvation, is confronted by his dogged self, the devil's attacks, and God's mysterious beauty. Therefore this salvific working-out embodies a triple encounter. These encounters can only be expressed by Antoninus in the on-rush of words, for that is his expressive way of satisfying himself and telling the world what self-discovery, exorcism, and sanctification mean. The poems are the mirror of himself, the signs of his relief from the exorcised demon, the witness of his faithfulness in engagement; they are the manifestation of every man in his struggle to meet God, to fight Satan, and to be himself.

Poetry must, in its very expressive quality (all other things being equal) first of all be a reflective image of its maker, and secondly, be so formed and shaped that it renders its meaning to other men. These two features correspond to T. S. Eliot's conception of the first two voices of poetry. Let me, then, indicate these two voices in Antoninus.

First, the poems must be looked on as they are the creatures, products, and expressions of this man called Antoninus, who must manifest himself in a certain way if his honesty and artistic integrity are to be maintained. Antoninus himself determines the structure of his poems, not solely by a free-will-act to produce this type of poem, but even more by an uncanny creative compulsion to say what has to be said.

Second, the poems are to be examined in their communicability to others and in the reaction they evoke from others.

First of all, let us look at the structure.

Order and Direction

Groping with the extremes of producing a work either for the sake of pure expression (so that the poem is really formless) or for the sake of absolute correctness (so that the poem is too-formed or rigid), Antoninus works for a coalescence of the two "... in which all relevant elements are synthesized into an indefinable whole." This indefinable totality cannot be perfect, for he cannot be. Yet the wholeness, despite any imperfection of part, is beautiful because there is <u>order</u> and <u>direction.</u>

The order and direction, although different in each poem, is the manifestation of movement toward God-discovery, struggle, and self-realization. In some poems, the motion is circular: the experience with life, self-discovery through grace, need for forgiveness, the return to innocence. For example, in "In Savage Wastes," the poet is tormented with guilt, making his penitential retreat in the desert until he is proved. Then he will go back to his people; he will look for the sinners so that he can show pity. He will return to his mother, to his father for a blessing, "... and again be made as a child."

That this poem has direction is plain, for it expresses the idea of return to innocence. The motion is circular, for in the Dream-Prologue to the poem, the old hermit who decides to leave his desert-solitude meets a young monk entering it. The old man sees himself in the young novice; he identifies himself with him and goes back into the world. The wilderness-retreat is like that of Job's. The poet has been "touched by God" and looks to others for pity--"at least you my friends." But there is no one there: no sound, no sight--except the bare encounter with himself and God. Unlike Job, he does not plead his innocence, but opens his address to God with these words:

I too, O God, as you very well know,
Am guilty.

This poem parallels and personalizes another poem, "Jacob and the Angel." Jacob the usurper must flee from Rebecca's fondness, from Isaac's frown, from Esau's anger. These three flights correspond to three angelic apparitions: the angels on the ladder, the angels at the Camps of God, and the angel of the wrestling-bout. With each angelic encounter Jacob is able to rid himself of a gnawing and false dependency; the final match brings him to self-awareness and courage. He is wounded, yet he is stronger. Renewed, he can meet his brother in "the siege of grace."

In "In Savage Wastes," Antoninus is Jacob, who can

go back after his wrestlings and complete the circuit to be born again. The beauty of order, the fulfillment of motion in man's life is thus captured by Antoninus.

Nature

Very conscious of order and perfection, Antoninus uses imagery and language as a craftsman. Rich cadences fall which capture nature in her pulsation and strength. As Francis attracted the forest birds to himself, so Antoninus is attracted to the winged creatures. It is the "small birds of a feather" who attend the Crucifixion, who are sent to watch until the end "after friend and foe had all alike gone over the hill." It is the "winged-spermed" birds who, with great precision, consume the carcass-remains of Paul's horse, the last link with the Apostle's former life.

In his canticle to Mary Magdalene, Antoninus, writing of Mary's love for Christ, heightens the description with a picture of the violent but clean thrust of the lance into Christ's side and with the figure of the love-flight of two eagles over Juda, forming "four wings, one cross."

In "A Canticle to the Waterbirds," he asks the birds of "... harsh and salt-encrusted beaks unmade for song [to] say a praise up to the Lord." Antoninus dubs these birds with a dignity which is not man's:

You keep seclusion where no man may go, giving Him praise;
Nor may a woman come to lift like your cleaving flight her
    clear contralto song
To honor the spindrift gifts of His soft abundance.
You sanctify His hermitage rocks where no holy priest may
    kneel to adore, nor holy nun assist;
And where his true communion-keepers are not enabled
    to enter.

Writers have for ages been stirred to capture the symbolic message of these mysterious fliers: the tragic heroine of Pagliacci is momentarily enthralled by the freedom of a flight of birds; the darkling thrush breaks the somber mood of Thomas Hardy, for the song of that bird had more "blessed hope" than he could ever summon up; the windhover's gliding-flight lifts Gerard Manley Hopkins' heart in ecstatic thoughts of Christ. Antoninus invokes these creatures to humble man, thinking his supremacy as absolute, to teach man much assured of his control of all things, and to say in their own necessary way what man cannot express in his freedom.

Violence

As if remembering Robinson Jeffers' line, "Violence has been the sire of all the world's values," Antoninus captures nature's violent upheaval to portray the upheaval and unrest in man's soul.

Although the concept of Christ as the Bread of Life in the sacrament of the Holy Eucharist is one of serenity and peace, Antoninus vividly portrays this reception of Christ in violently vibrant verse.

> ... I lay as one barren,
> As the barren doe lies on in the laurel ...
> As the eagle eats so I ate, as the hawk takes flesh
>   from his talon,
> As the mountain lion clings and kills, I clung and was
>   killed.

Christ makes His appearance in scenes of violence: the visage of a "great elk, caught midway between two scissoring logs" and of "the river, spent at last, beating driftwood up and down" give Christ a thundering entrance. Christ's birth in the soul is not a facile operation, but one of birthpangs, ocean-onrush, and body-gashes.

To sum up this point, let me say that Antoninus, like John Bunyan, is concerned with man the pilgrim reaching toward God. This progress involves awakening, experience, loss of innocence, gain of wisdom, encounter with grace, recovery of innocence, and return by way of retreat and wrestling to light. All this is conveyed in violent imagery. The image is expressed in words with hard celtic consonants, and Antoninus has an anglo-saxon hand at building up words, e.g., father-freed, hell-stench, heel-seized, which strike harder than they would if they read: "freed of father," "stench of hell," and "seized by the heel."

The Individual

The poems of Antoninus either comment on the life of Christ and the saints, or relate his own life. Thus he does not capture life on a photographic plate or imprison it within a frame, but he makes life pulsate with all his passionate and reasonable powers towards its fulfillment in God.

The course of life is predominantly described in terms

of the drama of the individual soul, the personal mystic enterprise:

> I cried to the Lord
> That the Lord might show me the thing I am.

It is the individual encounter with God which fills most of the poetic thoughts. For some reason, the Mystical Body, the Church, the Communion of all members with Christ their Head surprisingly is not sung about. In the "Waterbirds" it is the gulls and kingfishers which "sanctify His hermitage rocks," places "where his true communion-keepers are not enabled to enter." And it is true enough that God works His wonders with each singular man, and if Antoninus believes that every man is an island, he, at least in two poems, shows the concern of one sea-joined island for another. In "In Savage Wastes," the solitary retreatant will go back again to the city of man and "... will seek God henceforth in the shameful human face." In the "Hospice of the Word," the poet cries,

> O my brothers! ... At the grimed sink
> We fill the basin of our mutual use,
> Where our forty faces, rinsed daily,
> Leaves each its common trace.

All this gives one some indication of Antoninus' first voice. Let him speak for himself: "... The struggle with language is the struggle to make myself comprehensible to myself, to orient my inner and outer being."

But what of the readers and listeners? What must they expect from their self-comprehension and satisfaction of the poet? Certainly, they want to comprehend and to be satisfied as well. Since this expectation of the audience must be appreciated by the poet, he must labor to make his message penetrable; he must use his second voice to be heard by others. Let us, then, consider the message-impression.

All that has already been stated can very well be restated (and for that matter all that follows can be reinstated to fit that which has preceded), for the poet, although with different inflections and tonalities, says the same thing in his two voices. But for the sake of precision and conciseness, let me talk about the 'second voice' by way of the most predominant Antoninian motif--love.

How does a writer express love? A philosopher may

describe it as "velle alicui bonum"; a dramatist may set up
a balcony scene surrounded with "silver-sweet sounds"; a
poet may find the right word with "a many-splendored thing."
The poet Antoninus might ascribe to all these formulations,
but with his own special powers he sings about God's and
Man's love in terms which have very definite effects upon
the listener.

There's no doubt about it--Antoninus wants to proclaim
the wonderful ways of God's love. He cannot be content with
merely saying, "God's love is wonderful." He must use
words of wonder and images of fascination to tell it. He has
chosen the most venerable and hallowed vehicle of sexual
love to convey this mystery of God's love.

This should need no apology; yet for those of the un-
consciously "either-or" inclination and the "not-nice" frame
of mind, one is required, especially in the face of Antoninus'
writings. His imagery in fact is vivid and violent. I think
the reason can be found in what it images, the difficulty and
utter strain of loving God wholly--mind, soul, heart, and
strength.

Quoting a mystical adage, "The soul is feminine to
God," the speaker in "Annul in Me My Manhood" asks God
to transform totally his "bold possessive" masculinity into
a docile and maiden-like quiescence so that the mystical
union of God and man can be achieved. The man knows that
his "possessive instinct shoulders God aside." When he
says, "The use of sex is union,/ Union alone," he sees the
need for God's annulling in him all that prevents union with
God. As long as man is the impulsive pursuer, he is di-
verted and will remain forever needfully searching; man will
achieve the fulfillment of his love only when the lover is God.

The deep mystical-love union of Christ and Mary Mag-
dalene is richly and meaningfully unveiled through conjugal
love images, both in the symbolic image of the lance-thrust
into Christ's side and the beautiful picture of the love-flight
of eagles "on wakening wings." Mary goes forth from Gol-
gotha bearing "the stamp of a consummate chasteness."
There is no more vivid way of telling the world of the joy
and ecstasy of the "grappling of the soul in its God" than
through a heightened exposition of the natural forces of pas-
sion.

Antoninus sings to the Christ in the Holy Eucharist:

... On my tongue you were meek.
In my heart you were might. And thy word was the
    running of rain
That rinses October....
Thy word in my heart was the start of the buck that is
    sourced in the doe.

Again, a most intimate and loving gift of God is de-
scribed in terms of nature's generative act. The doe bears
the seal of the buck and she will guard in her womb his
sign; she waits, hidden, until she will give birth. The poet
too bears in his soul the seal of Christ and the poet will
treasure this secret and wait, hidden, until his time comes.

"The Song the Body Dreamed in the Spirit's Mad Be-
hest" opens with, "Call Him the Lover and call me the
Bride." The soul's utter incomprehension of its possession
of God through grace drives the imagination to evoke "...
the deepest resources of her sensuality, in order to achieve
in shamelessness the wholeness of being an age of shame
has rendered incomplete." Antoninus' imagination goes far
in that achievement. The plaintive and pastoral verses of
The Song of Songs swell into fierce and forceful lines in this
poem.

Some people have great difficulty in understanding why
God should choose to express His special love for human
beings in The Song of Songs by making use of poems of love
between man and woman. The occult contempt for the flesh
present in these people leads them to think less of God's
love for every man. This same difficulty will very well
arise in some upon reading "The Song the Body Dreamed,"
but the stumbling block becomes a menace only if they can-
not see further than the symbol. *

The portrayal of the siege of the soul by God leads
Antoninus in his "A Frost Lay White on California" to invert
God's activity as the Lover to His passivity as the Beloved.
God says, "I am your woman...." This love-reality of God
is so efficacious that its most poignant and delightful qualities
are best captured by the feminine image. Christ, it will be
recalled, calls himself "the Son of Man" but he also describes
himself as a hen, "gathering her chickens under her wings."

---

*For a development of this theme read The Third Revolution
by Dr. Karl Stern, and The Paradise Tree by Gerald Vann,
O. P.

Jahweh is both "a giant [who] shall go out to battle ... a warrior that stirs up his own rage...." and is also like "a woman in labor ..." (Isaias 42:13-14).

Antoninus has unburdened himself, and to use T. S. Eliot's concept, he has exorcised the demon within himself. The poet has not just thrown off before an audience some psychic material of his, but has transformed his inner conflicts in commanding, tough, and vibrating language. He uses terminology which at times runs counter to the traditional, and impresses an erotic imagery on the audience's imagination to drive home the grandeur of the personal contact God has with man. From out of the depths, into savage wastes, he has assimilated his days of serenity along straight paths and his nights of threat along crooked lines. The craft of the poet shows through when he can command the language to express the almost inexpressible. The song of the poet breaks through when he cannot make, in his powerlessness, the mysteries of life known in any other way.

--Albert Dosher, O. P.

POET FROM THE WEST

Thomas P. McDonnell. 1963

Perhaps the most telling aspect of the Beat Generation was
the revolution of the spoken word, restoring the poem from
the printed page to the poet's voice. Everson's emergence,
like that of Ginsberg, Snyder, Ferlinghetti, and McClure,
was so decisively effected by his public readings that this
collection would not be complete without inclusion of one of
the press notices which followed his appearances. Thomas
P. McDonnell's summary for Commonweal, March 29, 1963,
of Everson's first East Coast tour both captures the mood
and analyzes the aesthetics of the poet's extraordinary pre-
sentations.

> When this order of poetry reading
> is given by a poet of abundantly
> authentic gifts, it is not too pre-
> sumptuous to say that it is noth-
> ing less than a breakthrough from
> the poem as a platform recitation
> piece to the poem as the meaning-
> ful charismatic gesture in art that
> it was always meant to be.

Brother Antoninus' recent return to the east coast,
for visits to New York, Harvard and Yale, recalled the im-
pression I received from his first visit here last year when,
in a Jewish university on the eastern seaboard, Catholic po-
etry in the United States finally came of age. That Brandeis
University appearance was nothing less than the culmination
of an odyssey, which had started from St. Albert's Domini-
can House of Studies in California.

Actually, Brother Antoninus' first reading in New England occurred at Boston College on St. Valentine's night of 1962. It was on this night that one of the fiercest storms of the winter hit the Boston area, and though it was more than enough to hole me up in drifts on a side street, it did not keep Brother Antoninus from getting a standing ovation in Cushing Hall. Afterwards, however, Brother Antoninus suffered a fall (non-symbolic) which kept him on crutches for about a month.

At Harvard in an off-campus setting, Brother Antoninus' reading was given in the church hall of St. Paul's parish. Church halls have, of course, a generic identity which requires no further description beyond the usual disarray of collapsible chairs and the uniform obstruction of painted steel pipe uprights.

The poet entered the hall, declined the almost aloof stage behind him and stood before the audience at floor-level. His presence has not only a commanding quality but nearly an ominous one. Greater than average height and a seemingly stern countenance do not in themselves account for the immediately collective sense in the audience that a presence has been established. In the moments before speaking, it is as if he was gathering and ordering the resources of the psyche to the disciplines of art, that is, as these disciplines come to be involved in the genuine encounter between the poet and his audience.

At his off-Harvard Square appearance Brother Antoninus read chiefly from The Crooked Lines of God. "The Massacre of the Holy Innocents" was particularly effective, and from it he drew a most memorable discourse on the experience of reality through pain and human agony. It was this commentary, flowing naturally from the reality of the poem, which itself became woven back into the poetry of the actual moment--and this in a very literal sense.

Brother Antoninus spoke of pain and surcease. The siren of a prowl car sounded somewhere in the darkness outside. "There, you see," he said, "the night-cry, the summons to human agony in the streets of Cambridge." I do not think there were many there who disbelieved that a human life was truly in the balance. A few moments later the sound of a choir rehearsing in the upper church, almost ethereal in its connatural effects, drifted down to us. Surcease.

"Well, that's the way it is," the poet said very softly,

"and you can't fake it. " There were other instances of po-
etry made out of the actual moment: a dropped ashtray be-
came skulls as fragile as crystal, broken now all over the
world; knocking steam pipes became the taunting mockery of
devils for one's having revealed the pain of past life.

I later learned that this seizing of the moment--which
is itself perhaps an attempt to grasp the relevance of the
meaningful to the immediate, as well as evolving, creative
awareness--that this, too, occurred in a very pronounced
way at the Boston College reading. Indeed, Brother Antoninus
told me, the violence of the snowstorm both dispersed and
heightened the effects of what seemed to him one of the out-
standing readings of his experience.

The Boston University reading finally occasioned the
poem I had been waiting to hear--"A Canticle to the Christ
in the Holy Eucharist"--chiefly, I suppose, because I had
myself publicly described it as perhaps the finest "mystical"
poem yet written by an American poet. After the reading,
one noticed again the cluster of students that inevitably gathers
around the poet. The Salinger-syndrome embarrassment,
however, is lost in the simple fact of the cluster itself, stand-
ing there, as if reluctant to let the poet go his own way,
wherever it may lead him out of their lives.

This same rapport was immediately apparent at Har-
vard. But it was also clear that something quite different
was taking place, that this was not just another poet at the
lectern: poem, polite applause, repeat as scheduled, thank
you, good night. Rather, this was an organic experience in-
volving reality and poetry--perhaps of the poetry of reality.
Encounter. Yet there was something about it that I had not
myself fully clarified.

I arrived at Brandeis early, because I wanted to sit
as close as possible to the stage, since the volume of Brother
Antoninus' voice frequently drops to all but inaudible tones.
The strikingly effective Schwartz Hall began to fill steadily.
Despite the at first slightly disconcerting effect of so many
young students bearded in the beatnik mode, the general air
was charged with a genuine sense of communication and intel-
lectual curiosity. Even the affected dishevelment of dress,
here and there, did not detract from this. Of course, a
false emphasis has been placed upon the seeming relevance
of the beat to Brother Antoninus himself. Nevertheless, it
still remains true that all his sympathies are on the side of
the intuitively beat, whom in fact he does not hesitate to call
his spiritual brothers.

When the poet entered the hall, he immediately gained
that crystallization of attention which I had now witnessed for
the third time. "Well, now it begins again," he said. A
few students came quietly toward the front, sitting here and
there on the floor, and then at Brother Antoninus' invitation
a general exodus came forward from the rear hall and bal-
cony, one of the most intimate demonstrations I have ever
seen of the rapport between a poet and his immediate au-
dience.

His opening poem was the beautiful and powerful "A
Canticle to the Water Birds," the poem he invariably selects,
because it says at once so much about the art of his convic-
tions and the convictions of his art. He then went on to
read "The Song the Body Dreamed in the Spirit's Mad Be-
hest": "The Beheading of John the Baptist" and "Judith and
Holofernes," from The Hazards of Holiness. Occasionally,
the fulfillment of silence that followed each poem had nothing
to do with what might ordinarily be taken as an embarrassing
lack of applause. Yet I was still curious as to why a Brother
Antoninus appearance was so distinctly different from all
other poetry readings I had attended.

Then it came to me that, although assuredly not by
conscious design, Brother Antoninus had subsumed the method
of Bertolt Brecht's "epic" theater to the ritual of the poetry
reading. This he had done not so much through dramatic
presentation as in the encounter of dramatic awareness.

It would be fruitless to make excessive claims in this
matter, but elements of the "epic" mode are nonetheless
clearly present. They are seen in the rapidly shifting simul-
taneity of total involvement with momentary "alienation," and
especially in the astonishing relevancy of accidentals, out of
which the act of the poem is finally thrust. That is to say,
whatever spoken discourse follows from the poem--and this
again may be seen as the "epic" device of narration--it
evolves naturally from the act of the poem itself. When this
order of poetry reading is given by a poet of abundantly au-
thentic gifts, it is not too presumptuous to say that it is
nothing less than a breakthrough from the poem as a platform
recitation piece to the poem as the meaningful charismatic
gesture in art that it was always meant to be.

It was characteristic of Brother Antoninus, on that
first spring night at Brandeis, when the poetry of the Chris-
tian commitment in America reached a level of achievement

seldom approached, that he should have felt a sense of failure. I think that this is partly because he sees the offering of his poems as the ritual function in a cumulative gesture of love--a communion, no less, which obtains between the poet and listener.

This is, of course, an extraordinary burden to assume, and I do not know of any poet in the United States who has attempted to extend the reading of his poetry to that penultimate degree. It can readily be seen, therefore, that the ritualistic tensions attendant in such a commitment, might frequently leave the poet with a sense of unfulfillment. But always there is the great effort to achieve, however momentarily, the reality of the I-Thou encounter; and it is in the art of the poem that the effort is both subsumed and transmuted. In the art of Brother Antoninus the poem is not alone a terminal point in the artist's struggle, but a momentary liberation of the human spirit.

At the end there was sustained applause. As on other occasions, I saw the poet standing there as in both great gratitude and great loneliness. I knew that he longed very much to be where the Californian roots of his life strike deep, in that place where he now feels he most belongs. Then, the most disheveled of the disheveled, the archetypal beat student, made his way from the side amphitheater to the front of the stage, and he went up to Brother Antoninus, and they spoke to one another. The odyssey was over--and just beginning.

BROTHER ANTONINUS

Ralph J. Mills, Jr. 1965

By the mid-sixties, when Ralph J. Mills, Jr., published a
major study of twelve modern poets (Contemporary American
Poetry, Random House, 1965), Everson had gained sufficient
recognition to stand beside Robert Lowell without the raising
of eyebrows. Essentially Catholic in perspective, Mill's
chapter on Everson was nevertheless directed to the general
reading public, and is aesthetic and technical rather than
theological in scope.

> Words twist, surge, and lash out
> in his poems, or in other cases,
> they are formed into massive,
> hewn blocks. At times, Everson
> introduces unfamiliar words or
> coins them, not out of pedantry,
> nor with the idea of linguistic
> play we see in Wallace Stevens;
> instead he resembles an existen-
> tial philosopher, a Heidegger or
> a Sartre, who tries to wrest new
> and difficult meanings from his
> experience.

Catholic poetry, in the period of time this group of
studies attempts roughly to cover, originally saw its most
unique and accomplished practitioner in the person of Robert
Lowell. His first books, Land of Unlikeness and, particularly,
Lord Weary's Castle, revitalized orthodox religious verse in
this country, where one finds fewer poets committed to such
matters in their work than one does in England. With its
national church England continues to produce, even in an age

of diminishing faith and widespread agnosticism, poets who
write, and write well, from a firm core of Christian belief
and thought. America, on its side, has no persevering tra-
dition of orthodox Christian poetry, though a heterodox re-
ligious strain and a fierce moral sense are characteristic
of American literature. In the twentieth century various ex-
periments have been tried with religious poetry that involve
formal artistic innovation as well. T. S. Eliot epitomizes
this kind of experimentalist, but he has had no successful
imitators; and Lowell, as the separate discussion of him
will show, travels away from the apocalyptic religious vision
of his early poems to look more closely at human life con-
sidered in itself, within a completely historical and natural
context. Of the Catholic poets who arrived in the same gen-
eration as Lowell, or a later one, only a limited number
have made their Catholicism a central issue in their art or
have evolved a specifically religious vision of experience as
the distinctive source of poetic inspiration. Some of the best
of them--John Frederick Nims, Ned O'Gorman, John Logan,
Ernest Sandeen, Samuel Hazo--are identifiable as Catholics
on those occasions when they do bring their poems to bear
on the joys and vicissitudes of faith. The poems of Thomas
Merton, a Trappist monk, tend to be projected outward and
now chiefly to embrace, sometimes very forcefully and mov-
ingly, public and social dilemmas with their moral implica-
tions. By way of difference, the poetry of Brother Antoninus
builds its foundations in the problems and conditions of his
own life as an individual, both before and after his conver-
sion to the Catholic church.

Only a portion of Brother Antoninus' career as a
writer has been devoted to religious, specifically Catholic,
poetry. His earlier reputation was created under his actual
name of William Everson, and in examining this first part
of his work we shall call him by that name, which appears
on his books of those years. He made his debut with a small
pamphlet of poems, These Are the Ravens (1935), and this
secular half of his poetic career culminated in the represen-
tative volume of selected poems, The Residual Years (1948),
published in his thirty-sixth year. Everson was born in
Sacramento, California; his poetic vocation is undeniably as-
sociated with the Western states, where he has continued to
live, to hold a variety of jobs, and to write. There also,
for the past fifteen years, he has pursued his monastic vo-
cation. After sporadic studying and a period of employment
as a young man with the C. C. C. he returned to Fresno State
College in the autumn of 1934 and was introduced to Robinson

Jeffers' poetry, an encounter that signalled the beginning of his own poetic efforts. In a passage from a letter quoted by the publisher in his preface to These Are the Ravens, Everson says of his work:

> "I like to feel that these poems are, with two or three exceptions, inherently of Fresno County. Although it was never my purpose to write of Fresno County, and although most of these poems could have been written in any section of the country, nevertheless the luxuriant vineyards, the heavy orchards, the miles of desolate pasture-lands, and back of it all the tremendous mountains heaved against the east, hold for me an appeal that I hope has crept into my verse. "

Without any doubt this "appeal" is obvious in these early poems, and all to their advantage. In fact we should note here that many of the finest poems from both the secular and the religious parts of Everson's writing owe a great deal to their author's fondness for place and to his constant apprehension of what is involved in creation outside of man-- in other words, the existence of birds, animals, trees; of soil and rock; of the behavior of the elements. His startling sensitivity to the created world may suddenly intrude upon the imagery of poems not otherwise concerned with such things, and yet what intrudes will seem at once to authenticate and support the less tangible regions of experience the poet is investigating. Probably this lesson was learned from Jeffers, though there exist similarities in this technique to two other poets with whom Everson has some affinity, Walt Whitman and D. H. Lawrence, who frequently interrupt the abstract and speculative with the concrete and descriptive. The beginning pieces, already metrically loose, display a feeling for location, a responsiveness to nature, through the poet's occupation as a worker on the land. "Winter Plowing" is a lyrical evocation of his tasks and surroundings:

Before my feet the plowshare rolls the earth,
Up and over,
Splitting the loam with a soft, tearing sound.
Between the horses I can see the red blur of a far peach
    orchard,
Half obscured in drifting sheets of morning fog.
A score of blackbirds circles around me on shining wings.
They alight beside me and scramble almost under my feet
In search of upturned grubs.

The fragrance of the earth rises like a tule-pond mist,
Shrouding me in impalpable folds of sweet, cool smell,
Lulling my senses to the rhythm of the running plow,
The jingle of the harness,
And the thin cries of the gleaming, bent-winged birds.

Critics of Everson often speak of the presence of a
species of pantheism in his early work. While the regard
for earth, for the natural rhythms of life, or for the biolo-
gical cycle of birth, maturation, and death are especially
plain, there appears to be very little mysticism in the treat-
ment of these themes. That is to say, the poet does not
venerate the physical universe and its processes, or human
physical life and its processes, as if they were something
divine, but rather brings them into the midst of his poetic
vocabulary because they comprise the essential reality with
which he is involved and, at this point, indicate the extent
of the reality he knows and believes in. Poetry, for Everson,
should delineate his experience of this natural existence in
all of its required instinctive will and strength. The poet
has at his disposal for the artistic labor the spiritual energies
of consciousness, imagination, and conscience; thus a poem
turns into the occasion for an exchange between the spiritual
and the natural in himself. This exchange is maintained but
intensified in the later religious poems, where the spiritual
takes on the added force of the supernatural, of Divine grace
and command.

The dramatic tension arising from the interplay of
these powers, first in the poet and then in the poem, doubt-
less accounts for the forcefully articulated quality of speech
we meet everywhere in his writings. This poetic speech
bears considerable weight, a weight derived from the utmost
sincerity and a passionate desire for exactitude; Everson at-
tempts to grasp the ultimate truth his language may be capable
of yielding. But, we should understand, his motives on that
side are not primarily aesthetic; and so his poetic manner
is rough, sometimes even awkward or in poor taste. Words
twist, surge, and lash out in his poems or, in other cases,
they are formed into massive, hewn blocks. At times Ever-
son introduces unfamiliar words or coins them, not out of
pedantry, nor with the idea of linguistic play we see in Wal-
lace Stevens; instead he resembles an existentialist philosopher,
a Heidegger or Sartre, who tries to wrest new and difficult
meanings from his experience. In a poem entitled "The
Roots" from his third collection, The Masculine Dead (1942),
he contemplates the history of the English tongue from its

origins.   His attention fixes on the life that has given shape
and weight to the language through centuries, invested it with
untold emotions and significance.   As the poem unfolds, his
own relationship as a writer to that language becomes appar-
ent, and he finishes by defining his understanding of what a
poem's effect ought to be in the music of its words:

> And I, not English, in a level valley of the
>   last great west,
> Watch from a room in the solstice weather,
> And feel back of me trial and error,
> The blunt sounds forming,
> The importunate utterance of millions of men
> Surge up for my ears,
> The shape and color of all their awareness
> Sung for my mind in the gust of their words.
>
> A poem is alive, we take it with wonder,
> Hardly aware of the roots of compulsion
> Quickening the timbre of native sounds;
> The ancient passion called up to being,
> Slow and intense, haunting the rhythms of those
>   spoken words.

In the body of his own art Everson has given us what
he calls in this same poem "the core of existence caught on
the tongue," though we should add that it is his own existence
he puts into his work, the persistent, uninhibited investiga-
tion of himself as a man.   To be sure, such poems--and we
come across them in his religious as well as his secular
writings--are precursors, with many of Kenneth Rexroth's,
of the autobiographical tendencies prominent recently in the
poetry of Robert Lowell or Anne Sexton or Gary Snyder; but
there is an objectification of most of the admittedly personal
elements in Everson's verse that sets it apart from the confes-
sional bias of some later poets, and especially from the near-
ly hysterical ravings of a number of San Francisco Beat poets
with whom he was later--under the name of Brother Antoninus
--linked.   Then we must also acknowledge the fact that Ever-
son did not occupy a position from which to influence other
writers; he has always belonged to the company of writers
who had nothing to do with Metaphysical wit, Laforguean
irony, or with Symbolism and the use of mythology.   His is
a poetry of open statement, tortured and driven by the poet's
exhaustive probing of himself.

In the later poems from The Residual Years, Everson
includes a long sequence, "Chronicle of Division," which is

his most intimate piece of writing if we are thinking of personal or private detail. This sequence covers his marriage, the separation imposed on the couple by the poet's imprisonment as a conscientious objector during World War II, an attempted reunion following his release, and then a final separation. Painful, haunting, and absolutely authentic, these poems resemble a diary in which are recorded the torments and self-searchings, the brief moments of pleasure, the slow destruction of a relationship: in other words, they provide a lengthy account of the inner man attempting to create a balance with his external circumstances. Yet the poems are not apologies for their author but serve instead as the means by which Everson can take hold of his experience in all honesty and give it form. He does not depart from this aesthetic strategy in his religious poetry. In place of such subjects as his marriage and separation we discover in The Crooked Lines of God (1959) that he has taken his personal spiritual condition as material for poetry or that he seeks an equivalent for this condition in Biblical and religious story. The same may be said in general for his latest volume, The Hazards of Holiness (1962), where, in a "Foreword," he clarifies some of his views on the act of writing. "A poem," he says, "like a dream, is 'whole' to the extent that it registers the mystery of the psychic complex which produced it. My poem can never be 'perfect' because I cannot be. If I ever achieve a 'victory over language' it can only be partial, and only to the extent that I have achieved a 'victory over myself.'" Whatever we may think of this notion--which seems to me to identify mistakenly the formal aesthetic perfection of a poem with the difficult, improbable spiritual perfection of the poet's life--it states boldly the moral and therapeutic character of the creative process as Everson sees it. And so we are not surprised when aesthetic criteria are also rejected a little further on. "Thus," he continues, "I can say truthfully that I have no interest in the conquest of language, as understood by those who seek to achieve a hypostatized aesthetic object. The victories I seek, those of 'appeasement and absolution, and something very near to annihilation,' are one and all victories over myself, the unremitting attempt to exorcize the demon."

These convictions about the motives and processes of poetic creation have only recently been formulated; therefore they need adjustment in our minds when we consider the earlier, and secular, poems of William Everson with their emphasis on the biological nature of human existence, the compulsive sexuality, the loneliness and frustration of individual endeavor unrelieved by any religious hope. Those themes

echo throughout The Residual Years, and in the title poem of
The Masculine Dead, not later reprinted, they are strongly
combined. The speakers in the passage I shall quote are
"the masculine dead," men who, prematurely deprived of
life, lie underground like the dead of some Hardy or Housman
poem dreaming on their past and on earthly existence as a
whole. The device is highly artificial and purely poetical,
for we are not meant to assume that these souls of the dead
really survive in a spiritual realm by the will of a God.
Everson has not yet settled on his Christian outlook and the
position he takes here is fundamentally naturalistic. In the
stanzas below he summarizes the entire cycle of mortal life
as he envisages it during the first phase of his poetic career:

> And there rises before us the childhood moment
> When, staring out of wondering eyes,
> We saw the pattern open its folds,
> Show us the wide land lonely and broad between
>   the oceans,
> The little towns on the high plateaus,
> Making so tiny a light in the dark,
> We saw the forest of earth, and the long streets:
> We saw the wind in the frozen tomb of the north,
> And those tidal forces under the sea that alter the
>   future;
> And knew in the flare of that opening glimpse
> The sudden awareness of what we were.
>
> And it comes, it rises.
> We see ourselves in the good strength,
> Arrogant, loving our quick limbs and our wit,
> Ignorant, singing our bawdy songs,
> Shouting with pride and assurance in the plenty
>   of our health.
> Till over us crowded the load of darkness,
> Slipping like shadow across the sun.
> There was one long look of the turning sky,
> And our knees caved, the spring-tight nerves
> And the strained thews snapping and fraying,
> And we fell, urine burned on our legs,
> The broken lights and fragments of our dreams
> Raced on our eyes;
> Then only the night, shoreless,
> The sea without sound,
> Voiceless and soft.
>
> We lay for a time on the edges of death
> And watched the flesh slip into the earth.

We watched the eyes loosen their holds,
The brain that had hungered,
Known fury and pride,
Burned with lust and trembled with terror.
We saw our sex vanish, the passionate sperm,
All the future children of our loins
Be nothing, make mud,
A fertile place for the roots to plunder.
After a time the bones were chalk,
And the banded rings we wore on our fingers,
Corroded and green.

The distance from this vision of existence to the one
brought forward in the poems Everson began to write after
his conversion to Catholicism in 1949 is great in some re-
spects, and yet a decided continuity exists between the di-
lemmas posed by "Chronicle of Division," the ultimate pes-
simism of "The Masculine Dead," and their resolution in a
new way of life (fourteen months with the Catholic Worker
movement in 1950-51 and entrance into the Dominican Order
following that) and the poetry that grows out of it. None-
theless, we should not minimize the radical difference his
changed beliefs do make in his poetic themes and his human
concerns; if strains of somberness and of pain continue to
show themselves, they do so for altered reasons and against
an eternal rather than a temporal background.

The remarks quoted previously from The Hazards of
Holiness indicate that Brother Antoninus (as we shall here-
after call him in correspondence with his newer books and
his monastic vocation) does not aim at formal innovation or
aesthetic polish. In fact his poems frequently introduce ma-
terials that would seem to have outlived their poetic--which
is not to say theological or moral--value except in the hands
of an ambitious innovator and formalist. The materials I
refer to are Biblical story and incident, and the lives of the
saints. Yet Brother Antoninus has given them new poetic
spirit and force without sliding into the traps of banality and
cheap piety. The reason for his success is that behind the
retelling of familiar stories of the Wise Men and the shep-
herds, the birth of Jesus, the Flight in the Desert, the agony
of Gethsemane, and the Massacre of the Holy Innocents there
stands the poet's own inner or spiritual circumstance which
has, as he says, its peculiar relation to each of these stories
and the poems he has fashioned from them. This relation
can only become clear to us through a quality in the poems
themselves, for there we meet the same intense voice which

marks the earlier work speaking with an urgency, vividness, and singularity that give the stories a sudden life. Though certain of the poems articulate the sufferings and conflicts of a religious vocation devoutly obeyed, we still sense a deep and pervasive joy not present in The Residual Years.

Brother Antoninus writes poems that derive openly from his experience of the natural world as well as those dependent upon sacred history. In his love for the California coast and landscape there is no change except in perspective; he admires and marvels at the unspoiled life of creation, just as he did under the spell of Robinson Jeffers. But in a later poem such as "A Canticle to the Waterbirds," his new religious or supernatural perspective is surely alien to Jeffers'. This poem was "written for the Feast of Saint Francis of Assisi, 1950," and it is filled with the vitality and ecstasy we associate with Catholic visionary poets as different in other ways as Gerard Manley Hopkins, Paul Claudel, Edith Sitwell, and Ned O'Gorman, each of whom celebrates the particulars of God's creation:

Clack your beaks you cormorants and kittiwakes,
North on those rock-croppings finger-jutted into
     the rough Pacific surge;
You migratory terns and pipers who leave but the
     temporal clawtrack written on sandbars there
          of your presence;
Grebes and pelicans; you comber-picking scoters
     and you shorelong gulls;
All you keepers of the coastline north of here to
     the Mendocino beaches;
All you beyond upon the cliff-face thwarting the
     surf at Hecate Head;
Hovering the under-surge where the cold Columbia
     grapples at the bar;
North yet to the Sound, whose islands float like
     a sown flurry of chips upon the sea:
Break wide your harsh and salt-encrusted beaks
     unmade for song
And say a praise up to the Lord.

An awareness of nature as the actuality surrounding crucial events and actions in sacred history appears in those poems which treat aspects of the Christian story and also, according to the poet's prefatory notes in The Crooked Lines of God, obliquely reflect in their arrangement the developing stages of his own faith and monastic vocation. Natural detail is used in such a way as to create the impression of contemporaneousness in what is being described. In "The Flight in the Desert," for instance, the setting with which the poem starts is, strangely enough, some part of the American West; yet Brother Antoninus allows the figures of Mary, Joseph, and the infant Jesus to journey through this landscape without a hint of incongruity or falsity. The poem, in fact, gains substance and an atmosphere of reality from this unusual transposition:

The last settlement scraggled out with a barbed wire fence
And fell from sight. They crossed the coyote country:
Mesquite, sage, the bunchgrass knotted in patches;
And there the prairie dog yapped in the valley;
And on the high plateau the short-armed badger
Delved his clay. But beyond that desert,
Raw, unslakable, its perjured dominion wholly contained
In the sun's remorseless mandate, where the dim trail
Died ahead in the watery horizon: God knows where.

That is the first stanza. The poem progresses slowly, the long lines drawing each other on, reaches a section which portrays the fleeing family, and then proceeds to consider the effects suggested by the narrative. Once again the religious perspective reveals itself. Here the supernatural or Divine dimension of the story of the Flight, which contains its full meaning and importance, opens out beyond the human reality of the three travelers on their difficult journey and returns to it, for that, the poet seems to be telling us, is the manner of our understanding. The landscape of these later stanzas is still curiously modern and American, and the events that take place, like those involved in them, appear both to be historical and somehow to defeat history by coming to life over and over again and in different locations--or, it may be, everywhere and always. Brother Antoninus' other poems based on sacred story leave the same odd sensation.

But they, the man and the anxious woman,
Who stared pinch-eyed into the setting sun,
They went forward into its denseness
All apprehensive, and would many a time have turned
But for what they carried. That brought them on.
In the gritty blanket they bore the world's great risk,
And knew it; and kept it covered, near to the blind heart,
That hugs in a bad hour its sweetest need,
Possessed against the drawn night
That comes now, over the dead arroyos.
Cold and acrid and black.

This was the first of his goings forth into the wilderness
  of the world
There was much to follow: much of portent, much of
  dread.
But what was so meek then and so mere, so slight and
  Strengthless,
(Too tender, almost, to be touched)--what they nervously
  guarded
Guarded them. As we, each day, from the lifted chalice
That strengthless Bread the mildest tongue subsumes,
To be taken out in the blatant kingdom,
Where Herod sweats, and his deft henchmen
Riffle the tabloids--that keeps us.

Over the campfire the desert moon
Slivers the west, too chaste and cleanly
To mean hard luck. The man rattles the skillet
To take the raw edge off the silence;
The woman lifts up her heart; the Infant
Knuckles the generous breast, and feeds.

    Several poems in The Crooked Lines of God look to
the poet's private or inner experience rather than to the life
of Christ and the commemoration of saints as a fertile area
for imaginative concentration. "The Screed of the Flesh,"
"The Encounter," "A Penitential Psalm," "Hospice of the
Word," "A Canticle to the Christ in the Holy Eucharist,"
"Annul Me in My Manhood," and "Out of the Ash" focus on
a variety of spiritual problems in the poet himself. Some
of these poems, as well as a few addressed to saints, are
heavily indebted to what Brother Antoninus terms in his fore-
word "the erotic religious psychology of the Spanish Baroque,"
an overripe combination of sensuality and mysticism in which
the approach to God and the symbols of that approach are
boldly ambiguous. The better poems are, I believe, those
favoring austere renunciation and self-denial in a style that
is accordingly sparse and wiry. The erotic and baroque
poems appear heavy-handed and dull by contrast, bearing a
foreign element that remains alien and unassimilated. The
harsh, lacerating speech of such a poem as "Annul Me in
My Manhood," or of "Sleep-Tossed I Lie" (from The Hazards
of Holiness) proves the inappropriateness of the baroque
pieces:

        Sleep-tossed I lie,
        Midnight stemmed under,
        And the bloat moon
        Shut in its sky.

Lord, Lord of these tangled sheets!
My wrestling's witnesses
Certify my heat.

I have lain long, lain long,
Long in thy grasp am lain,
Lord of the midnight watchings,
The monk's tongue-shuttered groan
And the hermit's heart-ripped cry.

Somewhere the wanton lovers keep
Vigils of fecklessness,
Their hearts
Bursted on passion
And the body's blade
Plunged deep.
And in that death find sleep.

But I? Long have I lain,
Long lain, and in the longing
Fry.

Sleep-smooth this brow.
Bless with thy rippling breath
These anguish-awkward limbs.

Grant thy surcease.
Toy me no more, Lord.
Lord of the midnight wrestlings
Keep the peace!

This poem in its unabashed severity discloses the self-
scrutiny and the inward battles that generate some of the
best poems in Brother Antoninus' latest book. There is also
a very obvious infusion of violence in the new poetry, a vio-
lence the poet has defended in a "Dialogue on Holy Violence"
with Albert Fowler in the magazine Approach (Fall 1963), re-
marking that his religious experience has involved him in it,
and that he has consequently transferred it to his poems.
This defense seems to me perfectly legitimate in most cases,
though a few poems, and "The Hazards of Holiness" in par-
ticular, are pointlessly sadistic in detail. However, the
largest part of Brother Antoninus' recent work attempts to
objectify in word and image the poet's inner world where the
struggle for his faith is carried out. Internal division, the
endless demands imposed by the flesh, the desire for union
with God and the equally powerful instinct to escape Him,
self-assertion versus self-effacement: these are the themes
that inspire the most durable poems here. Biblical subjects
do appear a few times (in "Jacob and the Angel," "The Con-

version of St. Paul," and "The Hazards of Holiness"), but this vein was generally exhausted by the previous book and now has a slight air of irrelevance. The chief accomplishment in the most recent volume is not to be found in the longer poems, nor in a continued reliance on sacred story, but in those brief, taut poems--"I Am Long Weaned" is a good example--torn by suffering, self-doubt, and the pangs induced by true religious belief:

> I am long weaned.
>
> My mouth, puckered on gall,
> Sucks dry curd.
>
> My thoughts, those sterile watercourses
> Scarring a desert.
>
> My throat is lean meat.
> In my belly no substance is,
> Nor water moves.
>
> My gut goes down
> A straight drop to my groin.
>
> My cod is withered string,
> My seed, two fints in a sack.
>
> Some day, in some other place,
> Will come a rain;
> Will come water out of deep wells,
> Will come melons sweet from the vine.
>
> I will know God.
>
> Sophia, deep wisdom,
> The splendid unquenchable fount:
>
> Unbind those breasts.

These bare, tormented lines give full voice to Brother Antoninus' existence and to the faith he embraces; with the honesty characteristic of his poetry from its inception, he faces the realities in which he finds himself situated and those others, supernatural ones, which he hopes for and trusts in. His road as a Catholic poet has not been very easy, but his achievement must make us grateful that he chose it.

"SINGLE SOURCE": AN INTRODUCTION

Robert Duncan. 1966

When Everson's cumulative volume of poems, The Residual
Years, was published in 1948, the three earliest volumes
were heavily pruned by the poet's mentor, Kenneth Rexroth,
in order both to keep the volume within economical limits
and to mute the influence of Jeffers. Later, however, when
public acclaim threw interest back upon Everson's origins,
Oyez Press of Berkeley, California, reissued those first
three books in their entirety as Single Source. The occasion
enabled Robert Duncan, one of the poet's earliest associates,
to present in an introduction his retrospective impressions.

> By 1942 the character of Ever-
> son's poetry is set: all the ele-
> ments of his poetry--landscape,
> the war, his personal life--are
> drawn into the life of the psyche
> to form a drama he undergoes.
> He takes what revolts him, what
> apalls him, what terrifies him
> into his inner feelings, so that
> it becomes significant as some-
> thing happening inside.

Returning to these poems that were a source for me
in my own formative years in the early nineteen forties, I
am struck first by how solid a source they were. These
Are the Ravens, published in 1935, thirty years ago, and
San Joaquin (1939), have the austerity of single feeling and
single-mindedness and make in that simplicity for depth, as
we in our natural manhood are both simpler and deeper than
we are in the uneasy drama of our personality. The Everson

of this early work dwells in his animal being, a fellow of
the world in travail about him, having moods as the earth
has weathers and drawing self from an intense sympathy with
the self of the natural world. The growth of Everson's genius
is from this singleness of the youthful soul in its inner moods
and sympathies, awakening to identity in terms of seasons
and mountains, vineyards and tule fogs, the dripping rain
and the "scarlet smear" of a winter dawn, as he awakens
too to inherit a language of poetry and feeling in the single
source of Robinson Jeffers--from this singleness into the
duplicity and multiphasic experience of being a person in con-
troversy with his own nature. The earliest phase of Ever-
son's poetry has a consciousness that is not separated from
the world but taken in the world, so that in the title poem
of These Are the Ravens, the actual birds flying are "ravens
of my soul" and the poet exults in their nature as his own,
sending them "wavering down the sky," "Learning the slow
witchery of the wind." It was this deep sense of a participa-
tion in the world as soul that thrilled me in reading his work.
I realized that his vision came from a poetic conversion to
the world-view of Robinson Jeffers--not a literary influence,
but a conversion of spirit, as later, the poetic conversion to
the faith of Jeffers was to be succeeded by the religious con-
version to the faith of the Roman Catholic church.

By 1939 and 1940, when I, a young poet who would
not mature as an artist until the mid-nineteen fifties, first
read him, Everson was already a maturing poet. The first
signs of what was to be the ground of his poetry were at
work. The pagan unity of feeling is troubled, by the time
of his second book, San Joaquin, by the protestant voices of
self-accusation and yearning for release from man's sinful
condition. It is a protestantism that continues in the poetry
of his Roman Catholic conversion, for, as Brother Antoninus,
he is still torn by the antagonism between the natural man
and the ego that would take its self in a personality at war
with the natural man and that aspires to claim as its own
and only true one the purified body of the spiritual man.

In the early poem "I Know It as the Sorrow," he
takes his "ache," "weeping in the dark for no reason,"
"grief," "intolerable sorrow," to be his given inheritance in
the ancestral generations of experience. It is the feeling-
memory of nature in evolution, "deep in the bone, of the
flesh straining." He is still of the religion or life-vision of
his first conversion to Jeffers. The knowledge of "the bright
steel slashing the dusk" is absolute:

We have sprung from the loins of that mother, the past,
And got something but love from her dugs.

He sees man's making of war as a troublesome, a distressing
drive of his given species but not as a sin against his own
true nature; for man's true nature is identical in this early
period of Everson's work with his condition. But already,
in the poem "Love Song," where the gentleness of woman is
seen as confronted by the violence of man, something dif-
ferent from sorrow or grief appears, an anguish. I think
here there is forewarning of the anguish of Everson's develop-
ing sense of man's state, in which the gentleness of the wom-
an and the violence of the man are introjected as contending
elements of the psyche, and the violence of Man is no longer
true to him but a symptom of his deprivation and violation
of his true nature.

By trial, by suffering experience and by taking over
experience, incurring the burden of personality as an agony
of consciousness in adversity, yearning towards peace from
a war within that must increase his sense of the enormity
of actual wars without--the Second World War, that in 1939
already darkened our lives, for we saw that we were to live
as citizens in the adversity of the evil and false will of a
warring state--Everson entered the toils of a nature turned
against itself in order to force its conversion and redemp-
tion from itself. This is the drama of his poetry today, the
drama not of an eternal form presenting itself, but of man's
violation of and separation from the eternal--the drama that
lies at the heart of that Christianity that is centered in the
contest between the Adversary and the Redeemer. It is still
the heart of Brother Antoninus's intent today, and it appears
in its first statement in two poems included in this book from
as early as 1939 or 1940--"The Sides of a Mind" and the
title poem of The Masculine Dead.

Testing self to survive the overweening claim of per-
son, striving in the personal to twist the growth of person
towards an impossibility in which the simplicity once known
in the pagan unity of feeling with the world will be found
again but determined now only to be known in the death of
itself and the God-fire rebirth of salvation: this has been
the psyche-drama of William Everson into the poet William
Everson, then of the poet and person into the crucible-cruci-
fix of the man in Christ in which the identity of Brother An-
toninus must be refired. The beginnings of that psyche-
drama are presented in this book--a projection of the reality

of man's experience in terms of insatiable need to redeem itself, of painful self-immolation, of a sexual urgency violent in its revulsion from sensuality. Peace ceases to be "the poor dream," what pagans like Yeats or Jeffers must see it as, and is now the requirement of truth, which the Christian Everson-Antoninus still holds over himself, "as passionately as any," and man's making war is a continuation of the poet's acknowledged guilt in original sin. Yet, from the beginning, the poet had been fascinated by catastrophe, returning again and again to images of rape, murder, automobile wrecks, war.

In our period that is afraid or ashamed of mouthing its words then, Everson's poetry where a rhetoric that engages the reader in an active physical pleasure of alliterations and vowel shapings, sensual indulgences in the instrumentality of voicing, along with the pleasure to the ear of a fine music--such a poetry that combines knowingly oral as well as aural elements comes as a special thing.

But for the engaged reader of Everson-Brother Antoninus, the shaping of the poet and the person is the central thing. For these poems are the projection of a soul in trial. His spirit I hear in the music--and it seems a constant, a lasting resource in the poetry--returning again and again to lift, even in the midst of misery and pain, the poet into an ecstatic communion with the beautiful and the grand. But his soul, beginning already in These Are the Ravens and increasingly taking over in the following two books, San Joaquin (1939) and The Masculine Dead (1942) that are included in this volume of the early poems, his soul is in travail, suffering in the distortions and contortions of the person it projects. The poet writhes as if caught in the coils of his sexual needs, of his human lot. In tune with the cosmos, he is lacerated by the fact of man's cruelty, his brutality rather. By 1942 the character of Everson's poetry is set: all the elements of his poetry--landscape, the war, his personal life--are drawn into the life of the psyche to form a drama he undergoes. He takes what revolts him, what appalls him, what terrifies him into his inner feeling so that it becomes significant as something happening inside. So, the poet writhes with the writhing of men dying in automobile accidents, "the smell of misery and rot and the filth of the poor" is ingested to fill the soul with misery and the rot and filth, with the human condition. Later, as Brother Antoninus, in his Roman Catholic conversion to Christianity, he will fill himself with the labor of Mary or the agony of Christ so.

There will always come moments of sight. The Mas-
culine Dead in their litany tell us:

We saw the wind in the frozen womb of the north,
And those tidal forces under the sea that alter the future;
And knew in the flare of that opening glimpse
The sudden awareness of what we were.

In the drama of Everson's soul in travail, the drama of a
painful and insistent need, two poems in this volume, "The
Sides of a Mind" and "The Masculine Dead," are important
early statements or scenes. "But the theme! the theme!
Every motive I try/ The thin mind stooping above it searches
and tests ..." "A dry fury eating our lives," he feels.

BROTHER ANTONINUS: THE WORLD AS METAPHOR

William E. Stafford. 1967

It was not until the poet was in his mid-fifties that a non-Catholic critic undertook to appraise in an extended essay Everson's work as a whole. Written as an introduction to a selection of poems across the entire body of Everson's verse, The Achievement of Brother Antoninus (Scott, Foresman, 1967), William Stafford uses the poet's original anarcho-pacifism to bring his witness into focus. Also of note is Stafford's attempt to reclaim Everson from Rexroth's anti-academic platform.

> Those who have found this poetry
> realize its distinction. But it is
> not for everyone. For some, it
> is too disturbing. For all, how-
> ever, it is phenomenal, a refer-
> ence point of the modern sensi-
> bility.

Racked out in the spread of poetry to follow is one of the most notable, extreme, jagged figures of modern American poetry--the intense, religious, wholly committed persona of Brother Antoninus, and his earlier self, the aggressively secular anarchist rebel William Everson. Between these two selves, or aspects of one self, there hums a line of poems held closely along a sustained documentary sequence, portraying, overall, the slow turning of a character under duress.

> I speak from a cold heart.
> I cry out of a cold climate.
> I shake the head of a cold-encrusted man.
> I blow a blue breath.

74

I come from a cold place.
I cry out for another future.
--"The Blowing of the Seed"

The progression of the sequence is from the young man in-
fluenced by his farm background in the California valley:

You cannot shake it, the feeling of mountains, deep in the
    haze and over the cities,
The mass, the piled strength and tumultuous thunder of
    the peaks.
They are beyond us forever, in fog or storm or the flood
    of the sun, quiet and sure,
Back of this valley like an ancient dream in a man's mind,
That he cannot forget, nor hardly remember,
But it sleeps at the roots of his sight.
--"Walls"

Through early love and its recollection:

The bruise is not there,
Nor the bullying boy,
Nor the girl who gave him the bitter gift,
Under the haws in the hollow dark and the windless air;
But the rue remains,
The rue remains in the delicate echo of what was done;
And he who labors above the lines,
Leans to an ache as old almost
As the howl that shook him in his own birth,
And the heavy blow that beat him to breath
When the womb had widened.
--"The Answer"

Into the clash with the warring state:

And I vow not to wantonly ever take life ...
And seek to atone in my own soul
What was poured from my past.
--"The Vow"

Coming to adult love:

Under my hand your heart hits like a bird,
Hushed in the palms, a muffled flutter,
And all the instinct of its flight
Shut in its wings.
--"The Blowing of the Seed"

And into announced faith:

> The light woke in the windows.
> One by one the saints existed,
> The swords of their martyrdom healed in their hands.
> The linnet opened his voice;
> He blistered his throat in the seethe of that rapture.
> The suddenness split my skull.
> --"A Frost Lay White on California"

Pressures in the long development spring from the distinguishing issues of our time--World War II, the moral crises incident to war and the uprootings that go with it, the political turmoil felt by a whole alienated group, and the emotional revulsions of a conscientious and sensitive human being subjected to such pressures. And the solution or re-solution, or asserted prospect, hacked out in the poems is most abrupt, emphatic, and extreme. Finally, the unifying element is an announced faith, a religious commitment main-tained forcefully in the struggle and sweep of modern chal-lenges.

Those who have found this poetry realize its distinc-tion. But it is not for everyone. For some, it is too dis-turbing. For all, however, it is phenomenal, a reference point of the modern sensibility.

The poetry of Brother Antoninus confronts the reader with two main hazards, the first an immediate and obvious quality, and the second a more pervasive demand. The im-mediate quality is that of bleakness and insistent emotional involvement, lying at an extreme from prettiness, and even from recent, more generously updated conceptions of poetry's content. Modern poetry is no valentine, but Brother Anto-ninus has done more than leave off the lace:

> ... the great elk, caught midway between two scissoring logs,
> Arched belly-up and died, the snapped spine
> Half torn out of his peeled back, his hind legs
> Jerking that gasped convulsion, the kick of spasmed life,
> Paunch plowed open, purple entrails
> Disgorged from the basketwork ribs
> Erupting out, splashed sideways, wrapping him,
> Gouted in blood, flecked with the brittle sliver of bone.
> --"In All These Acts"

This passage is from a late, religious poem, and in the de-velopment of Brother Antoninus' work it seems that the more

intense his religious commitment becomes, the more violent
the content of his poetry. But even the earliest work has
this quality, as a glance at the sequence cited earlier will
show: "... howl that shook him ... heavy blow." Even
the linnet's song "blistered his throat."

This bleak aspect of the work impressed critics from
the first. Kenneth Rexroth, in an article which helped to
launch "the beat generation" into public notice ("San Fran-
cisco Letter," in the second issue of Evergreen Review),
calls William Everson "probably the most profoundly moving
and durable poet of the San Francisco Renaissance," and
continues: "His work has a gnarled, even tortured honesty,
a rugged unliterary diction, a relentless probing and search-
ing, which are not just engaging, but almost overwhelming."
And Rexroth goes on to say, "Anything less like the verse of
the fashionable literary quarterlies would be hard to imagine."
The implication is meant to be honorific: "rugged unliterary
diction," not like "the verse of the fashionable quarterlies."
But that implication, though understandable, is quite mislead-
ing. Rugged as the poems are, they are lavishly literary.

Consider the organization of sound in the following
passages. The striking words and pictures may pose as un-
literary but are in fact elaborate with repeated sounds and
varied, rhymed, slurred progressions:

> They came out of the sun with their guns geared,
> Saw the soft and easy shape of that island
> Laid on the sea,
> An unwakening woman,
> Its deep hollows and its flowing folds
> Veiled in the garland of its morning mists.
> --"The Raid"

> "No pride!" cried God, "kick me I come back!
> Spit on me I eat your spittle!
> I crawl on my belly!"
> --"A Frost Lay White on California"

It is clear that the immediate quality of bleakness and shock
looms here, but everything is tuned and heightened and artful,
even relentlessly artful. Consider the syllables and their
sounds, no matter where they come in the lines, no matter
how casually they seem to fall--the sun-gun-geared of the
first line, the saw-soft, easy-shape of the second line. Think
of the hovering erotic implication of the scene in "The Raid."
How could you find in any "fashionable quarterly" any verse

with more density of repetition than pride-cried-God-kick-come-back? The reader may trust his sense of something special in the language of these poems; they are both rugged and literary. The immediate quality of feeling, the shock, derives from something other than just rough words, and in order to identify the cause of the obvious bleakness and shock, we must cast back to the first statement made about the self, the persona, which is created out of contrasts.

One kind of poetry--and the poetry of Brother Antoninus is a distinguished example of it--flourishes because it expresses many impulses which practical, politic life coerces most of us to avoid. That is, many of our everyday actions and sayings we adjust to calculations about effects on others; we are purposeful and instrumental with language. But there is another way to live, a way to stay honest without staying silent; and the poetry of Brother Antoninus demonstrates this other way--it is a shock and a delight to break free into the heart's unmanaged impulses. All literature lives in one way or another with this freedom, but the Everson-Antoninus poetry lives openly--even flagrantly--by continual recourse to shock.

Brother Antoninus has committed his whole life to conduct and communication which maintain independence, a stance of accepting what the immediate being can find, and a readiness to reject anything else; he is a passionate romantic. As a radical in politics, as a conscientious objector in war, as a recklessly individual spokesman in his religion, Everson-Antoninus exemplifies to an extreme degree a quality which marks current literature--the exhilaration of rebellion. A reader must accept a certain view if he is to read such a writer sympathetically; he must relish how the literature stiff-arms the genteel, how the author delights in presenting abruptly topics often avoided. Brother Antoninus requires this kind of acceptance immediately and repeatedly.

The shock method is evident in the following passages, chosen from early and late work. Note that the passages do not necessarily prove anything unusual, nor do they have to consist of inherently shocking materials; but each one deliberately confronts the reader with a certain almost electric realization that the writer has shoved against commonly slurred-over or conventionalized human expectations. After an introductory poem, the selection in this text begins with the line: "These verses are lies." Immediately the writer has begun his attack on the reader's expectations. The following demonstrate the prevalence of this challenge as a way of writing; the author subjects his reader to a world that hurts:

When they rode that hawk-hearted Murietta
down in the western hills
They cut the head loose to prove the bounty....
--"Lines for the Last of a Gold Town"

He is a god who smiles blindly,
And hears nothing, and squats faun-mouthed
on the wheeling world....
--"Circumstance"

Churchill: the sound of your voice from the eastern air ...
Who listen beyond the hammering tongue
For the eloquent fallacy wound at its root
Are not to be wooed....
--"The Unkillable Knowledge"

These are typical passages. They demonstrate the punishing quality in the poems: the reader is to suffer while he receives something that promises an eventual, bitter, satisfying reward.

Bleak, rugged passages, though extreme in the work of Brother Antoninus, and hence an immediate hazard to some readers, do not constitute so much of a barrier as does his other main distinction, the more pervasive quality mentioned earlier. That quality is, bluntly put, didacticism. Brother Antoninus takes a conspicuously unfashionable stand on the issues of belief, assertion, and authority in literature. The results of his stand pervade his poems, which consequently baffle or estrange some readers.

We are accustomed today to accept for the duration of a literary experience all kinds of moral reversals, anti-universes, and ordinarily outrageous assumptions. We ride with the work, accepting the author's most emphatic statements temporarily, without yielding ourselves in any vital way to his assumed authority. We accept his tone as part of the literary experience, but we know that the writer cannot through personal authority coerce our belief. He can only provide us with experiences which we can value for their shimmer and excitement. The fine arts cannot impose; they have to appeal.

However, a generation ago, or longer, an author was a sage, sometimes almost a prophet, a model of some kind.

Brother Antoninus is in that tradition, and his poems take on a prophetic, oracular tone. What he presents, he presents as an insight, a truth, not merely as an exercise of the imagination. In his work his voice is direct; he does not turn aside to flirt with fancies and baffling temporary allegiances; there is no Emperor of Ice Cream in his poetry, no Raven saying "Nevermore" to enhance a temporary feeling chosen for literary exercise. Brother Antoninus sets up to be a thinker and guide, a statesman of letters. His stance is that of responsibility. "These verses are lies," yes; but only because they come from a limited intelligence and will, not because the writer is setting out to create passing sensations for the reader.

So the reader of Everson-Antoninus finds himself presented with metaphors intended as truth. The world that is asserted must be linked in its largest events and in its details with a belief that is asserted triumphantly, but then subjected to the terrors and horrors and weaknesses of our existence, and then asserted again. It is the vicissitudes of this faith, surviving in the modern world and in the particulars of the author's life, that have become more and more central in the work of Brother Antoninus.

Even his earlier work is tied to the soul's program of development: his poetry inducted him into his religion, and his religion shapes his poetry. The reader who is unwilling to accept that pattern, who is reluctant to suspend his disbelief in the significance of the particulars of the author's life as the author sees them, will be continually under a strain in reading the poetry; for it asks the reader's participation and makes the author's discoveries into the central rewards of the later poems:

> And I crawl.
> I will get there.
> Like a clubbed snake
> I hitch toward freedom.
> Out of this skin, this slough,
> Across these illusions,
> Upon this blood.
> --"The Face I Know"

In addition to the evidence in poem after poem that Brother Antoninus is using literature deliberately for purposes other than just the literary, the author himself, outside his poems, declares his objectives. He says in a letter about his work, "I strive for spiritual perfection and make the

striving the subject and the themes of my poetry." The Fore-
word to his 1962 collection, The Hazards of Holiness, elab-
orates:

> "This is not to say that I despise craftsmanship,
> but only that the struggle with language is the
> struggle to make myself comprehensible to my-
> self, to orient my inner and outer being....
> Thus I can truthfully say that I have no in-
> terest in the conquest of language, as under-
> stood by those who seek to achieve a hyposta-
> tized aesthetic object. The victories I seek,
> those of 'appeasement and absolution, and
> something very near to annihilation,' are one
> and all victories over myself, the unremitting
> attempt to exorcize the demon."

Important as the author's attitude is, and pervasive
as its effect is, in the work of Brother Antoninus, the dis-
claimer of literary ambition need not greatly change the
reader's approach. For Brother Antoninus--whatever his
explicit intention--is manifestly and even almost helplessly
poetic. He maintains creative momentum partly because he
continues to be surprised at his own religiousness; he con-
tinues to make the kind of visionary statement a discoverer
makes. The world says straight to him what it is supposed
to say, and for the reader it is the intensity, rather than
the validity, of the statements that counts. Almost to the
pitch of a Saint Francis, Brother Antoninus encounters the
intricate sermons of God acted out by the creatures around
us:

> Curlews, stilts and scissortails, beachcomber gulls,
> Wave-haunters, shore-keepers, rockhead-holders,
>   all cape-top vigilantes,
> Now give God praise.
> Send up the articulation of your throats
> And say His name.
>   --"A Canticle to the Water Birds"

The rugged shock effect of his writing and the per-
vasive didactic or moral tone are, then, the most distinctive
qualities in the poetry of Brother Antoninus; but two further
characteristics--both having to do with the distinctive content
of the poetry and both related to the struggle of the self
which runs through all the work--may distance for many
readers the poems in this text. One characteristic is the

extreme alienation modern war has forced on him, and the other is the decidedly personal focus of many of his poems relating to the breakup of a marriage.

In the content of his poetry, and in his life, Brother Antoninus demonstrates forcefully how intense, abrupt, and devastating to the soul modern war is. His distinction in this regard is somewhat blurred by a common supposition that war literature must come from participants, like Wilfred Owen, or Siegfried Sassoon, or Ernest Hemingway; but the young William Everson was even more of a casualty; he did not have even the relative immunity to war which is necessary for reluctant involvement; he did not survive the vision of mass destruction, and was a soul casualty. In common with Robinson Jeffers, who greatly influenced his topics and his style, William Everson saw modern war, from its first flare upon the imagination, as demanding that participants abdicate their humanness; he found himself a spokesman for a kind of being from whom modern warriors cannot be fashioned.

It is difficult to overstate the alienation this writer works from: he gives ordinary readers a view of the place of the absolutist, of the principled rebel. This is not to say that his stance is one of moral superiority; but he has taken the much-contemplated step of saying no to the state, and has been imprisoned for it. That passionate individuality referred to earlier resulted in long-suffering rebellion, in circumstances which continue to test individual values. It is unlikely that many readers even today can participate emotionally, without some qualms, in such a poem as "The Unkillable Knowledge" or, as expressed more simply, in this passage from "The Vow":

> I flinch in the guilt of what I am,
> Seeing the poised heap of this time
> Break like a wave.
> And I vow not to wantonly ever take life;
> Not in pleasure or sport,
> Nor in hate ...
> And seek to atone in my own soul
> What was poured from my past....

This pronounced alienation from the "national purpose" when the main group of citizens were mobilized for war has marked one section of our society, and the work of Brother Antoninus is in regard to pacifism probably the most representative of all that the "beat" poets of the San Francisco group have produced. After World War II the Bay Area in California became a center for many who had been uprooted and had come to know the attractions of the place. Brother Antoninus--then William Everson--had been a prisoner in isolated Civilian Public Service camps during the war years, and he had seen many of his friends taken away to prison. The society around him was alien enough to bring about in-group solidarity among the students, conscientious objectors, and political radicals who began to identify themselves and each other during the postwar years. That background of disaffection with a warring society is worth mention in order to point out that the literary renaissance in San Francisco, as well as later campus and political events of the Bay Area, stems partly from the kind of position exemplified by this poet.

The other markedly distinctive content in what follows comes mostly in the poems about the breaking up of a marriage. One whole section, "The Blowing of the Seed," provides a very ambitious working out of the complex relation between man and woman. They are mutually attracted; they can save each other by the welcome they give to each other's needs. But even that relation carries an implied danger, for all such relations are unstable balances--precarious and disturbing.

Earlier, the poet's "Chronicle of Division" (printed in part here) documents an estrangement between a man and a woman, and something more than a particular estrangement--the poem becomes a religious, psychological drama of attraction and repulsion, complicated by separation enforced by war. So intense are the feelings back of "Chronicle of Division" that some natural image can best serve as a quick indicator; it is convenient to glance at a poem like "Lava Bed" to see how the intensity of vision can reveal itself through the choice of scene and a bitter selecting of components to be held up to view:

Fisted, bitten by blizzards,
Flattened by wind and chewed by all weather
The lava bed lay.
Deer fashioned trails there but no man, ever;
And the fugitive cougars whelped in that lair.
Deep in its waste the buzzards went down to some
    innominate kill.
The sun fell in it,
And took the whole west down as it died.
Dense as the sea,

Entrenched in its years of unyielding rebuff,
It held to its own.
We looked in against anger,
Beholding that which our cunning had never subdued,
Our power indented,
And only our eyes had traversed.

In this poem a part of the world wonderfully suited for the
poet's most fundamental vision is simply held up and de-
scribed; in appearance, the world is delivering its own mean-
ing by existing in materials and patterns which speak drama-
tically of struggle, hardness, enduring rebellion. The world
is a hard bed, fisted, bitten, flattened, chewed; mankind
finds itself confronting that kind of Garden of Eden in the
poems of Brother Antoninus. Even when what the world of-
fers has appeal, the greater that appeal, the more poignant
its brief existence; and even a poem about childhood allows
a quick, strangely erotic glimpse, and then loss:

And what lumps in the throat is the music's magic,
Its exquisite trill
At the October fairs,
Where the painted horses
Bridled in gold,
Leap up, leap up in that lifeless lope,
With the little girls
Who shriek with joy
And shake out their ribboned hair ...
And the dream will go....
--"The Springing of the Blade"

This bleak view of love, and the forceful stand against
war, along with the rugged bluntness of the poems and their
uncompromising moral stance--all of these characteristics
become pyramided and intensified as Brother Antoninus forces
his poems to take upon themselves a big, coherent program--
he uses the writing of poetry as a way to master emergen-
cies in his own experience; he writes his way through crises
and undertakes to wrestle down the ills of our time by means
of what he encounters in his development as a poet. All of
the poet's encounters are made valid and valued parts of the
soul's venture through the world. In recognition of that large
purpose, the poems in this text are selected and ordered to
help the reader see three main steps in the content of the
writer's career. Moreover, it is content that Brother An-
toninus talks about when he considers his own work. But
before settling for a quick, clear pattern of content, we
should emphasize that this poet's technique, his characteris-
tic procedure in writing, also deserves attention.

The "rugged diction" and the shock tactics discussed
earlier are like the "personality" of this writer; but his
character remains for deeper discovery. Note that in the
largest, decisive maneuvers of his poems he exercises con-
tinuous firm control. He provides constant assurance for
the reader, who is guided unswervingly, even as the poem
gives the appearance of casual progression. The study of
a poem like "The Raid" will demonstrate this constant, as-
sertive control:

They came out of the sun undetected,
Who had lain in the thin ships
All night long on the cold ocean,
Watched Vega down, the Wain hover,
Drank in the weakening dawn their brew,
And sent the lumbering death-laden birds
Level along the decks.

They came out of the sun with their guns geared,
Saw the soft and easy shape of that island
Laid on the sea,
An unwakening woman,
Its deep hollows and its flowing folds
Veiled in the garlands of its morning mists.
Each of them held in his aching eyes the erotic image,
And then tipped down,
In the target's trance,
In the ageless instant of the long ascent,
And saw sweet chaos blossom below,
And felt in that flower the years release.

The perfect achievement.
They went back toward the sun crazy with joy,
Like wild birds weaving,
Drunkenly stunting;
Passed out over the edge of that injured island,
Sought rendezvous on the open sea
Where the ships would be waiting.

None were there.
Neither smoke nor smudge;
Neither spar nor splice nor rolling raft.
Only the wide waiting waste,
That each of them saw with intenser sight
Than he ever had spared it,
Who circled that spot,
The spent gauge caught in its final flutter,
And straggled down on their wavering wings
From the vast sky,

From the endless spaces,
Down at last for the low hover,
And the short quick quench of the sea.

    Consider the recurrences in sound and structure, the
funnel-shaped action, and the turn signals in this poem:

They came out of the sun undetected,
Who had lain in the thin ships

They came out of the sun with their guns geared....

The action is in a clear, explicit pattern: they came out ...
they came out ... and then tipped down ... they went back ...
at last.... The reader knows from the first that the poem
is sweeping along toward a definite, summarizable conclusion.
Further, the world of this poem is again the typical Antoninus
miracle of metaphorical rightness, with war, moral judgment,
the erotic images of nature, and final retribution for pre-
sumptuous man.

    Brother Antoninus' poems are not wandering and ex-
ploratory; they drive forward with an assured pattern loom-
ing throughout. Consider an early example, "On the Anni-
versary of the Versailles Peace, 1936." This example typi-
fies the poems; it links to social and political issues; it looks
rambling and baggy on the page; it is sustained by the pattern
of the natural background, the scene; it subjects the reader
to shocks of sensation:

Low is the light;
No red in the sky but a yellow stain;
And that killed snake the sierra all angles and humps
   on the filled east....

Alliteration recurs throughout this poem; the design is a pat-
tern almost as steady as in Old English verse, with balanced
alliterative assertions. And the world spreads itself before
the human actors as a delphic lesson:

There is no warring nor fury nor flame, but the hush
   and the balance;
And one watching can nearly accept with hope that gospel
   of love which was Christ's.

But the truce fails; the light spreads, hurling west,
And the sun bursts roaring from the rough hills,
Trampling up the sky, and is free.

Even the alternation between long and short lines adds
to the reader's sense of a controlled speaker in these poems.
For a time in his development Brother Antoninus shortened
his lines, to maximize the kind of come-to-the-end-and ...
drop-over effect continually available to the poet, but for the
most part he varied the lengths of the lines and thus attained
an extreme effect with abruptly bobbed utterances:

I call to mind that violent man who waded the North.
He imagined a slight,
Killed for it;
Made outlaw, lay in the echoing wastes;
Fled to far cities;
Knew dangerous about him the subtle strands of communication
Ticking his doom.

--"The Outlaw"

Many of his later poems fill the page from left to
right, unloading with detailed care the full reasoning of the
writer; but the intermittent short lines continue to mark the
style; and often that bobbed line of the early poems turns up
again as the ritual intonation of later religious poems:

Now give God praise.
Send up the articulation of your throats,
And say His name.
--"A Canticle to the Water Birds"

These stylistic distinctions will sustain a reader: the
language promises sure advancement through the structure,
and the pressured swerve of the lines carries on the assur-
ance.

A further enhancement--so frequent as to become by
anticipation a part of the reader's appetite--is intensity as
communicated by strains and displacements in the language.
For instance, often scenes or actions become illuminated
for the reader by a word or phrase which indicates immediate
technical involvement on the part of the speaker, a flashing
out with terms used by adepts--a crane waits to "gig" fish;
or a small bird, "the swart junket," "skits" in the thicket;
a river "cuts" its way to the sea. Events come into the
consciousness with immediacy, signaled in and accommodated
by a writer who feels his closeness to the action.

Sometimes this effect of closeness derives from forc-
ing the language to accept adjustments which appear to be
necessary because of emergencies in stating something felt

too distinctly for communication in ordinary language: a noun may be forced to become a verb, for instance. At times this procedure is like a mannerism, though it always creates an intensity:

> All gone, all broken,
> Smashed and smithereened....
> Speak from the bloodied past, the failured venture.
> --"The Blowing of the Seed"

The effect of this custom-made wording is to induce in the reader a realization of tension. The poems are never allowed to become inert, are never standard formulations. The effort of the self to attain its place, its soul's rescue, is reflected in the effort of the poems to attain the resolution intimated by their apparent strain. In effect, the poems act out, even in the details of their wording, the whole effort intimated from the first of this discussion, the progression of Everson to Antoninus, the evolution of the persona animating the successive poems.

Strangely, it is this very feeling of effort that has led some critics to assume that the fox is not cunning. Whether cunning is the right word or not, an examination of Brother Antoninus' work will certainly show that he treats the language with that same confidence and control which distinguishes the work of the most elaborately "literary" writer.

One other distinction in the style of this poet deserves recording here: he has carried all of his force and individuality into public readings; and again he qualifies as an important representative of the San Francisco group of poets in that he has helped to establish poetry reading in its current popularity, through many readings locally and in a number of trips across the country. His appearances are striking. He is tall, and though he appears to understate his posture, he is still tall. In the long robe of the Dominican, he dramatizes his stance. He adjusts to different audiences, apparently finding his manner as he goes along, but the effect is always that his poems appear to come from a need to communicate directly; in the reading as in the writing, a personal message dominates. His voice is piercing, a reed instrument. And he intones and invokes as he moves about the stage. He has confidence in his poems, and he is capable of putting the audience under a strain as they have to wait for him to begin. He challenges and taunts. He jolts and teases the audience. As he writes for purposes larger than the literary, so he reads with apparent intention of using poems for changing the lives of his hearers.

Directly using poems for the sake of his hearers, as part of his life applied to the immediate situation, is typical of the career of Brother Antoninus: he has carried from farm to camp to home to monastery the accumulation of his work and even the means to print it. As he himself was a printer and as his friends were often engaged in writing and publishing, and as they often considered their work to be independent, outside the mainstream, his bibliography has become very much tangled. His writing and publishing make an elaborate puzzle, with partial printings of certain large works, and with consequent gaps in the material he considers continuous. The selection presented herewith weaves as best it can with a range of work from the earliest to the latest in book publication; and the sequence draws into itself material not yet in book form. The acknowledgments page will enable a reader to trace some of the main strands of the bibliographical puzzle, but because the line of his development lends itself to certain simplified clarifications, it has been thought best to group the poems into the three imposed sections indicated in the Contents, and to offer a somewhat elaborated explanation here.

Each section marks a stage in chronology identified by a phrase which to a fair degree indicates a stage in the poet's development. In the later 1930's and into the 1940's, while the writer was farm worker, student, and then prisoner in a camp for conscientious objectors, he was writing what he has classed as poems of "the natural imagination," that is, poems which rely for their value on sense impressions as guides for the self. He was at this time much influenced by Robinson Jeffers. Though always alerted to overtones in natural experience, William Everson, before his change of religion and name, was not identified with any church. In fact, some of his poems from the conscientious-objector camps accurately depict a certain distance he maintained from the professedly religious objectors; in particular, the sequence called "Chronicle of Division" reveals that distance and some traces of rebellion against the program accepted by "conformers" in the camps:

> The newcomer marvels,
> Beholding about him wherever he enters,
> The direct head,
> The declarative face,
> That wears its look like an open hand.
>
> . . .
>
> Till time taught him less,

Revealing the brittle bias
The unseen error that makes human the saint. ...

His official listing in the directory of the camps identifies
him as a "farmer, poet, printer," and his religion is listed,
"none. "

      Overlapping the first period and extending into the
1950's, was a period here labeled that of "metaphysical
search. " This term merely serves to identify poems which
appear to move from confusion and discouragement and so-
cial indictment toward some achieved sense of direction.
This division is probably the most schematic and least valid,
chronologically, of the three divisions offered here for the
convenience of the reader. The difficulty of achieving help-
ful groupings is apparent from the date appended to "The
Vow," which ends this section. That date is 1940, but no
later poem more appropriately takes up into itself the scene,
the sense of direction, and the religious overtone later to
become predominant:

Delicate and soft,
The grass flows on the curling palms of my hands.
The gophers under the ground
Fashion their nests in the cool soil.
I lift up my eyes,
And they find the bearing that swings the sky,
And I turn toward home,
Who have gathered such strength as is mine.

      The last section, representing the current stage in
this poet's development, contains the Roman Catholic religious
poems. They celebrate, beyond the detailed suffering, a
security--a continuing struggle but in some respects a reso-
lution of the author's long struggle to achieve a coherent
self. The poems hammer a direct, religious view, and they
even approximate ritual patterns at times; but they do not
mark a complete change from the tone and technique of the
earlier work: the writer has brought his metaphors, and
his general sense of the world as a metaphor, into the frame
for repeated assertion of his Roman Catholic faith. He has
found it possible to view himself as one of the "crooked
lines" with which God writes straight.

"THE RESIDUAL YEARS": AN INTRODUCTION

Kenneth Rexroth. 1968

It was fitting that when Everson finally collected his pre-
Catholic poetry in the enlarged Residual Years (New Direc-
tions, 1968), he should ask Kenneth Rexroth to write the In-
troduction. It was Rexroth who stood behind that book from
the beginning, securing its publication, editing its earlier
portion, and writing its challenging jacket quote which threw
down the gauntlet before the New Critics. In this piece,
however, Everson's mentor is nostalgic and tender, content
to muse on the vindication of his discovery.

> Everson has been accused of self-
> dramatization. Justly. All of
> his poetry, that under the name
> of Brother Antoninus, too, is
> concerned with the drama of his
> own self, rising and falling along
> the sine curve of life, from com-
> edy to tragedy and back again,
> never quite going under, never
> quite escaping for good into tran-
> scendence.

It's long ago now, another epoch in the life of man-
kind, before the Second War, that I got a pamphlet of poems
from a press in a small California town--These Are the Ra-
vens--and then a handsome book from the Ward Ritchie Press
in Los Angeles--San Joaquin. They weren't much like the
poems being written in those days, either in New Masses,
Partisan Review or The Southern Review. They were native
poems, autochthonous in a way the fashionable poems of the
day could not manage. Being an autochthon of course is

something you don't manage, you are. It was not just the
subjects, the daily experience of a young man raising grapes
in the Great Valley of California, or the rhythms, which were
of the same organic pulse you find in Isaiah, or Blake's
prophecies, or Whitman, or Lawrence, or Sandburg at his
best, or Wallace Gould, or Robinson Jeffers. This, it seemed
to me, was a young fellow out to make himself unknown
and forgotten in literary circles. The age has turned round,
and the momentary reputations of that day are gone, and
William Everson, now Brother Antoninus, is very far from
being unknown and forgotten.

I say this, not in a spirit of literary controversy, but
to try to bring home to a time that accepts his idiom and
his sensibility, how unusual these poems were thirty years
ago. Everson has won through, and in a very real sense
this whole book--a new edition of his early poems--is a
record of that struggle. It is a journal of a singlehanded
war for a different definition of poetic integrity. There is
nothing abstract or impersonal about these poems. They are
not clockwork aesthetic objects, wound up to go off and up-
set the reader. T. S. Eliot and Paul Valéry told the young
of the last generation that that's what poems were, and the
young dutifully tried their best to make such infernal ma-
chines, never noticing that their masters never wrote that
way at all. Everson paid no attention. He cultivated and
irrigated and tied up the vines and went home in the sunset
and ate dinner and made love and wrote about how he felt
doing it and about the turning of the year, the intimate rites
of passage, and the rites of the season of a man and a wom-
an. He used the first person singular pronoun often, because
that, as far as he could see, was the central figure in the
cast of the only existential drama he knew. And what is
wrong with that? Nothing at all, the critics of the last gen-
eration to the contrary notwithstanding. It wasn't an alarm
clock that meditated in the marine cemetery or suffered in
the wasteland of London.

Everson has been accused of self-dramatization. Just-
ly. All of his poetry, that under the name of Brother An-
toninus, too, is concerned with the drama of his own self,
rising and falling along the sine curve of life, from comedy
to tragedy and back again, never quite going under, never
quite escaping for good into transcendence. This is a man
who sees his shadow projected on the sky, like Whymper
after the melodramatic achievement and the tragedy on the
Matterhorn. Everything is larger than life with a terrible
beauty and pain. Life isn't like that to some people and to

them these poems will seem too strong a wine. But of course life is like that. Night alone, storm over the cabin, the sleepless watcher whipsawed by past and future--life is like that, of course, just as a walk on the beach is like "Out of the Cradle Endlessly Rocking," or playing on the floor while mother played the piano is like Lawrence's "Piano." Hadn't you ever noticed?

Something terribly important and infinitely mysterious is happening. It is necessary to hold steady like Odysseus steering past the sirens, to that rudder called the integrity of the self or the ship will smash up in the trivial and the commonplace. This is what Everson's poetry is about--but then, sometimes less obviously, so is most other poetry worth its salt.

I don't think there is any question but that William Everson is one of the three or four most important poets of the now-notorious San Francisco school. Most of the people wished on the community by the press are in fact from New York and elsewhere. The thing that distinguishes Robert Duncan, Philip Lamantia, William Everson and their associates is that they are all religious poets. Their subjects are the varied guises of the trials of the soul and the achievement of illumination. Everson's poems are mystical poems, records of the struggle towards peace and illumination on the stairs of natural mysticism. Peace comes only in communion with nature or momentarily with a woman, and far off, the light is at the end of a tunnel. So this is an incomplete autobiography--as whose isn't?

How deeply personal these poems are, and how convincingly you touch the living man through them. I have read them for years. Brother Antoninus is one of my oldest and best friends and the godfather of my daughters. As I turn over the pages, some of them thirty years old, I feel again, as always, a comradeship strong as blood. Evil men may have degraded those words, but they are still true and apposite for the real thing. Blood brotherhood.

THE REBEL'S METAPHYSIC OF EXISTENCE

Ronald F. Webster. 1969

William Stafford delineated Everson as the highly motivated
protestor against the claims of the status quo, directing his
passion and his craft in a prolonged effort of counter-affirma-
tion that is essentially a denial of the conventional world.
In his 1969 master's thesis at Gonzaga University, "Mimesis
of the Absolute: The Revolt of Brother Antoninus," Ronald
Webster takes Camus' The Rebel as a bearing-off point of
modern sensibility and measures the revolt of Everson against
it. The essay that follows reproduces chapter four of the
thesis.

> The soul's center of affinity is
> its own world of subjective con-
> sciousness, its own interior
> wasteland with no boundaries,
> wherein the ravages of evil rise
> and struggle against the will and
> the heart, trying to find God.

Camus never attempts to reduce the word "metaphysi-
cal" to a simplistic definition. It is understandable that if
he had subscribed to a dictionary definition, he would have
had little need to write The Rebel. But for Camus meta-
physical reality in its fundamental structure is more than the
relationship of one being to another: it is an unequivocal
relationship of rebel to rebel. This relational stance reveals
the philosophical methodology of Camus. Though the rebel
Baudelaire is not the rebel Nietzsche, both are authentic
metaphysical rebels; both delineate their own metaphysical
world view. This methodology is Camus' means of interpret-
ing the notion of existence as well as metaphysics; yet under-

standing why both Baudelaire and Nietzsche are authentic
metaphysical rebels, while individually they manifest obvious
differences, is not so difficult if the problem is approached
in the light of Jacques Maritain's ideas of existence and the
existent.

Maritain's analysis of subjectivity formulates an im-
portant notion which Camus does not explicitly deal with in
his study of metaphysical rebellion. Though Camus enumer-
ates a multiplicity of authentic metaphysical rebels, he does
not specify a normative principle by which their authenticity
can be at once highly particular as well as universal in sub-
jective expression. But Maritain's analysis of subjectivity
is a useful context for understanding why metaphysical revolt
becomes authentic in terms of the rebel's own experiential
ideal. If the nature of metaphysical revolt is decided in
terms of subjective, individual consciousness about varying
value systems, then the empirical ideal of metaphysical
revolt according to Albert Camus stands beyond the empirical
moral system of metaphysical revolt that another experiences.
This is true because each rebel is at the center of his own
infinity. Maritain says:

> "By sense or experience, science or philosophy,
> each of us, as I said a moment ago, knows the
> environing world of subjects, supposita, and
> persons in their role as objects. The paradox
> of consciousness and personality is that each of
> us is situated precisely at the center of this
> world. Each is at the center of infinity."[1]

What Maritain clarifies is that subjective consciousness gives
the spirit an identity from which emanates an inexhaustible
variation of knowing and experiencing reality. No matter
how much alike two subjects may be, then, their subjective
consciousness remains autonomous in an absolute sense.
This Maritain principle is a philosophical tool for under-
standing why Camus has no trouble in equating Nietzsche,
Baudelaire, Rimbaud and Lautreamont as metaphysical rebels,
though individually each symbolized a form of rebellion not
imitable beyond the phenomenon of revolt "motivated by the
concept of complete unity."

At the core of subjective consciousness (this limitless
variable of experience exemplifies what Maritain means by
infinity) Brother Antoninus experiences metaphysical rebellion
just as authentically as Nietzsche, Baudelaire, Rimbaud and
Lautreamont. Because Brother Antoninus is bound to revolt

"motivated by the concept of complete unity," his form of
rebellion is consistent with the same principle guiding the
others. Yet Antoninus succeeds in discovering what he seeks
in revolt at the point where they refuse to search. Though
the nature of both forms of rebellion places Antoninus at the
furthest possible pole from them, a common denominator
still exists between the factions: subjective consciousness
as the principle of unity motivating their rebellion.

This common denomination clarifies the "Love and
Violence" unit of The Hazards of Holiness in that Brother
Antoninus' poems can be experienced as symbolic infinities,
autonomous worlds of subjective consciousness. And the
form of expression that is subjective consciousness exists
not only as the whole poem per se but as the man within
the poem. The moral revolt of John the Baptist against
Herod and the moral revolt of Judith against Holofernes are
metaphysical rebellions whose subjective consciousness vali-
dates the believer's choice of God, while on the other hand
Rimbaud's subjective consciousness of a principle of unity
(extolment of evil) validates the agnostic's choice of a sea-
son in hell.

Brother Antoninus' poem "The Conversion of Saint
Paul" also recapitulates the symbol of revolt as a metaphy-
sical reality experienced in the form of subjective conscious-
ness; in Saint Paul's conscience, rejection of the supreme
outrage takes the form of accepting Christ as a redeemer.
Yet Brother Antoninus enters this metaphysical reality on an
empirical level when he thinks of himself as being a soul on
the road to Damascus out in the savage wastes. Saint Paul's
conversion becomes in essence Antoninus' form of subjective
consciousness whose autonomy, in his own confrontation with
Christ, is absolute. Precisely because this experience at
the deepest core of his soul is unique, his experience alone,
it becomes symbolic of God's being, Infinity. This personal
experience of subjective consciousness Maritain clarifies in
his interpretation of what his interior world is: "With regard
to my subjectivity in act, I am the center of the world ('the
most important person on the world'). My destiny is the
most important of all destinies. Worthless as I know myself
to be, I am more interesting than all the saints."[2] This
empirical view of reality explains why as a subject, isolated
in his own center of infinity (the core of the soul), the rebel
is able to judge the limits of his own form of rebellion.

The metaphysical rebel's form of rebellion is absolute
in the sense that it is altogether personal. Antoninus' sub-

jective consciousness to his inner world, then, creates the
conscience by which he judges his responsibility to the prin-
ciple of unity. He says:

> ... [I] thought myself to be the Christ
> And am found the Devil.

Antoninus' theological misunderstanding about his iden-
tity creates the lacuna of subjective consciousness where he
discovers the fullest extent of his rebellion: that he had in
fact extolled evil just as the romantic rebel Karamazov had
diabolically extolled it. This admission of guilt is the seed
out of which springs an absolute affirmation of belief:

> ... [I] will find my God in the thwarted love
> That breaks between us....

And it is important to see that Brother Antoninus' refusal of
this spiritual death by thwarted love exists in terms of spatial
proportions analogous to T. S. Eliot's wasteland concept.

The soul's center of infinity is its own world of sub-
jective consciousness, its own interior wasteland with no
boundaries, wherein the ravages of evil rise and struggle
against the will and the heart, trying to find God:

> And the desert gorges, those hacked
> Untendered waste-worlds of the soul--
> What buzzard's eye from its sun-skewered height
> Has peered such places,
> Pierced such deeps?

Brother Antoninus suggests that the soul's identity, bound to
a wasteland, is more than archetypally fulfilled in God when
it admits that its own waste-worlds need the purgation of di-
vine grace; but seeking the unity of God the spirit recognizes
at the same time that it is metaphysically limited; at its
core the spirit understands what the terror of an authentic
wasteland is so long as God cannot be found:

> In terror,
> Who gazed in the poisonous pool,
> In dread,
> Who sucked of its jet.
> Am sick and am sick
> Who have seen to myself,
> Begging forgiveness of my own self
> In what I have done.

Brother Antoninus exposes the spirit's intuitive recognition
that it is warring at the center of its own wasteland, a war
in which the soul's struggle for God is a mimesis of Milton's
Paradise Lost theme. Like Paradise Lost "In Savage Wastes"
assumes the epic proportions of what occurred between Adam
and Satan; but in realizing that spiritual existence is pitted
against the unprecedented thrust of man's fallen nature, draw-
ing him down into the darkness of hell, Brother Antoninus
exposes the rebel's psychology of learning to love God:

> For if You, O God, can pardon a man,
> Should himself be less merciful?
>
> Let me forgive myself of my terrible sins
> That I may have peace.

Accepting the peace of God, allowing God to forgive are
Brother Antoninus' form of unifying what was the chaos of
a deficient faith in God's infinite mercy; this leap of faith
is a symbolic referent through which Brother Antoninus not
only attacks unbelief, but also opposes his won identity against
an unjust master.

As rebel, he assimilates what exists in the subjective
consciousness of God. And this is not an absurd act on his
part when the metaphysical revolt of Saint John the Baptist
is no more than the expression of God's absolute commitment
to man's redemption by the sacrifice of self through death.
Brother Antoninus seeks to make clear his commitment to
this spirit of metaphysical revolt by revealing the terror of
the unjust master trying to kill man's soul in his pursuit of
pure Justice. Antoninus expresses this paradox in the im-
agery of Apollinaire:

>   "Give me the head
> Of John the Baptist!" cried the violent girl,
> Her eyes like an eaglet's blazing behind her
>   unbrooched hair,
> Mouth insolent with wine, throat panting
> Those covetous gouts that howk toward murder,
> The dauntless breast beating that oath up
>   out of her blood,
> Her sovereign demand. "On a plate! On a plate!"
> She turned, imperious, her legs spread like
>   a man's,
> One naked arm distended, the savage bracelets
> Aclash on her wrist.

What Brother Antoninus observes of Salome becomes the
spiritual symbol of his interior war, only to be evoked more
clearly in the accusation that Saint John the Baptist's decap-
itated head symbolizes against her sins of lust and hate:

> On a plate, held high, tilted to the arrogant
>   zest of life,
> The great face of the innocent rides somberly in,
> Black-mouthed, a terrible hole of condemnation
>   cracked in the jaw,
> Rebuking the confrontation of ecstasy and sin,
> The dangerous edge teetering yet in those
>   coinless eyes.

Where does Brother Antoninus' experience, as an objective
correlative underlying metaphysical revolt, define the empiri-
cal center of infinity in this poem? Its center of infinity
lies at the core of the moral judgment which he directs to
Herod and Salome; they become spiritual mediums through
which he directs his prayer towards gaining inner conscious-
ness, perception of metaphysical value. The cleavage be-
tween their two worlds is the archetypal center of infinity
representing the soul's spiritual wasteland--its war between
good and evil.

In the sense that Brother Antoninus recognizes the
existence of this wasteland at the core of his inner life, he
has theologically premised a reason for spiritual conversion.
But this conversion is one which promises the trial of travel-
ing through an Unreal City before it promises the light and
peace of God:

> For the light is lost.
> Great darknesses drop over the waste.
> The hostile stars burn green as cat's eyes
> In their depth of dread.
> There is not an owl on the greasewood,
> There is not a saw-whet on the creosote bush
> To keep a man company.

Yet seeking a moral explanation for what has occurred in
the Unreal City, Brother Antoninus admits the cause of this
spiritual rupture; such an admission makes real the power of
sincerity before God as a spiritual source of illumination;
now the rebel can see his own metaphysical value before God:

> I too, O God, as You very well know,
> Am guilty.

> For I sought and found not,
> I searched, but was not successful.
> When I failed, You drew back the veil,
> And I am in terror.

Confessing the terror of having revolted against the goodness of God, and affirming too that he had sought God so that this ruptured order might be realigned, he considers that the only means of achieving authenticity is to do what Christ had already done:

> For I will make friends of the sinner
> And comfort him in his plight.
> I will pick the evildoer up from the ground
> That he may take heart from his evil
> And hunger the good.

That Christ is central to this spirit of compassion makes meaningful what Martin Heidegger affirms in An Introduction to Metaphysics as a clarification of Maritain's thesis about the metaphysic of subjective consciousness; for the Christian subjective consciousness is an empirical fusion of man's spirit to God's.

According to Heidegger, when the psyche truly becomes itself it no longer needs to reflect upon what it appears to be but merely upon what it inexorably is. That Brother Antoninus is a metaphysical link between Maritain and Heidegger encompasses an interpretative referent through which one can understand his view of reality as an assent of becoming and being, rather than an archetype of Heidegger's term appearance. "In All These Acts" Brother Antoninus synthesizes, as if it were some Parmenidean image, the unity existing in the flux of creation, in the multiplicity of events, for he asserts that at the metaphysical core of all reality exists Christ:

> In all these acts
> Christ crouches and seethes, pitched forward
> On the crucifying stroke, juvescent, that will
>   spring Him
> Out of the germ, out of the belly of the dying buck,
> Out of the father-phallus and the torn-up root.
> These are the modes of His forth-showing,
> His serene agonization. In the clicking teeth
>   of otters
> Over and over He dies and is born,
> Shaping the weasel's jaw in His leap
> And the staggering rush of the bass.

That Brother Antoninus portrays the rebel spirit of God's order in the form of earth's evolutionary gestation and growth allies him with the anthropological system of Teilhard de Chardin, for Chardin visualizes the work of God as existing at the core of all material change, waging war against the forces opposed to Omega.

But the metaphysical significance of Brother Antoninus' view of earth's metaphor of birth is that Christ is at the core of this reality, the absolute Affirmation in whom the rebel discovers his identity. Understanding through faith that the work of God is itself the revolution of absolute justice, he is able to argue the cosmic value of his revolt against all that contradicts God's divine truth. Metaphysically, he is able to revolt because he has synthesized through his recognition of God's ontological good a reason for knowing that this God rebels against Satan's forces which oppress man's spiritual consciousness reaching out towards truth.

Notes

1   Jacques Maritain, Existence and the Existent (New York: Image Books, 1956), p75.

2   Ibid. , p84.

THE LOVE POET

Harry James Cargas. 1969

By the mid 1960s the shock of Everson's identification with
the Beat Generation had resided, and he was being accepted
in poetry circles as a powerful new voice. But the publica-
tion of The Rose of Solitude in 1967 put him before a broader
public in a new and sensational light: that book's narration
of the love affair of a monk was avowedly autobiographical.
In several interviews the poet sought to provide perspective
by reference to the theme of erotic mysticism. Here Harry
James Cargas, a commentator then with St. Louis University,
translates the poet's views for Marriage and Family Living
(February 1969), a Catholic family magazine out of St. Mein-
rad, Indiana. It appears here in a slightly revised form.

> In my life the love of God has
> been so intensely bound up with
> the love of woman that in a way,
> it's always been through a wom-
> an's hands that I discovered God
> at ever deepening levels.

The male albatross, we are told, has a peculiar rit-
ual while courting. He makes himself completely vulnerable
to his partner as a show of his trust. There is a lesson to
be learned here by those of us who are too frightened to
bare our true selves to those we love. As one psychiatrist
put it, "Only those human beings who bring their deepest,
inmost reality to love can have any experience of its true
joy and fulfillment. This truth is often forgotten by those
modern young people who think that they know all about love
because they have had a fine salad of erotic experience.
Actually, what they cynically call their realism is only a

cloak for a complete ignorance of everything below the sur-
face. They have been too greedy for pleasure, too unwilling
to face pain...."

One writer who understands the pain of giving oneself
in a love relationship is, surprisingly to some, a religious,
Brother Antoninus. This Dominican is frequently identified
as a beatnik poet. Traditionally, other men of the cloth have
written poetry about married love. Perhaps the best known
is the seventeenth-century British Anglican priest, John Donne
who felt that the body is the book by which love's mysteries
are revealed. (Donne, of the "Metaphysical School" of poets
was humorous as well as profound. One poem begins "For
Godsake hold your tongue, and let me love.")

An American poet and preacher, Edward Taylor, who
bridged the seventeenth and eighteenth centuries, endeavored
to show in a love letter to his future wife how conjugal love
represents "that which is betwixt Christ and his church."

Of course all such Christian love poetry has its bib-
lical source and that is in The Song of Songs from the He-
brew Testament. What can only be described as the lush
primitive imagery is seen as extremely rich and obviously
inspiring to other writers such as St. John of the Cross whose
Dark Night of the Soul has been called the culmination of
baroque erotic mysticism. One is reminded too of Richard
Crashaw, the English Catholic baroque poet and Henry Vaughan
as well, who died in 1695.

But few good poets, religious or lay, contemporary or
past, use sensuous language or imagery as Antoninus does.
He frankly admits that the somewhat notorious novels, Lady
Chatterley's Lover (D. H. Lawrence) and Tropic of Cancer
(Henry Miller) "were the crystalizing force in my pre-Catho-
lic formation." With this in mind, readers may better under-
stand his writings which shock so many. In "A Canticle of
the Great Mother of God" the line: "Pale opals on the move-
ment of your breasts, or your womb" has raised eyebrows.
Some object to "Her limbs! Her limbs! the witchery of her
excellent legs," while more question the propriety of

> I held it against my raddled groin
> My jewel of pain on which Christ died.

But passages read out of context are passages read
out of context. That Brother Antoninus has recourse to shock
is certain. One admiring critic calls his poetry flagrantly

shocking.   This does not make it less relevant, less impor-
tant, less excellent.

Much of Antoninus' work is very personal and bio-
graphical information is of some importance to readers who
would understand him.   He is apparently writing of this great
love in his life in much of his most recent book of poems,
The Rose of Solitude.   (Its subtitle is "A Love Poem-Se-
quence.")   Readers need to know that for him a relationship
with a woman may be the fulfillment of a man (and vice-
versa, of course).   This is a far cry from St. Paul's "Bet-
ter to marry than to burn."   Antoninus believes as psychia-
trist Carl Gustav Jung believed that the wholeness which we
all seek comes from a union of opposites.

One particular symbol of this for the Christian is
that of Christ who unites not only heaven and earth but death
and life in his crucifixion and resurrection.   More immediate
to our concern here is Jung's notion of the integration of
man and woman.   Briefly, Jung taught that each man needs
to objectify a feminine principle and each woman a masculine
one.   As one analyst put it, "the unconscious of a man con-
tains a complementary feminine element."   What this boils
down to is that each man hopes to "complete himself" by
finding in a woman that which comes closest to the comple-
mentary feminine element in his unconscious.

True marriage for Antoninus, a follower of Jung, is
therefore a rebirth into wholeness.   As he puts it in "Black
Christ":

> Make me a marriage,
> Death, my master, my Christ.
> Keep thy bed holy,
> My cross.
> Kill me.

But it is "Kill me" that I may be resurrected more perfectly
in you.

A Jungian understands that a woman "can give him a
sense of rootedness and of all the color, vitality and magnetic
allurement of life, without which his mind is cold and for-
bidding."   The first lines of poetry in his latest book are
these:

> The dark roots of the rose cry in my heart.
> They pierce through rock-ribs of my stony flesh.

Antoninus is aware of his need for a relationship with a woman. That he recalls a particular woman with whom he, as William Everson, had a passionate sexual relationship is not something to be judged--it is simply so.

In one poem he sees her thus: "She is all passion, all fire and devotion. She is all woman, in love of God bitten by the rapture of God." That passion, fire and devotion are not strange bedfellows is seen when we consider that the most passionate of devoted lovers, the mystics, could say as Jakob Boehme did: "I will tell you what God is; he is fire."

Antoninus' work may be discussed under the heading of erotic mysticism, just as that of St. John of the Cross may be in a poem like "Romance IV" wherein God's creation is seen in terms of a palace for his bride. Or the suggestion in "Romance VII":

> There is in every perfect love
> A law to be accomplished too:
> That the lover should resemble
> The beloved: and be the same.
> And the greater is the likeness
> Brighter will the rapture flame.

Henry Vaughan observes that deep, in the center of the heart, the Bridegroom seeks his nuptials with his spouse --elaborating on the image of Christ as groom, the Church as his bride. And he can utilize the kiss, in some of his work, to symbolize the union of God and persons or even to suggest a Jungian union of opposites as with the finite and infinite, the physical and spiritual.

Likewise Antoninus uses sexual imagery to render the mystical. In "Black Christ" we read:

> My body, thy cross,
> Make pregnant with thy seed,
> Swell into definition,
> Stalk of thy desire.

And there are poems like "The Way of Life and the Way of Death" in which the persona is crucified and resurrected through love for a woman.

What we have to recognize, in justice to Antoninus, and to ourselves as readers of his creations, is the validity of what he told me in our interview, "In my life the love of

God has been so intimately bound up with the love of woman
that in a way, it's always been through a woman's hands
that I discovered God at ever deepening levels. And this I
trust. I trust this movement...."

He put it dramatically in "Immortal Strangeness":

> On her lips
> Her lips,
> In the agon of a bird,
> I seize salvation.

Later in the poem he talks of the "wisdom of the flesh" as
redeeming element. In another poem it's almost like a syl-
logism:

> To love her more
> Is to love self less.
> To love self less
> Is to love God more.
> To love selflessly
> Is to love:
> Him in her.

At another point we read:

> So she: I
> In us: He is.
> We Three:
> Free.

Antoninus has a significant fondness for using crucifixion
imagery to illustrate the relation he describes. He can say
for example:

> On the blade of the crimson poinsettia
> She has gashed my side.

or

> Between the two thieves of her eyes,
> I nail my life.

He is not so naive as to fail to see dangers inherent
in a man/woman relationship. However, he refuses to begin
with the assumption that such a situation is automatically
evil. To end one stanza he quotes the old bromide "When
the devil/ can't find a way/ He sends a woman." This he
follows simply with "So does God."

I hope that I am not giving the impression that Brother Antoninus is writing poems of the theme of sexual love or of some facet of unholy egotism. He wrote in one letter, "I strive for spiritual perfection and make the striving the subject and the themes of my poetry." One perceptive critic recently wrote that "his poetry inducted him into his religion, and his religion shapes his poetry."

Novelist Graham Greene seems to feel that grace results from sin (no Fall, no Redemption) and perhaps this is Antoninus' position as well. Two questions he asks in poems hint at this:

> Is sin
> Transformed in ecstasy,
> In love reprieved?

Or again,

> When does a sin
> Become ·its virtue?

There is no doubt for Antoninus that he feels a woman's love brought about a religious resurrection for him. He says as much in many of his individual works. And he has a holy pride in what a woman did for him. He asks "Is it any sin/ I cry out a woman's name?" and later

> Do you call it disaster
> That under the white
> And the black of the friar
> Burns a woman's name?

Antoninus has already furnished his own answer in his poems. The love relationship that led him to God, he seems to say., is the sin become its virtue. Sexual love as an expression of love for God is very real for Antoninus and exceedingly meaningful.

The Middle Eastern poet Kahlil Gibran once wrote, "For even as love crowns you so shall he crucify you." Brother Antoninus' poetry reverses the emphasis here. He sees perhaps what the albatross instinctively knows when he makes himself vulnerable to his mate, that even as love crucifies, it crowns.

BROTHER ANTONINUS: "IN THE FICTIVE WISH"

Samuel Charters. 1971

Although Everson had gained something close to celebrity
status with his erotic mysticism following the publication of
The Rose of Solitude, the appearance in 1968 of the complete
version of The Residual Years turned attention back to his
earlier verse. In a critical study a few years later, Some
Poems/Poets: Studies in American Underground Poetry Since
1945 (Oyez, 1971), Charters responded to Everson's erotic
sequence, In the Fictive Wish, written in the closing days
of World War II (but published by Oyez in 1967).

> It could be that the difference
> between Antoninus and most of
> the other poets of the last twenty
> years is that his blood runs
> closer to his skin, and that his
> involvement with the emotional
> realities of his life is more in-
> tensely felt than theirs.

How can a poet like Antoninus be made to fit any
group of American poets or poetry? It's hard to believe that
at this point there could even be an Antoninus, that somehow
out of the doubt and the questioning of much American poetry
of the last twenty or thirty years there could still be a poet
as fervent and as stripped bare as Antoninus. He has fully
invested himself in each of the dimensions of his work--from
the first nature elegies that were his early response to the
poetry of Robinson Jeffers to the complex, passionate poems
that marked his conversion to Catholicism and his acceptance
of Dominican vows. It is almost as difficult to place Jeffers'
work into any kind of perspective; so it isn't surprising that

the work of a disciple--as Antoninus has always described
himself--has some of the same problem. The surprise is
that there could be poetry like this being written.

It isn't only the insistence on the urgency of the poet's
self that sets Antoninus's work apart from other poetry of
the last twenty years. There have been other poets who have
tried to scrape away as many layers of the skin. Antoninus,
in a period when the poetic idiom has become dry and under-
stated, has an almost seventeenth century richness of language
and expression. He has a closer affinity to Vaughn, Cra-
shaw, Alabaster--the Christopher Smart of A Song to David--
than he does to the insistent objectivity of Robert Creeley
or Denise Levertov, or to the complex allusiveness of Charles
Olson or Robert Duncan. I don't think he was influenced by
the metaphysical poets--he was from the beginning a Jeffers
disciple--but the feeling in the poetry is of a man, like the
earlier poets, who has been driven by the torment of his
life to the most intense poetry he can find language to ex-
press.

Antoninus's language is so intense, so vivid, that the
poems can almost be read in clusters of words and phrases--
"Far trumpets of succinctness," "a treading of feet on the
stairs of redness," "I think moons of kept measure," "I felt
the new wind, south/ Grope her tonguing mouth on the wall,"
"The wind breaking its knees on this hurdle, the house,"
"Birds beak for her!" "In the high peal of rivering lips,"
"The low freighters at sea/ Take in their sides the nuzzling
dolphins that are their death...." He has a brilliant sense
of alliteration. From In the Fictive Wish,

> Wader
> Watcher by water,
> Walker alone by the wave-worn shore
> In water woven.

And he doesn't hesitate to extend the flash of phrase into a
poem's inner tensions. He uses a long, wavering line at
points that near the stillness of a moment of contemplation.
From The Rose of Solitude,

> For what blooms behind your lips moves ever within
> my sight
> the kept diffusion of the smile;
> And what dawns behind your brow subsists within
> my thought
> the somnolent mystery of mind;

And what trembles in your words lives on forever in
                                  my heart
    the immutable innerness of speech

But at moments of deepening intensity the line tightens to an abrupt, insistent rhythmic unit. From earlier in The Rose,

        I crept

        I brought Him gifts
        Hushed in my heart

        I brought what I had
        I crept.

None of this has the flat speech rhythm that sets the dominant tone of most contemporary poetry. Duncan has his own kind of rhetorical verbosity, and Ginsberg has some of the rhythm of the synagogue chant, but the modern poet has usually been less emotional--his own responses kept at an objective distance from the poem. Antoninus has none of this restraint--the phrase, the phrase rhythm, function as a direct expression of his emotions. Part of the felt affinity with the earlier group of metaphysical poets is this emotional extravagance, this sense of poetic hyperbole. From The Rose,

        Heart to be hushed.
        Let it howk and then hush.

        Let the black wave break.
        Let the terrible tongue
        Engorge my deeps

        Let the loins of ferocity
        Lave my shut flesh.

From "The Song the Body Dreamed in the Spirit's Mad Behest,"

        Born and reborn we will be groped, be clenched
        On ecstasies that shudder toward crude birth,
        When His great Godhead peels its stripping strength
        In my red earth

The image and the language could almost have come from Donne's sonnet,

        Divorce mee, 'untie, or breake that knot againe,
        Take mee to you, imprison mee, for I

Except you 'enthrall mee, never shall be free,
Nor ever chast, except you ravish mee.

It's true that of all the contemporary poets Antoninus
is the only one with some kind of persona--his identification
with his holy order--that he can put between himself and his
work, and it could be that this has given him the situation
he needed to open his emotional stance. When he took his
vows in 1951, after more than a dozen years of publication
as William Everson, he had, as Brother Antoninus, a reach
of expression opened to him that had been inhibited while he
was still writing as William Everson. Nothing in his secular
poetry has the grinding fervor of his religious writing. But
is the poet William Everson? Is the poet Brother Antoninus?
The two persons of Antoninus have never fully merged--even
now that he has left the order and married, and the complex
currents of his poetry express this continuing duality. Not
confusion--I don't think there is any confusion of his separate
identities in Antoninus, only a deep consciousness of their
differences. But the emphasis of the poetry has moved--
since 1951, when he was thirty-nine--from the pre-occupa-
tions with the self to the more specific emotions of his re-
ligious self. Everson is still present in Antoninus, as the
man who is Antoninus was a presence in the poems of Ever-
son.

It is the poems from his deepest point of spiritual
crisis that in some ways most intensely involve anyone read-
ing his poetry. The poems from this point of decision, from
about 1945 and 6 to 1948, have a desperate, immediate poi-
gnancy. It is possible to be unmoved by the religiosity of the
later work, and to pass over the Jeffers-like cadences of
the first poems, but this period of his life was one of deep
personal unhappiness, and the humanness of his loss is di-
rectly, and strongly, moving. So much seems to be slipping
through his hands, and one moment of loss slides uncertain
and confused into only another moment of loss. Artistically
they become some of his most fully formed poems. The
images of his earlier work--earth, the sea, the smells of
weeds, the distances of hills and fields--have spread and ex-
tended through the lengthened lyric impulse of his dominating
unhappiness. Since the poems come near his moment of
crisis their resolutions are temporary--their sense of immi-
nent despair tangled and heavy through their loping lines.
In the Fictive Wish, from Oregon, 1946, has perhaps the
most fully realized flowering of beauty, since it centers on
one of his points of almost complete resolution. The Blowing
of the Seed, from Sebastopol, California, in 1946, is agoniz-

ing in its pained cutting of his body in its sudden despair.
"There Will Be Harvest," from Berkeley the next year, in
the collection The Springing of the Blade, is dominated with
the weight of his life's details, and its involvement with the
crisis of his physical love.

In the Fictive Wish is a sustained lyric outburst, its
syntax and form left ambiguous, but its emotional clarities
brilliantly sustained. From its opening lines the difficulties
of understanding are obvious, but the poem's great beauty
also begins to unfold with its first hesitant breath.

> So him in dream
> Does celibate wander
> Where woman waits,
> Of whom he may come to,
> Does woman wait
> Who now is
> Of his.

Instead of "So he in dream ..." the other pronoun form "him"
for its alliteration with the final m of dream; the first sound
of the s of So returning in the soft c of celibate, the two
opening lines making a loosely conjoined phrase of four ac-
cents ending on the feminine cadence of wander. The lan-
guage has an almost medieval sense of word usage in its in-
versions of sentence structure, "Of whom he may come to,"
"Does now the Lord retain," "Of that they then came to,"
and there is a suggestion of the medieval poem of physical
rapture in his description of the woman's body,

> Of such body and of such croft,
> Where ache of sex could so conjoin,
> Could so sink,
> As dreams sunken;
> Of such cunted closure
> Built broad in the love grip;
> As of bed,
> Broad,
> As of width for woman;
> And of belly
> Broad for the grapple.

The language could be from Skelton, or an anonymous 15th
century carol. The poem's ending is one of his most beauti-
fully moulded series of enfolding alliterations--the opening
lines of the last section,

Wader
Watcher by water,
Walker alone by the wave-worn shore,
In water woven.

with their soft sounds of w̲, w̲a̲, w̲o̲--in the next line mingling
the w̲ with a beginning m̲ sound

She moves now where the wave glistens,

and in the next line it is the m̲,

Her mouth mocking with laughter

then the s̲ of glistening returns again with,

In the slosh unheard

the sound opens to

When the sea slurs after;
In the sleepy suckle

and the verse ends with a long rhythmic unit developing the
l̲ of sleepy and suckle--and leaves the sound poised for the
opening line of the next verse.

That laps at her heel where the ripple hastens,
And the laughing look laid over her arm

The final lines are one of his most intensely moving images
of loss and unhappiness.

Lurker,
She leaves with laughter,
She fades where the combers falter,
Is gone where the dream is gone
Or the sleeper's murmur;
Is gone as the wave withdrawing
Sobs on the shore, and the stones are shaken
As the ruined wave
Sucks and sobs in the rustling stones,
When the tide is taken.

The physical insistence of the poetry has continued
since this period of his life. The pain was only briefly re-
solved in the certitudes of the Church. On some levels of

his expression there has even been an intensification. The
poetry that emerged from his years in the Dominican Order
increasingly shared the violent physicality of the metaphysical
poets--the acerbation of celibacy on a body that is unable to
deny its desire for fulfillment. In his book The Rose of
Solitude the violence of desire and its turmoil becomes the
central problem of the poem--and the desire expressed in
the poem is open and explicit, forced in on him by the real
embrace of a woman, the rose, on the floor of a San Fran-
cisco apartment,

> Now up from down under
> The long stitch of manflesh
> Goes suckering in.
>
> All that fretfulness
> Shucked now,
> Purled shuddering under.
>
> It is the make of the male.

He even questions the meanings of his continence.

> O God and Riddler,
> Why?
>
> Is this sin?
>
> I seek no sin.
> I would never offend Thee.

In an earlier verse,

> Is truly a sin
> That her name is written,
> Stroked in primal fire,
> On my stultified heart?

In "The Song the Body Dreamed in the Spirit's Mad
Behest" it is a sublimated desire suffusing his response to
God.

> Call Him the Lover and call me the Bride,
> Lapsing on the couch of His repose
> I heard the elemental waters rise,
> Divide and close ...
> He is the Spirit but I am the Flesh
> Out of my body must he be reborn,
> Soul from the sundered soul, Creation's gout

In the world's bourn ...
Mounted between the thermals of my thighs
Hawklike He hovers surging at the sun,
And feathers me a frenzy ring around
That deep drunk tongue.

The poem has an indelible, raw energy. But in all of his
mature work there has been this same sense of urgent need,
and it has been as strong a force in the poems not immedi-
ately physical in their confrontations. It could be that the
difference between Antoninus and most of the other poets of
the last twenty years is that his blood runs closer to his
skin, and that his involvement with the emotional realities of
his life is more intensely felt than theirs. The guarded tone
of most modern poetry does give the impression of a cautious
withdrawal from a social environment so hostile that anything
except a kind of guarded mistrust seems too naive as an emo-
tional response. Whatever anyone has believed in as a kind
of center for himself or the society has turned out to be
mostly useless. This doesn't mean that other poets haven't
been involved with the implications of sexuality, haven't brood-
ed over the failure of what Antoninus would call Man and
Woman to resolve their differences--it only means that they've
decided to let less of themselves be measured against the
force of this confrontation. Antoninus refuses to step out of
the way, just as he has refused to deny any of the physical
implications of his mature work.

At points in the poetry Antoninus seems to be over-
whelmed by some of the forces he's thrust himself against.
The texture of the line becomes strained, the force of the
language becomes excessive. The experience of the sexual
embrace is almost beyond any verbal expression, but he
keeps trying to find an explicit imagery that would break
through to the physical reality.

... In my emptiness
These arms gall for her, bride's mouth,
Spent-breathed in laughter, or that night's
First unblushing revealment, the flexed
Probity of the flesh, the hymen-tilted troth,
We closed, we clung on it, the stroked
And clangorous rapture!

The imagery is so forced that it loses its effect of
moving through to the experience itself. Sometimes his de-
spair cries out too strongly--almost with a kind of self-in-
dulgence.

The face I know
Becomes the night-black rose

And I cry out of a shambling of pain,
A clothing of anguish ...

                              Great tongs
Tear rents of speechlessness
Cut from my lips ...

I drunkenly stagger. I flay
Segments of numbness,
A stuff of wretchedness
Tatters my shanks ...

But the outburst is no more naked than Shelley's,

As thus with thee in prayer in my sore need.
Oh, lift me as a wave, a leaf, a cloud!
I fall upon the thorns of life! I bleed!

Even when the imagery is most strained, the language most driven, these moments in the later work only more deeply etch the complex portrait of himself that the poetry gives us. It is poetry that meets us so strongly--even when it looms at us from directions where we hadn't expected poetry to come. And the only thing that matters now is that the poetry has come, that he has written the poems, that there is, almost unbelievably, an Antoninus.

THE WOMAN OF PREY

Allan Campo. 1966

Everson's recourse to the themes of erotic mysticism in
order to unify his instinctual and religious drives inevitably
touched the negative as well as the positive aspects of the
self. This condition is known as the Dark Night of the Soul,
and is most often depicted in art as the Temptation of Saint
Anthony. In an unpublished thesis for Loyola University of
Los Angeles, "Soul and the Search: Mysticism and Its Ap-
proach in the Poetry of Brother Antoninus" (1966), Allan
Campo devotes a chapter (here slightly revised) to this dis-
quieting element in the poet's work.

> <u>Surprising and contradictory as</u>
> <u>she is, the "woman of prey" is</u>
> <u>formidably real, and Everson's</u>
> <u>poems of portrayal are no less</u>
> <u>formidable in their own right.</u>

The most startling poem in William Everson's <u>The
Hazards of Holiness</u> (published in 1962 under his religious
name, Brother Antoninus) might well be "The Song the Body
Dreamed in the Spirit's Mad Behest." That the poet was
aware of the problematics of the poem's impression--which
are due to its graphic and elemental portrayal of the Body
and the Spirit as Bride and Lover engaged in sexual union--
is indicated by the brief introductory note he gave to it,
wherein he stated:

> "The Imagination, unable to grasp the reality of
> pure Spirit, conceives of their union under the
> modality of her own nature. Longing to respond
> totally to the divine summons, and convinced in

faith that the Redemption has rendered this pos-
sible, she struggles to cast off all the inhibitions
of original sin, and evokes the deepest resources
of her sensuality, in order to achieve in shame-
lessness the wholeness of being an age of shame
has rendered incomplete. "[1]

Citing "The Song the Body Dreamed" as "one of the finest
poems in the book," Herbert Kenny, in his review of The
Hazards of Holiness, added his own explanation for the es-
sential validity and effectiveness of this poem:

> "As the modern age has debased sex as a re-
> sult of rightly rejecting the false standards of the
> Victorian but failing to grasp the theological sig-
> nificance of sex, so Brother Antoninus has re-
> stored it to its proper and significant role in this
> poem. A faith which calls the Church the Bride
> of Christ, and Christ, a bridegroom, cannot
> shrink from the obvious corollaries, properly
> handled. For these are metaphors that Cathol-
> icism has sanctified by applying them to Christ,
> a simple but inevitable consequence of the Word
> having been made flesh. "[2]

**

A poem like "The Song the Body Dreamed" may in-
deed be made possible by the apprehension of "the obvious
corollaries" or by being "convinced in faith," but what en-
ables such a poem to move from the possible to the actual
is rooted in something of a deep interior liberation. Some
of the poetry surrounding "The Song the Body Dreamed"
strongly indicates that such a liberation has to do, in its
sources, with the poet's particular encounter with and integra-
tion of the feminine pyschic reality, the anima, in her less
attractive aspects. This consideration brings us to three
substantial poems: "The Beheading of John the Baptist" and
"Judith and Holofernes"--which were paired as the title-work
of the collection--and "The Last Crusade," written in 1958
but withheld from The Hazards of Holiness, not to appear in
print until 1969.

J. E. Circlot summarizes the varied facets of the
feminine archetype:

> "She has three basic aspects: first, as a siren,

lamia or monstrous being who enchants, diverts
and entices men away from the path of evolution;
second, as the mother, or Magna mater ... re-
lated in turn to the formless aspect of the waters
and of the unconscious; and third, as the unknown
damsel, the beloved or the anima in Jungian psy-
chology.... All allegories based upon the personi-
fication of Woman invariably retain all the impli-
cations of the three basic aspects mentioned
above. "[3]

Actually, Jung generally uses the term "anima" as equivalent
to the archetype of woman, and it is in this more compre-
hensive sense that I employ the term. The point is, in any
event, that if the anima may fittingly be portrayed in her
more elevated aspects--as Sophia or the "Great Mother" or
the Mother of God, aspects which, of course, Everson used
for "A Canticle to the Great Mother of God"--she may no
less be portrayed in her undesirable or fearsome aspects,
as we see in such familiar Homeric figures as Circe, the
beautiful enchantress who transformed men into swine, or
the Sirens, who lured men off their intended course to be
dashed upon the rocks. In fact, to portray the sublime char-
acter of the anima is virtually to necessitate the encounter
with the dark side of that archetype, the anima steeped in
the shadow, so to speak. In this regard, Jung's comment
on the Apocalypse of St. John is worth noting:

"The pièce de résistance is the destruction of the
Great Whore of Babylon, the counterpart of the
heavenly Jerusalem. Babylon is the chthonic
equivalent of the sun-woman Sophia, with, how-
ever, a reversal in moral character. If the
elect turn themselves into 'virgins' in honour
of the Great Mother Sophia, a gruesome fantasy
of fornication is spawned in the unconscious by
way of compensation. "[4]

We can see the same type of development by looking ahead
to the introductory episode of "In Savage Wastes," the poem
which concludes The Hazards of Holiness:

"A hermit who has lived a long time in the de-
sert experiences great dearth of spirit, and one
night, exhausted, falls asleep over his prayers.
He is awakened by a knock at the door, and open-
ing it beholds two nuns. They explain that they
are on pilgrimage and have become separated

from their company, and beg of him shelter for
the night. He graciously shows them into his
cell, and prepares to spend the night outside so
that they may have its privacy to themselves.
However, once inside they lock the door and
throwing off their habits reveal themselves as
naked succubi. They cast a spell over him,
and seduce him, and there is not a shred of
sensory excitation which they do not stimulate
within him and gratify.

"In the morning the monk wakes up and rea-
lizes he has dreamed."

In the three poems to which we must now turn, Everson por-
trays, through objective narratives, the anima in her capac-
ity for ferocity, sensuality, and destruction--not with the
unqualified simplicity of legend, but with something more of
the complexity that belongs to this figure. Coming, then,
to the two poems that form the title-piece of The Hazards of
Holiness, let us note Ortega y Gasset's comment that "Judith
and Salome are two variations of that type of woman which
is most surprising because it is most contradictory: the
woman of prey."[5] Surprising and contradictory as she is,
the "woman of prey" is formidably real, and Everson's poems
of portrayal are no less formidable in their own right.

**

In "The Beheading of John the Baptist," the first of
the pair, Salome is the means of breaking the stalemate be-
tween the male antagonists, for in the face of John's unyield-
ing accusatory stance, Herod maintained his politically cau-
tious handling of the prophet, even against his wife's unbend-
ing desire for vengeance. The poet takes special notice of
this in the course of the opening stanza:

Herodias, that corrosive female wrath,
Black grasp of the invidious breed,
Blanched, swore blooded reprisal.
But the Tetrarch, sensitive, winnowing
    those careful
Cross-fertilizing fears, that tease of
    the politic heart,
Smelled dangerous fire in the prophet's blood,
Checked his hand. Dungeoned deep, a claw
    of conscience

Repressed in the brutal heart of the State,
The Baptist dreamed implacably on,
Manacled but unmaimed.

In his epigraph to the poem, Everson had included Herod's promise, given in the aftermath of Salome's dance: "Ask of me what thou wilt, and I will give it thee." In her response, the girl dashes the tense triangle which Herod had attempted to sustain:

                              "Give me the head
Of John the Baptist!" cried the violent girl,
Her eyes like an eaglet's blazing behind her
    unbrooched hair,
Mouth insolent with wine, throat panting
Those covetous gouts that howk toward murder,
The dauntless breast beating that oath up out
    of her blood,
Her sovereign demand. "On a plate! On a plate!"
She turned, imperious, her legs spread like
    a man's,
One naked arm distended, the savage bracelets
Aclash on her wrist.

Salome has razed Herod's masculine prudential formulation, and, trapped by the unforeseen rashness of his promise, he is rendered impotently acquiescent:

He smiled, squirmed, lifted
            the hand of lifeless assent,
Concurred.

It is at this point that Everson takes up the dance itself, to show how it was that the astute pragmatist was undone, overpowered by the unerring shaft of female sensuality made more delicious by the incestuous overtones that were present. It is important to note that it was not merely John the Baptist who suffered the mortal consequences, but Herod, too, who was beheaded, his political stratagem unraveled and his rulership overcome--accomplished by a girl's dance:

She had danced, had she not? Twirling
    her loose skirt,
The nubile thighs flashing the ringlets
    of excitation,
Flamboyant, the inflammable gestures of a
    crude sexuality

Nascently alive, a virgin gambling away
    her maidenhead
In the crouched animality of arrested
    stupration,
That thrust of blood in the heart's valves
    when treasure is spewed,
The toothed heels stuttering out a mirthless
    crescendo,
Rapacity unflexed, the impossible strut
    of childish excess,
Astute circlings of consanguinity, most
    ancient of inversions,
Blood calling to the blood.

In her triumph Salome is as ferocious as the warriors of
Israel:

                    Clash the spears, warriors!
Throw down those drinking goblets onto
    the stones,
You sunburned fighters, swart treaders of Asia,
Dirk-fierce drinkers of barbarous life--
    behold your own!

Before the men gathered there, Salome flaunts her trophy,
the Baptist's head, and the poet emphasizes the victorious
feminine power:

Strutting, the outrageous, excessive girl
    confronts them,
Brandishing into the aghast male faces, flattened
    on the nexus
Of the opposed female will, her bloody pledge.

There is only the stunned male discomfiture, as Everson
makes a deft narrative ploy:

                    Nobody laughed.
In the choked silence someone kicked a
    musician, and the zither
Screeched, a shrill hysterical bleat of
    masculine consternation.
Smoldering, her face flushed with aggression
    and contempt,
The umbrageous girl flounced menacing
    out, dragging her prize.

The poem concludes with a long reflective stanza on

the relation of the Baptist as precursor to the redemptive
emergence of Christ, for that is, finally, the transcendent
dimension against which the episode itself is measured. But
it is the narrative, so effectively marshalled and carried out
by Everson, that portrays the fearsomely indomitable feminine
capacity for overturning the masculine purposiveness, a ca-
pacity actualized through her irresistible sensuality making
a mockery of the man's rational disposition.

**

If holiness, with its hazards, like a two-edged sword
cuts both ways, threatening the unholy no less than the holy,
it may be wielded in fatal consequence by either as well.
The second of these poems, "Judith and Holofernes," relates
the grisly assassination of the pagan chieftain by the Hebrew
widow who employs the most fundamental of feminine wiles
to accomplish what the masculine ruling contingent could never
effect. The poem is not only somewhat longer than its com-
panion-piece, it is, more importantly, greater in the force-
fulness of its portrayal.

The narrative takes place within the tent of Holofernes,
where just the two persons are present, each pursuing the
pathway of a leisured seduction, though for widely contrary
purposes. Early in the poem, Everson presents a descrip-
tion of the most telling sort. Back in the brief poem "Sleep-
tossed I Lie," referring to lovers engaged in their sexual
act, he had written of "the body's blade/ Plunged deep."
Here, he makes a formidable application of that image as he
pictures Judith dallying with the sword of Holofernes:

> She toyed with it, binding her scarf on the
>   ponderous hilt
> For favor, fondling the pendulous tassels she
>   found there,
> Curling finger and thumb round the thirsting point,
> A spidery tickle. "Let it bring down the proud.
> For which I have come to you, a woman's weakness
> In the stitch of God's grace ..."
> She mocked her mouth at him over its edge,
> The razor-stroked steel. "When my lord
> Has pinked at last his terrible blade
> I will quench my desire ..."

As for Holofernes, he is utterly taken in by the woman--the
sexual innuendoes of her gestures heightening the phallic sug-

gestiveness of the sword, his sense of sexual prowess fatten-
ing upon the widow's seductive tones, his male self-esteem
basking in her flattery.   And all the while Holofernes is
utterly deaf to the terrible irony of Judith's words and blind
to the doom toward which she is leading him.   The poet
shows him in his complete ease of complacency:

> The conqueror grinned,
> Lolling his muscular hams on their print,
> The double indentation of crushed cushions,
> Where his strong legs spread, and blinked sidewise.

Thinking himself master of the situation in which he is truly
the hapless victim, Holofernes is shown in a remarkably
pointed etching of the man in the coils of the fascination of
the anima.

Everson builds and elaborates upon the scene and the
progress of the two persons toward the fulfillment of their
separate intent.   He comes then to the climax, presenting
the infernal aftermath in a strange paradox and a ghastly
image:

> God uses the devil, Job proved that.
> But does the devil use God?   Holofernes, headless
>   in hell,
> Will twist forever on the demon's nail,
> Crucified on the splayed tree of the sexual act,
> Ejaculating out of the dismasted shoulders
> The orgastic splurge of neuric excess.

Shortly thereafter, the poet gives us the act itself:

> Holofernes, divided on his own blade,
> His swart head slewed back and chopped off,
> Hewn loose in two hacks, and the bloated trunk
> Stiffening in the cerement of his own arras,
> His head balled up, stashed away in a woman's purse,
> Never again to gloat in triumph on the proud neck
> When battles are joined and maids deflowered,
> Sings his own requiem, the terrified bellow
> Of distempered blood.

After some further embellishment of the incident and the di-
vine aegis of the widow's mission, Everson tells of Judith's
leaving the camp and returning to her people:

> The strange woman
> Glides through the camp like a young goddess
> Bearing her gifts, back through the thorn
> And the desert gravel, over the flints,
> Picking her way through camel dung and the
>   urine of mules,
> Drifting back to the beleaguered city that gave
>   her birth,
> Where the greybeard fathers, impotent,
> Sit on their mats, invoking the inscrutable God,
> Of whom in fact they have quite despaired,
> To make in this hour some bland interpolation,

an "interpolation" which is not to be made, and could hardly be "bland," for their liberation is not to come fortuitously, but only to be attained by the unflinching directness of the woman's act.

**

The fact that Everson made of these two poems the combined title-work of The Hazards of Holiness indicates the centrality with which he regarded them. At the same time, these poems epitomized the principal reservations on the part of the reviewers. Consequently, they doubly deserve some reflection on our part, beyond the consideration which I have just given them.

John Logan, in his review of the volume, complains that

> "one is hurt by the relentless succession of poems
> violently written on violent subjects: the wrestling
> of Jacob, the encounters with Christ as witch or
> dog-woman (Sphinx), aggressive or fawning female;
> the beheading of John the Baptist; Judith and Holo-
> fernes; the violent conversion of St. Paul."[6]

There seems little doubt that Logan's reaction would have been quite otherwise if the third part of the book had been milder. If Logan recoils from the excess of violence, Robert Creeley, writing in Poetry, takes exception to the excessive character of the poet's rhetoric, for, according to him,

> "it is, at times, a rhetoric that is present apart
> from demands of specific content; I find this most

the case, for example, in the more dramatic
poems, as Saints and the two parts of the title
poem. "[7]

And he quotes from "The Beheading of John the Baptist" to
exemplify the matter. Yet, both reviewers, directly in the
face of their objections, acknowledge that the poetry is power-
ful and that they are greatly impressed by it. In a sense,
they seem reluctant to make the connection that exists be-
tween the means to which they object and the effectiveness
which they applaud. The impression that ensues is that the
poet is righter in his methods than are the reviewers in
their strictures.

In any case, such reservations seem closely related
to the objections voiced by Ralph Mills in his more considered
appraisal of Everson's poetry--written outside the circum-
stantial limitations of producing a book review. In regard
to The Hazards of Holiness, Mills reserves his praise for
the shorter, more directly personal poems, as he comments:

> "Biblical subjects do appear a few times (in 'Jacob
> and the Angel,' 'The Conversion of St. Paul,' and
> 'The Hazards of Holiness'), but this vein was gen-
> erally exhausted by the previous book [The Crooked
> Lines of God] and now has a slight air of irrele-
> vance. The chief accomplishment in the most re-
> cent volume is not to be found in the longer poems,
> nor in a continued reliance on sacred story, but in
> those brief, taut poems.... "[8]

Just prior to this observation, Mills has raised another ob-
jection which, on the face of it, may seem unrelated, but it
is actually quite pertinent. Referring to "A Dialogue on
Holy Violence," which featured a review of The Hazards of
Holiness accompanied by an extended commentary from the
poet in explanation and defense of the violence present in
the poetry,[9] Mills states,

> "This defense seems to me perfectly legitimate
> in most cases, though a few poems, and 'The
> Hazards of Holiness' in particular, are point-
> lessly sadistic in detail. "

What is especially striking is that Mills can proceed to re-
mark that "the largest part of Brother Antoninus' recent work
attempts to objectify in word and image the poet's inner
world where the struggle for his faith is carried out." It is,

in fact, on the very basis of this purpose that the biblical subjects decidedly avoid the "air of irrelevance" and their details are not at all "pointlessly sadistic."

Appearances to the contrary, I am not primarily concerned with rebutting these critical comments. They do show the misunderstanding to which this poetry is liable and provide a background for a more accurate appraisal of the poetry and the particular achievement which belongs to it. When Mills points out that the poetry "attempts to objectify ... the poet's inner world," he is not far from Everson's own statement in his foreword to The Hazards of Holiness, where he explains that

"the struggle with language is the struggle to make myself comprehensible to myself, to orient my inner and outer being. As Claudel says, 'Every word is the expression of a psychological state, caused by attention to an outside object.' Between the 'heresy of expressive form' (shape-lessness) and the 'heresy of a priori correct form' (rigidity) one gropes toward the ineluctable authority of synthetic form, in which all relevant elements are synthesized into an indefinable whole. I say indefinable because only that which possesses mystery can manifest the character of wholeness. A poem, like a dream, is 'whole' to the extent that it registers the mystery of the psychic complex which produced it."

Furthermore, Everson's understanding of rhetoric is along these same lines, as, in the course of a printed interview, he once stated that "rhetoric for me is the device by which the consequentiality of the emotional situation and the mood is in some way registered."[10] Somewhat further on in the same interview, Everson says,

"To me that unconscious power, or rather power rising from the unconscious, is recorded in what I call rhetoric. It's possible to be rhetorical in an academic way, but it won't register anything."

If these citations point the way to what it is that Everson is seeking to accomplish and the means by which that accomplishment is attained, it remains for us to see whether his intentions are truly actualized.

Where Mills goes significantly astray is to have seen

the biblical narratives as further instances of what had been done in The Crooked Lines of God. Despite the similarities involved, the earlier and later uses of biblical narratives are fundamentally different. In The Crooked Lines of God these materials served to portray inner dispositions or attitudes. In The Hazards of Holiness, however, the biblical narratives serve the purposes of myth, as understood by Jung and others. They are narratives, conceived at a more than ordinary scale, the function of which is to carry the projections of deeply interior psychic events ("psychic complexes" and the archetypal realities upon which they are founded). The energy driving these narratives is precisely the "power rising from the unconscious" and therefore calling for uses of language and detail that would not normally be tolerable. Far from being work of a "vein" that has been exhausted by the earlier biblical uses, these later narratives are mining a new and extraordinarily rich vein.

I think that there is, in that "Dialogue on Holy Violence," a particularly revealing statement by Everson in this regard, when, addressing himself to Albert Fowler, the reviewer, he writes:

"You note that I 'take comfort in the thought that its [the Bible's] violence appears in the service of God.' Actually I am not comforted but appalled by this fact. My chief purpose in writing the book was to come to terms with precisely this issue, for I can conceive of nothing more awesome and fearful, nothing more fascinating, than the uses of violence, especially sexual violence, in man's redemption."

For the poet to say these things is not enough. The feelings and reactions must be validated in his poetry by the presentation he makes of such biblical episodes as account for his response. Therein lies the basis for the rhetoric, melodramatic or excessive as it might seem, and for the details, which are thus quite purposive.

That the appalling realities are not exclusive to the biblical sources is clear, for Everson is able to seize upon these external episodes because they answer to the interior drama of the archetypes--in this instance, the terrifying facets of the anima being encountered--and therefore give him the means to integrate that drama within his art and his religious perspective, as well as in terms of conscious realization. Even a relatively cursory survey of ancient myths would demonstrate the extremity to which such portrayals can go. The same could be said of those great dramas of the Greeks, with their stupefying violations of the normal perspectives. Closer yet are the terrible visions of saintly contemplatives, especially those earlier Desert Fathers, and particularly well-known those "Temptations" of St. Anthony the Hermit. Such are the exemplars for what Everson seeks to accomplish.

In his comparison of a poem with a dream, we can see the necessity for the manner of his narratives. The dream achieves its wholeness only in virtue of its details, for every detail serves its significance, its purposiveness. So, too, must the poem in its details be true to the reality giving it birth. It is in its details that the poem's rhetoric is given substance, just as by its rhetoric the poem's details are made to register their impact. Even before the poetry of The Hazards of Holiness came to be written, Everson had stated his belief in the fullness with which a poem must be composed. In his autobiography, he declares:

> "In the joy of His creation God does not stint Himself. Nor does the poet, in his great vision, renounce the fullness, the vivification and the impetus of his art. Rather it is only out of his whole intensity that the deeper art is fashioned. He fashions out of the magnitude of the abundance pouring through him, and if he so much as taints that abundance with his inhibitive scrupulosity, his very art will suffer."[11]

When that vision is of the violent and the erotic, there is a special problem that comes forward. For the religious man who is a poet, the considerations of that "inhibitive scrupulosity" include the matter of sin and therefore the ultimate matter of salvation. In a later instance, Everson took up this problem and presented its intellectual solution:

> "The tendency of the religious artist is to shy away from the most acute imaginative demand because of the fear of the imagination, and the danger of falling into sin. This is what I meant by the inner censor, the artist's first problem. I call it a pseudo problem because the Thomistic principle is clear: 'Now the delectation of the thought itself results from the inclination of the appetite to the thought. But the thought itself is not in itself a mortal sin. Sometimes, indeed,

it is only a venial sin, as when a man thinks of
such a thing for no purpose; and sometimes it is
no sin at all, as when a man has a purpose in
thinking of it; for instance, he may wish to preach
or dispute about it' (ST, II-II, q. 179). Or, I
might add, he may, if he is a religious artist,
seek to transform it in the universality of the
life of man in God, purged of its decadent soft-
ness, and epitomized in the extremes of moral
consequence through the projected truths of the
aesthetic vision. "[12]

By following the "most acute imaginative demand," Everson
is enabled to create his poems of great power. Logan's
remark that "one is hurt by the relentless succession of
poems violently written on violent subjects" is actually a
confirmation of that power. Furthermore, it is precisely
by such a "relentless succession" that Everson can fully
wrestle with the interior realities in all their ferocity. Only
through this complete engagement does the interior liberation
emerge by which the total and shameless response can issue
in "The Song the Body Dreamed in the Spirit's Mad Behest."
By the same token, the humbled and penitent concluding poem,
"In Savage Wastes," has its validity only in view of the en-
countered realities graphically and unsparingly articulated in
the poems which precede it. That, taken all in all, these
poems are pre-eminent artistic achievements, Herbert Kenny,
in the review cited earlier, once again provides an apt obser-
vation when he points out that

"if the sexual imagery startles and if the brutal
images repel, the whole is redeemed by the over-
all artistry which, to use one of the Brother's fa-
vorite words, subsumes the barbed parts into the
magnificently textured whole. "

One could take this discussion, the basic lines of which
I have set down, much further. However, to conclude my
particular attention to the matters involved, there is a final
point to be made. Beyond the artistic achievement and be-
yond the psychological revelation which Everson's poetry sus-
tains, these poems with which I have been concerned make
emphatically clear the ultimate proportions of his verse, even
when--or, especially when--it appears most excessive. Neither
truly excessive nor fundamentally pointless, his verse goes
inexorably onward, limning the deep contours of his humanity
and measuring them, not in terms of his own limited nature

but--and here Everson attains what his contemporaries hardly attempt--against the absolute dimensions of the Divine.

**

When "The Last Crusade" appeared in print in 1969,[13] seven years after the collection to which it actually belonged, it served to emphasize what had already been discernible, particularly in the "Love and Violence" section of The Hazards of Holiness. In addition, except for a further theme to be pointed out below, the poem and the essay which accompanied it in its independent printing confirmed the observations which I have just discussed and which were formulated long before the appearance of "The Last Crusade." In his essay on the poem, Everson draws upon some of the same texts I have already cited. For these reasons and in deference to space limitations, I will give "The Last Crusade" a rather brief consideration, although the poem, taken on its own, could easily accommodate a substantial discussion.

Fundamentally, "The Last Crusade" serves the same mythic purposes as the biblical narratives included in The Hazards of Holiness, and particularly the projection of the dangerous potential of the feminine reality, as it emerges from the unconscious as well as in its objective counterparts. Where it differs from those narratives is in its much more violational character--in its material, in its details, and, most importantly, in its underlying theme. Furthermore, instead of being based upon a biblical episode, the poem is an imagined narrative set in the period of the Crusades.

Baldly stated, the plot is sensational. A beautiful young duchess, wandering in the upper areas of her husband's castle during the early morning, comes upon a sleeping nobleman who has stayed the night in a turret-room as a guest of the Duke. The Duchess lingers in fascination over the man. Stirred sharply out of his sleep by her presence, the man pulls her down to him, and they engage in a sexual encounter which becomes, as the poem proceeds, a titanic contest between them. Before they have done, the pair come to the awesome recognition that they are, in fact, father and daughter, thus compounding the adulterous with the incestuous. This is especially devastating for the man, who, as a knight, was on his way to engage in the Crusades. No sooner does he determine that he must now turn from his original purpose in order to do penance for his transgression than, in the final

lines of the poem, the Duke's men suddenly and without warn-
ing smash through the door of the room.

In its opening section, the narrative is presented from
the point of view of the Duchess, recalling the event, seeing
about it something fated, and retracing her movements that
dawn.   The section has a leisurely pace and is marked by
some beautiful passages of natural description.   The middle
sections of the poem, concerned with the tremendous sexual
encounter, are as unrestrained in rhetoric and as uninhibited
in detail as anything Everson has written.   Quite likely, had
the poem been reviewed it would have been subject to such
objections and reservations as was the case with the poems
paired as "The Hazards of Holiness."

As this central part of the poem proceeds, and each
of the partners becomes alternately dominant and overpowered,
the action takes on increasingly transpersonal dimensions as
it leads toward its final and complex revelation.   One would
have to read through the entire part to truly grasp the rising
power of the encounter, but a couple of brief passages will
at least intimate the scope it attains.   Here is the man:

> He reared, the stallion-man,
> His head neighing the sky,
> The flared nostrils, frightful
> His sex the red ruiner, monstrous,
> Ran at her.

And here is the woman at her most elemental:

> All infidel and beast
> She screamed, clawing, the skewered cat.
> As the female fights.
> As the she-snake toils her prey.
> As the she-lion claws the bulked head down
>   of the trampling bull, the goring horn.
> As the she-beast ...

As layer after layer of limitation and restraint gives way,
the action arrives at its revelatory conclusion:

> All the daughters of Eve
> Stamped and twisted
> Swinging the final insuperable subjugation:
> The phallus of God.
>
> More than virtue,

More than delight,
More than the intellect's
Conceivable beatitude,
The terrible consuming splendor
Of archetypal sin.

Stripped, the blaze of its actuality
Sheathing them round,
Father and daughter
At last confront.

. . .

From the brain's deep mystery,
From the heart's black hole,
From the pit beyond delusion,
They stared, they knew.

The poem thus confronts not only one of humanity's most
hardbound taboos, but also a terrifyingly awesome awareness
that sin is somehow committed with God. To speak exclusive-
ly within the context of the poet's narrative, we can say that
behind any man there resides, for the woman, the psycholo-
gical image, the imago, of the father; but beyond the human
father there lies the supreme Father, God Himself. In his
essay, Everson makes it clear that this matter is truly meant
to be carried by the poem. And he claims it not only as a
generalization derived from the specific situation depicted--

"for in her confrontation with God the Father im-
plicit in every male all of humanity is subject to
the law that relates them to each other: the law
of desire. The buried lust of the father for the
daughter and the daughter for the father from the
ultimate equation inducing the stripping away of
the masks. As Father, God knows and loves.
As daughter, humanity desires and responds.
And in the violational encounter, in the depths
of the sin, they recognize what they are...."

--but also "in every sin we commit":

"He is there in our depths, behind our mind's
deceptive particularization, despite the concrete-
ness of the individuals involved, or the immediacy
of whatever the situation we are engaged in. It
lurks behind the facade of all violation, an obses-
sive compulsion, a lust of our disordered thought
--God-lust--and, like all lust, denotes the intem-

perate good we seize upon as a short cut to
finality.

"And I saw that in some way God is complicit
in this. I say 'in some way' because if we are
forbidden to entertain the idea theologically it
emerges no less powerfully in all its psychologi-
cal force."

Powerfully indeed. It is worth pointing out, however, that
at the most conservative and orthodox level, it is axiomatic
that man seeks and does in accordance with some aspect of
good; and, further, that every good is reflective of the Su-
preme Good, again God Himself. Once more, Everson has
taken an accepted position to a far-reaching conclusion,
working out one of the implicit "corollaries," if this time
not so "obvious" as Herbert Kenny had commented in regard
to "The Song the Body Dreamed in the Spirit's Mad Behest."

To have recognized the archetypal reality of her en-
counter was the woman's triumph. It was a triumph lost
when she recognized the specific physical reality of her indi-
vidual father:

And she broke, terrified,
Sheared sideways,
Doom-spun, spitted on bone,
The fell lance gutting.

It is from this lapse that, psychologically, she evoked her
doom, first in the fierce rejection of the self-recriminating
father and then in the closing of the poem with the entrance
of her husband's men. Nevertheless, the recognition was
made, and with it the great surge of psychic energy unleashed
--as much for the poet himself as for the heroine of his tale.
Although the feminine has shown her great power in over-
turning the aims and structures of the masculine, she has
also given to the poet the impetus out of which could be writ-
ten the remaining poems of The Hazards of Holiness, enabling
him to make his way artistically as well as personally out
of his Dark Night of the Soul.

Finally, we must note that even in the face of her
lapse and the father's condemnation, and on the verge of her
apprehension by her husband's men, the heroine maintains
an incredible unselfconsciousness, the true feminine insouci-
ance. The poet describes her on the final page of the poem:

She lay on the bed
Her eyes like a fawn's
Great listening pools of unperplexed silence,
Gazing out of a measureless regard,
Subsumed in the complex infinity of
    serene comprehension,
. . .
She opened her lips to say Go then,
A syllable utterly without rancour
    or condemnation,
Transparently feminine in its unreflecting
    acceptance of him and of her,
The deed, the castle,
The moment and the world,
The last crusade,
Contained in them and containing them,
At peace, the winey ardour
Quelled in her loins,
Instinct with seed . . .

Combined with this personal quality is the "purity" of the
act itself, something very like the natural acts Everson de-
picted in "In All These Acts." Whereas both Salome and
Judith are shown to be acting for ends beyond themselves,
for the Duchess the act is its own justification. In these
two features, she appears as a reflection of the feminine
archetype, the anima, more perfectly than the other women.
This same twofold character will re-emerge in The Rose of
Solitude and be amplified there, but the fact of the poet's
portrayal of it here, as though preparatory, is important to
note.

Notes

1 Brother Antoninus, The Hazards of Holiness: Poems
      1957-1960, with a Foreword by Brother Antoninus
      (Garden City, N. Y. : Doubleday, 1962.)

2 Kenny, Herbert A. , "The Hazards of Religious Poetry:
      A Shocking Book," The Catholic Reporter (Kansas
      City, Mo.), September 21, 1962.

3 Circlot, J. E. , A Dictionary of Symbols, translated by
      Jack Sage (New York: Philosophical Library, 1962),
      p356.

4 Jung, C. G. , Answer to Job, translated by R. F. C.

Hull ("A Meridian Book"; Cleveland: World Pub. Co.,
1960), p160.

5 Ortega y Gasset, José, On Love: Aspects of a Single
   Theme, translated by Toby Talbot (New York: Meri-
   dian Books, 1956), p173.

6 Logan, John, "Poetry Shelf," The Critic XXI, No. 5
   (April-May 1963), p86.

7 Creeley, Robert, "'Think What's Got Away,'" Poetry:
   A Magazine of Verse CII, No. 1 (April 1963), p43.

8 Mills, Ralph J., Jr., Contemporary American Poetry
   ("Studies in Language and Literature," No. 2; New
   York: Random House, 1965), p99.

9 "Dialogue on Holy Violence," Approach: A Literary Quar-
   terly, No. 49 (fall 1963), pp40-44. The review is by
   Albert Fowler.

10 "A Conversation with Brother Antoninus," The Harvard
   Advocate XCVII, No. 3 (spring/summer 1963), p32.

11 "Prodigious Thrust," unpublished typescript, pp368-69.
   The autobiography was completed in 1956.

12 "The Artist and Religious Life," The American Benedic-
   tine Review XI, Nos. 3-4 (September-December 1960),
   232, n. 14. The article itself is a printed transcrip-
   tion of an interview with Brother Antoninus, to which
   he added amplifying footnotes for its appearance.

13 Brother Antoninus, The Last Crusade, with a Commen-
   tary, "A Note on The Last Crusade," by Brother An-
   toninus (Berkeley, Calif.: Oyez, 1969).

14 Ibid., "A Note on The Last Crusade," pp24-25.

THE INNER WAR

Paul A. Lacey. 1972

It is perhaps to be expected that the extended commentaries
on Everson's verse have been confined almost wholly to those
who have been favorably impressed with his work. His
many vociferous critics (like James Dickey and Leslie Fied-
ler) have contented themselves with blistering attacks in re-
views of individual volumes as they have appeared. It re-
mained for a Protestant critic to mount the only sustained
indictment that Everson has received, operating not so much
from an anti-Catholic position as from an anti-doctrinal one.
In this essay appearing in his book, The Inner War: Forms
and Themes in Recent American Poetry (Fortress Press,
1972), Paul A. Lacey denies the contention that Ev-
erson emerges untrammeled from the confrontation between
poetry and dogma.

> If his poetry achieves the victory
> over himself that he wishes, we
> must be grateful for that, and
> wish him well. But if we bring
> to our reading the expectation
> that form and content support
> each other in such a way that
> poetic problems are solved po-
> etically and not doctrinally, we
> must remain dissatisfied with
> much of Brother Antoninus' work.

Two stages are readily discernible in William Ever-
son's life as a poet. For fifteen years he published poetry
as William Everson--farmer, printer, conscientious objector
of no particular religious persuasion in World War II; for
nearly twenty years he was Brother Antoninus--convert to

Catholicism, Dominican lay brother. That second stage represented by the name in religion is now over, since he has given up his annual vows as an oblate, left the Order, and married.

The pre-Catholic poetry reflects the same preoccupations which mark all his later work. It is rooted in awful awareness of nature and history, the two matrices in which man either finds himself or knows himself trapped. Both nature and history are violent; both represent outwardly and universally the inner war which Everson experiences. Kenneth Rexroth says in his introduction to The Residual Years that all of Everson's poetry, including the later, Catholic poetry, "is concerned with the drama of his own self, rising and falling along the sine curve of life...." Coming to terms with the self also means coming to terms with the savagery of men and the savagery of the natural world. And poetry is both a means of coming to terms and the product of the conflicts out of which the self is being shaped. Poetry has pattern, created by the tug and pull of emotions and events, refined and perfected in the frustration of human fallibility and incapacity. "The Answer," a poem from "The Impossible Choices" (1940-1946), explores these themes. The poet labors over his lines, drawing on the pain which has afflicted him from birth--failure, guilt, the tyranny of sex--but no poem comes, "nothing converges." Only later, when some sense experience or casual word evokes a response from the inner depths, do "the inner locks open." Conscious labor is replaced by unconscious growth: "The thought stirs in its seed;/ The images flower"; and the poem emerges,

> Freighted with judgment,
> Swung out of the possible into the actual,
> As one man's insight matches mankind's at the
> midpoint of language;
> And the meeting minds reduplicate in the running vowel
> Their common concern.

The inner war is a necessary prelude to the act of creation, but creation itself comes from those depths in the self where individual and race meet, where convergence occurs. The poem does not belong to the poet alone; it confirms and is confirmed by the language of the race.

> Then here rides his triumph:
> Caught in his doom he had only his anguish,
> But the human pattern imposes across his
> stammering mind
> Its correctional hand.

"Delicate structure," "midpoint of language," "the
human pattern": all speak of the individual's link with others,
but for Everson these links are most frequently created by
guilt and violence, the outer wars which reflect the inner.
In "Attila" and "Fish-Eaters" Everson speaks of the violent
past from which individuals and social forms alike spring.
Attila's outer wars failed--though only because there have
been so many others--but he has made his mark on the deeps
of life, in the genes of the race and in the unconscious. The
poet cannot trace his blood to its single source; it has min-
gled in thousands as a result of conquest, war, and lust.
But, thinking of the fish-eaters, he knows that what he wants,
his longing for peace, somehow has its roots in that past he
must explore and affirm: "I, the living heir of the bloodiest
men of all Europe."

What has made structure--the human pattern, language,
social institutions--is violence. In "The Roots" the poet
meditates on the English, gaunt raiders, broken in turn by
waves of conquest, who shape the words of our language from
their history: "... The single rhythm of the ancient blood/
Remembers the anguish, the hate and desire." Trying to
write, the poet feels behind him this trial and error, the
shaping of sounds for experience, the awareness of genera-
tions coming to form in his mind.

A poem has both structure and freedom; it is both
personal and universal; it is made from the stuff of violence
but transformed into peace and beauty; it is a midpoint of
language where minds meet. A poem grows out of the tangle
and struggle of opposites. Light comes out of darkness:
"I feel the power rising out of the dark sources,/ Those
unknown springs in the sea-floor of the self." War is a
constant motif in the poetry, whether Everson is writing
about the act of making poetry, his consciousness of history,
or his response to the natural world. The poem "Sun"
begins "Season on Season the sun raiding the valley/ Drowns
it in light." The storms speak "furious words" and "sylla-
bles of thunder"; the music of nature, like the music of po-
etry, grows out of the dark impulses, danger, destruction.

Everything is at war, but the poet's end is to find
peace without sloth. The early acts of Everson's drama of
the self are played out against the backdrop of the rise of
fascism in Europe and the approaching world war. Two
poems in particular memorialize the drama: "The Sides of
a Mind" and "Invocation." In the first, the spiritual struggle

expressed in the conflict of sides of a mind parallels the
physical struggles being played out in war, the march of
squadrons, and "the smell of misery and rot and the filth
of the poor." Behind the battle to build shining cities and
obliterate poverty there still lies the doubt that any human
action matters. "But there is no God, nor was ever a God,/
And that is the root of our trouble." Working over his
futile poem, the poet feels the power to write surging in
him but lacks a theme: "Belief made foolish, the pitiless
hunger unfulfilled,/ The mind crying for anchor." He sur-
veys his heritage and knows only guilt and inadequacy; he
turns to nature and sees only the destruction on which his
life is predicated. Working in the fields, breathing, eating,
his body is inescapably engaged in warfare against other creatures.

> Every sucking breath that I drew
> The long border of warfare ran down my lungs,
> Furious soldiers of my blood warring and killing ...

The poet turns inward so radically that he becomes
conscious of the oozing of his pores, the sloughing of dead
skin from his feet, and the growing of his nails, and asks
whether this ugly decay can justify his poetry. The poem
reaches two conclusions, the first that "life feeds on life,"
so that what we make of our existence means everything and
nothing. This thematic rounding off leaves unresolved the
conflict represented by the "sides of the mind." The second
conclusion loses the conflict in a lyrical celebration of the
close of a decade and the opening of something new. Nature
for itself, not as a symbol of any inner meaning, soothes
the poet; the night flows and the river rolls, "the decade
wears itself out," and the unsubstantiated hope for the future
closes the poem.

"Invocation" also sums up a decade, in this case the
completion of the poet's third decade. Now, however, he
has made his affirmations, recorded for example in "The
Vow," never to take life wantonly, to atone in his soul for
the past he had no control over, to show pity and mercy to
all life precisely because he knows its ultimate dissolution.
He now sees the spring fructification, the summer fulfillment
of nature, and asks for himself a part in that fertility and
harvest. He is still at war, "in which neither the foe nor
myself is known," a war within the self which finds its double
in the war between men. To answer his question "And I?
What am I?" the poet must strip away the ease and pleasure,
the lack of imagination, the habitual frameworks which conceal
the warfare.

There runs the war,
In the half-perceived but unattended,
There at the marginal edge of perception,
There must it be met.

He promises his pity for all living things, so that the
spirit will be cleansed, the ego chastened, the senses hushed.
He pictures the terrible struggle of evolution, where the self
is locked in its inner struggle and "the extensional conflict,"
but where the perception of its need and its partial attainment
can partially redeem the waste of the past. And out of that
vision of the war of evolution he prays that his thirtieth year
might yield him fulfillment.

Of Everson's early poetry it might be said that his
theme is finding a form, while his forms express a persis-
tent struggle to find a theme. The war in the self has as
its purpose finding a truth to speak and to live by. But war
is always destructive; Everson's poetry is marked by disgust
for the physical--especially human sexuality--shame, guilt,
imperfectly controlled violence. That this should be so in
the writing of one so sensitive to the times in which he lives
is not to be wondered at. What he longs for is meaningful
pattern, a framework within which life makes sense. History
provides one framework, nature another, and many of Ever-
son's poems grow out of the attempt to measure and value
the self against the patterns of family history, racial history,
or natural history.

The verse patterns and language he uses in these
poems illustrate the theme-form problem. He favors long
poem-sequences where the separate stanzas and parts often
relate to each other like separate poems within a book. End-
rhyme or regular metrical patterns rarely occur; instead
Everson uses alternations of long and short lines to represent
the rise and fall of emotion or activity. Lines are frequently
built up in the loose parallelism of the Hebrew Psalms.
Phrases and words modify each other simply by being placed
side by side. The poetry frequently tends toward slackness--
in the line, the stanza, and poem--which duplicates the emo-
tional sprawl. The language he uses serves to counteract
this effect, but not without exacting its own price. Anglo-
Saxon monosyllables predominate, often harsh, blunt words
which convey images and feelings through tactile impressions.
Nearly every noun has its adjective, but often they are past
participles which lend a sense of physical action to the phrase.

The whispering wind,

The erect and tensile filaments of weeds,
The fallen leaf,
Half-consumed near the igneous rock,
All keep accordance,
Strung on the rays that leave no trace,
But sift out the hours
Purling across the deaf stones,
While the exactitude of each entering star
Chronicles the dark.

["A Privacy of Speech" IX]

Intense but unfocused emotion, language in which physical reality and intellectual abstractions jostle with one another, form and theme in search of one another, an aura of violence surrounding even the most pastoral poems: these are the characteristics of Everson's earliest verse. Perhaps no recent poet better exemplifies the longing for and resistance to form.

In 1949 William Everson became a Roman Catholic, in 1950 he began working with the poor as part of the Catholic Worker movement, and in 1951 he entered a Dominican monastery. An intense conversion led to a series of callings, first away from secular success, and finally away from the secular life itself. With his new name, symbolizing a new life and changed nature, Brother Antoninus also received a new, tight, and finely articulated framework into which he needed to fit his whole life. His next book of poems, The Crooked Lines of God: Poems 1949-1954, testifies to the importance of that framework, as do the "Pages from an Unpublished Autobiography" which appeared in Ramparts in September, 1962, and the interviews he has given.

"The first thing about a vocation is that there is a need for perfection.... If you come to the religious life, you come to do sacrifice. This is imperative. If this is not understood, woe to the man who comes; if his inner search, his grasp of reality, does not exceed his other concerns, even his art becomes a trifling thing."[1]

The terms in which Brother Antoninus describes the religious life set the conditions for a more intense inner war than he has experienced before, except that the adversaries cannot claim an equal right to win. To practice the vocation of artist in opposition to the religious vocation is to commit the sin of disobedience. The dedication of the artist becomes willful pride. God writes straight; man--the poet--writes crooked. "My crooked lines, tortured between grace and the depraved human heart (my heart) gouge out the screed of my defection. Everywhere about me the straight writing hems me in, compresses me, flattens my will. "[2]

The Crooked Lines of God shows a number of organizing principles at work. There is, of course, Roman Catholic theology, stressed and heightened by the convert's zeal. Following that organizing principle, Brother Antoninus has arranged the poems in three parts, "each corresponding to a particular phase of spiritual development, and each dominated, more or less, by the psychology of a particular saint. " The first section he sees dominated by the psychology of Saint Augustine, focusing on guilt, repentance, and the contemplation of the Passion; the second section, corresponding to his time with the Catholic Worker, he sees as Franciscan in psychology; the third is Dominican, moving through "the full development of the erotic religious psychology of the Spanish Baroque. " This three-part division also roots in Brother Antoninus's development chronologically, taking us from the conversion through its first fruits, to the monastery and to the point where the clash of crooked and straight choke out poetry. Finally, Brother Antoninus set the type for the book, giving, as we shall consider later, yet another important shaping influence on the poetry, "concretizing" the spiritual states it testifies to.

The book opens with "Triptych for the Living," the first poems of his conversion, and they reflect the intense compression of that subjective experience in the form of the Christmas story, the mature, skeptical mind reflecting on and appropriating the most naive elements of the Christian mythos.

"The Uncouth" is a meditation on the shepherds to whom the angel announced the birth of Christ. The subject is almost mandatory for the Christian poet, but for that reason a successful handling is difficult. The story always raises the same questions, approached and answered in hundreds of poems and thousands of sermons each Christmastide: Why were these simple people first given the Good News? What does this story say to our own time? Unfortunately, the range of responses to these questions has narrowed down over the years. W. H. Auden makes the shepherds represent the Lumpenproletariat, a void to be filled, a force to be given direction. That is one kind of updating. Brother Antoninus gives us another kind--straightforward, unironic--making the shepherds a symbol for the perennial

outcast, the uncouth who is unknown and unknowing. Once
this connection is made, however, there is nothing more to
do with it--no shock of recognition, no admiration of a witty
comparison, nothing but the working out of details.

Recognizing this, Antoninus paints a picture reminis-
cent of an altar-panel, where our interest is engaged more
by craftsmanship than by the story. The scene becomes
California, the shepherds become the sheepherders, "in the
folklore of the West ... of all types the most low. "

As for them, the herdsmen,
They'd rather hug out the year on a juniper ridge
Than enter now, where the hard-bitten settlers
Fenced their acres; where the merchants
Wheedled the meager gain of summer;
Where the brindled mastiffs
Mauled the wethers.

They become types of the "prime, animal amplitude
for life," the representation of unchanneled energy, the body
and "naked intelligence" awaiting a soul. Grace comes first
to them, in Antoninus's poem, because they have retained
the purity of ignorance and have no knowledge of either the
world or the angel.

Since Antoninus leaves the story untouched, except to
place it in an American setting, we must look to the details
of form to determine whether he has made something new.
The poem has six stanzas of varying lengths, from one line
to thirteen, loose verse paragraphs built on irregular iambic
lines. Only the diction gives any sense of energy to the
poem, and it is rooted in physical description, monosyllables,
and strong verbs. Some coined words effectively surprise
the reader: "pastures/ Greened again with good verdure,"
"Wind northed for cold," "wilderness-hearted earth. " Al-
literation and assonance operate to give the poem a quiet mu-
sic.

When we compare this poem, a quiet, pious rendering
of a traditional Christian story, with the prose account of its
genesis, we see some of the difficulties Antoninus faces in
working with the framework he has chosen. In "Pages from
an Unpublished Autobiography" he speaks of attending mid-
night mass, Christmas of 1948, sitting in the church and
feeling his customary estrangement from it. He smells "the
resinous scent of fir trees" coming from the crib which the

nuns had set up in the cathedral. He seizes on the scent
with "true realization," and without the rebellion it would
ordinarily call up. "Now out of the greatness of my need
I sensed in it something of a verification, a kind of indeter-
minate warrant that I need not fear, were I to come to Christ,
that He would exact the dreaded renunciation of my natural
world."[3] The verification, only a scent mixed with the in-
cense, draws him into meditation on the scene in the crib.
He reflects on the shepherds until "I saw the correlation."
This, the key to his conversion, is also the key to the poem;
the California sheepherder becomes a confirmation of the
meaning of the Incarnation, for the Good News comes first
to the man of the wilderness, the ignorant sheepherder sub-
dued to what he works in. All this Antoninus renders for
us through constant reference to the odors of the fir and
the recalled odors of the sheepherders. The evidence which
wins his assent to Christianity comes through "the odor of
fir, the memory of sheepdung and mutton grease, cutting
across the closed interior air of the Cathedral." After the
logical structure of a faith has been affirmed, he says,
there remains a blankness of those areas of association
"which make in the mind the living thing a religion must be,"
and this blank filled for him when the odor of fir persuaded
him that Christ would not deprive him of "the natural king-
dom and the great sustaining Cosmos...."[4]

Turning from the crib to the woman beside him, whom
he loves, the poet reflects on the feminine receptivity to the
Mystery. The woman becomes a symbol for intuition, open-
ness, "vibrant expectancy." Alternating between her innocent
waiting and the crude primitive subjectivity of the sheepherder,
Antoninus weaves his mediation, searching for the correla-
tions. In turn he stands in the Mystery of Christ and the
Mystery of the Church: "The once sinister Church, seen
only as evil, becomes in a trice the resplendent Mother of
Men, the Christ as pure beneficence, and he skips in sing-
ing."

Paraphrasing his description of the moment of conver-
sion cannot do Antoninus justice. In a few pages he shows
us the convergence of forces and experiences and the dis-
covery of "correlations" so vividly that we stand within the
conversion situation with him. Intellectual insights and af-
firmations of faith receive some final confirmation for him
through his senses; the smell of fir and the remembered
smell of sheepherders become signatures for a spiritual
truth. And we participate in this with him. Unfortunately,

the poem which grows out of this experience is thin and abstract by comparison. Perhaps the simplest explanation for the difference is that the autobiographical passages must be in the first person, the discoveries must be personal, while the third-person telling in the poem distances events. But, more importantly, there is a world of difference between discovering a correlation or link in one's past which brings a truth home to oneself, and elevating that correlation into a general truth. Antoninus tries to translate the emotional and spiritual profundity of his experience into a rational profundity in the poem, and it does not work.

In this we see the chief difficulty facing Brother Antoninus as a poet and us as his readers. The conversion has been accomplished and is in the past:

"Nothing remains to show now but the poetry, and what is that? Something of the energy is contained there, but also something of the shapelessness, something persisting in the mystery of form, the mystery which blankets and obscures the outline of its temporality, but somehow releases the abiding energy, the force, and the inherent motive that made the act what it was."[6]

Form is ambiguous for Antoninus. Energy and shapelessness come together; the mystery of form stands over against them, acting to release energy but also to obscure and blanket the "outline of its temporality," which apparently means all the slight details of sensory experience, the stuff out of which poetry, and conversions, is made. Form comes, ab extra, imposed by a theory or a theology. The poems must be introduced with a Foreword to blanket and obscure the torment of unworthy thoughts and human temptations by announcing that the crooked lines will eventually be made straight. The Foreword reports that the inner war, out of which the poems come, is over, or has ended in armistice.

"The Coming" and "The Wise," the other poems of the Triptych, are like "The Uncouth" in employing vigorous, kinesthetic language to explore relatively simple correlations between past and present. The "freshness, raciness and energy of immediate observation," which Samuel Johnson demanded of poetry, are there in abundance, but we must conclude, also with Johnson, that so far as theme is concerned "there is no nature, for there is nothing new." What is said is familiar, orthodox.

A number of problems arise in any treatment of biblical stories. The most obvious is that one has little latitude with a sacred fable; the details must be faithfully reproduced or any deviation thoroughly justified by its clever contemporaneity. Of course, in the richest literature, details occur for themselves and for the deeper significance they offer the rest of the work, but when the details of a story are so sacred that the only acceptable use of the artist's imagination is to make every one of them plausible in a new telling, no matter what the demands of the new work are, we see the heaviest weight of tradition.

Perhaps a more difficult problem to deal with for the artist who wishes to explore Christian themes is one we find in the New Testament itself, namely, that every action and speech must be explained through the benefit of hindsight, by reference to types and prophesies. So every surprising act or word of Jesus is explained by reference to the crucifixion and resurrection which are in the future, from the narrative's point of view, but already accomplished for the narrator. Or the hard sayings are explained as fulfilling a prophesy from the Old Testament. Saint Paul's reading of the Old Testament as providing types and shadows of Christ illustrates the difficulty of reading a text free of this sacralizing tendency.

A third problem in dealing with a sacred fable is that it must be made to bear theological or spiritual freight. It must mean more than the events themselves. Frequently the artist meets this demand by a resort to dramatic irony of the "had-we-but-known!" kind, underplaying the events while hinting at their cosmic significance. T. S. Eliot's "The Magi" is an example of the type, as are "Triptych for the Living" and other poems in The Crooked Lines of God. The generalizing of "The Flight in the Desert" illustrates the point:

This was the first of his goings forth into the wilderness
    of the world.
There was much to follow: much of portent, much
    of dread.
But what was so meek then and so mere, so slight
    and strengthless,
(Too tender, almost, to be touched)--what they
    nervously guarded
Guarded them. As we, each day, from the lifted chalice,
That fragile Bread the mildest tongue subsumes,

To be taken out in the blatant kingdom,
Where Herod sweats, and his deft henchmen
Riffle the tabloids--that keeps us.

The look forward here requires turning the infant
Jesus and Herod into symbols at the cost of their humanity.
So much is made of the deeper significance of the flight into
the desert that we lose sight of the personal drama, and even
the final stanza, picturing the Holy Family around a camp-
fire while Jesus feeds at his mother's breast, fails to per-
suade us that these are real people. Anyone reflecting on
his sacred stories will discern in them both a universal and
individual significance; seeing the world's history and the his-
tory of his own life converging in each story. It is harder
to recognize that what gives them their vigor is that they
are first of all the history of the people they speak about.
In "Gethsemani" Brother Antoninus describes Christ fainting
with fear as He contemplates the approaching crucifixion.
The language is vivid and excites our compassion, but then
the theological tidying-up begins. "Power had proved his
Godhead," the poet says,

But that the God was man,
That the man could faint,
This the world must know,

The human suffering becomes an object lesson and
loses its credibility in the process. "Whatever the world
will suffer/ Is here foresuffered now." The second and
third parts of this long poem become steadily more discursive
and correspondingly less interesting poetically. Rhetorical
questions and exclamations become the chief devices for im-
porting excitement into the poem. Finally the object lesson
swallows everything else.

His subject has deep importance to Brother Antoninus,
and he clearly has brought to it a wealth of reading and re-
flection. He is personally engaged throughout the work, but
the poem is not personal and fails to engage the reader per-
sonally, for where there should be discovery and revelation,
there is only explication.

When Coleridge published his "Reflections on Having
Left a Place of Retirement," he attached to it the epigraph
sermoni propriora, "in his own voice," which Charles Lamb
preferred to translate as "properer for a sermon." For
though Coleridge was deeply engaged with his reflections--

tentative religious opinions and ideas and resolutions for fu-
ture action--poetic form was more a convenience than a
necessity for them. For the poet to speak "in his own voice"
will not make the result poetry, if the voice he uses is a
schoolteacher's or the village explainer's. A constant dif-
ficulty with Brother Antoninus's poetry is precisely that what
matters most to him, what brought him to his faith and his
vocation as a Dominican Friar, cannot be directly translated
into poetry. When he speaks sermoni propriora as a Domini-
can, what he says may be "properer for a sermon." At
least, in the practice of his art, a tension actually exists
between the demands of form and those of content.

The short, choppy line and a largely Anglo-Saxon vo-
cabulary characterized Brother Antoninus's pre-Catholic po-
etry, as it does much of his later work. In The Crooked
Lines of God he also tries a number of canticles, songlike
poems composed in long, flowing lines. Here the influence
of Catholic liturgy is most clearly seen, but it is enriched
by other streams which have fed the poet, including Robinson
Jeffers, Whitman, and the Song of Songs which has such a
direct influence on the liturgy. The long accentual line and
loose parallelism of the canticle form offer an ideal medium
for one of Antoninus's favorite themes, celebrating the pleni-
tude of nature. His "Canticle to the Waterbirds" in the sec-
ond section of the book, glories in the creation, symbolized
by the strange waterbirds of California. The early stanzas
of the poem illustrate what Gerard Manley Hopkins meant
when he spoke of "stress" and "idiom," whatever strongly
accentuated individuality and set one thing off from another,
and "inscape," how the details of external nature reflect an
inner, spiritual shape.

Clack your beaks you cormorants and kittiwakes,
North on those rock-croppings finger-jutted into the
rough Pacific surge;
You migratory terns and pipers who leave but the
temporal clawtrack written on sandbars there of
your presence;
. . .
Break wide your harsh and salt-encrusted beaks
unmade for song
And say a praise up to the Lord.

Detail, difference, individuality, and their beauty take
the center of the poem, but once again Antoninus turns from
describing things as he sees and loves them to explaining

what they are there for. And a long, loose line is the worst possible medium for discursive writing: "But mostly it is your way you bear existence wholly within the context of His utter will and are untroubled."

In the final section of his book, Brother Antoninus explores most freely the sensual language and compressed intensity which were common to his earliest poetry. Here he takes his warrant from the Spanish Baroque and particularly from Saint John of the Cross and Saint Teresa of Avila. Saint John can be a particularly lucky influence on a poet still newly converted enough to suffer from scruples about literary creation, for he was able to separate the system-building aspects of his theology from the intense personal experience from which it drew its evidence. The Ascent to Mount-Carmel and The Dark Night of the Soul are prose treatises on the spiritual life; the poems render the sensual and emotional experience of religious ecstasy. And, as Saint John says in the preface to The Ascent to Mount-Carmel, all the stages of the spiritual journey to be explicated in the prose work are revealed in one poem in which the soul perceives itself as the Bride of Christ.

His influences allow Brother Antoninus to write about violence and sex, subjects which have always held a threatening fascination for him. Now he can bring them together, as in his canticle for Mary Magdalene, and speak of "A Savagery of Love." Mary Magdalene's saintly purity, her sacrificial love of Christ, are the redirecting of her sexuality, not its abnegation. The crucifixion becomes truly the Passion of Christ as we view it through her eyes, taking on some of the sexual significance of suffering for love of others. As Mary Magdalene poured out her body for the delight of others, she poured out the oil to anoint Christ's feet and finally pours out her grief at the foot of the cross. As her sexual nature is completed when her body has been penetrated, so Antoninus makes the lance's penetration of Christ's body a symbol for the completion of His Passion, love of mankind.

> What plenitude of power in passion loosed,
> When the Christ-love and the Christ-death
> Find the Love-death of the Cross!

If sex and violence threaten Brother Antoninus, following the example of Saint John of the Cross gives him a way to exploit the themes and still keep distance between this poetry and his earlier, pre-Catholic work, for in these poems

he imagines himself feminine, receiving the mark of God as
the barren doe receives the blaze of the buck. In "A Can-
ticle to the Christ in the Holy Eucharist" he speaks of Christ
as the mark, the kill, the wound, and describes himself
sucking the wound as a fawn sucks milk from its mother.
"Thy word in my heart was the start of the buck that is
sourced in the doe." Sexual conquest unites violence and sen-
suality; when God is the conqueror, the man who must other-
wise assert his aggressiveness through sexual conquest may
justify his passivity and even pray "Annul in me my man-
hood, Lord, and make/ Me woman-sexed and weak." At
the risk of appearing to psychoanalyze or explain away Brother
Antoninus's poetry, we may say that these poems of the final
section of the book attempt to sublimate material and person-
al drives which have been the source of both anxiety and in-
tense power in his earlier work. These personal issues are
by no means resolved through the poetry, though the intensity
of the struggle confirms his wish to change his nature. They
are among the most striking of his poems, but they testify
eloquently to the constrictions which finally shut off the poetic
flow with which his conversion began.

Brother Antoninus wanted to create a double work of
poetry which would balance out his earlier work. In this
plan either his inspiration or God failed him. What stands
out clearly is how the claims of the religious life and those
of the artistic impulse interact to provide what he calls "cre-
ative tension," the "tension which is union."

Whether speaking about the religious life, artistic cre-
ation, or the structure of the human psyche, Brother Antoni-
nus always begins with paired opposites: active and contem-
plative, conscious and unconscious, rational and nonrational,
intellect and imagination, male and female. In discussing
the tensions which beset the artist in a religious community,
he develops an extended and evocative contrast between the
institutional and the charismatic. This becomes the key dis-
tinction for talking about all the creative tensions he exper-
iences; the tug between these two characterizes the church
as well as the individual within it. "Any religion can only
develop by refining the tension between its charismatic and
institutional elements.... When the charismatic finally breaks
through an institutional matrix and makes its pronouncement,
it brings down upon itself the whole wrath of an almost un-
conscious terror from the opposite side."[7]

It would be unfair to treat this distinction as an at-

tempt to speak with philosophical precision, for Brother An-
toninus is using it to discover how the conflicts and interac-
tions of opposites have fructified his own life and where they
have caused paralysis. "Charismatic" as he uses it always
roots back to the literal meaning of the word, a divinely in-
spired gift of supernatural power or a capacity to lead others.
The charismatic side he identifies, therefore, with the Diony-
sian, the irrational, the artistic, the creative, and the mys-
tical. Inwardness, contemplation, and the imagination are
all associated with it. "The artist is an imaginative man,
and the whole mode of an artist is freedom. The imagina-
tion, strictly speaking, knows no laws."[8] The charismatic
must always be ambiguous and dangerous; it always threatens
to dissipate its gifts in the pursuit of freedom.

For Brother Antoninus the struggle between religion
and art seems far less the result of a tension between the
charismatic and the institutional, though that plays its part,
than between contrary aspects of the charismatic itself. The
charisma presses toward fulfillment of its own nature, toward
some kind of perfection. Here is the source of a deep con-
flict within the charismatic as Brother Antoninus understands
it, for if the artist fulfills his gift through freedom, the re-
ligious man fulfills his through restraint. The Dionysian
man, opening himself up to the mystical even at the risk of
madness, stands opposed to the contemplative, whose goals
are calm vision. "The problem for the spiritual man, the
man seeking perfection, is to curb the sensibility; for the
artist, to liberate the sensibility."[9] But the artist too seeks
perfection of his gifts.

In his interview with David Kherdian, however, he
describes a complex attitude toward perfection in art. As
his poetic craft matured until it became something unconscious,
he turned to printing so that he might have another craft to
develop in. He speaks of approaching facility in a craft,
having it become unconscious, but perfection seems more
threatening than encouraging as a goal, perhaps because it
suggests a willed achievement which consciousness controls.
He speaks of perfecting the work as an act of concretizing or
memorializing the craft. "You write a perfect poem, a per-
fect book of poems, and concretize it in a perfect format
established on absolutely authentic materials."[10]

He renounces the search for perfection in either print-
ing or poetry, however, arguing that the norms of perfection
finally work against themselves and become a demand for

perfectionism. "To go beyond it is worse, believe me, than
to fail to reach it.... What is over-done is more than fin-
ished, it is finished off, 'finalized'--the thing that has hap-
pened to so much modern poetry."[11] Perfectionism is the
violation of the tomb, he says, whereas imperfection, "as
for instance in the gash, actually liberates the charisma."

The terms "memorialize," "concretize" have to do
primarily with finding the right form for what he wants to
do or say in art. But form means something more than pat-
terns created by technique here, for facility in the craft only
signals an intermediate stage in the artist's development.
"The craft has to be memorialized in the flesh, and the flesh
has to be memorialized in the spirit, the life principle. Then
you are free.... She, perfection, delivers you."[12] Perfec-
tion, Sophia, Divine Wisdom, and the Muse become the same
figure, the feminine principle, the receptor of the charisma.
When he speaks of learning to print, Brother Antoninus speaks
of it as having to do with what Jung calls Sensation, the con-
crete side of experience. He needs first to learn techniques,
which means to be straitly confined by them, but only so
that at a later point he will have internalized them sufficiently
to be free even to violate them. Form, whether it derives
from a religious commitment, a theological framework, the
liturgical year, a schema tracing his conversion through the
psychological stages represented by Saint Augustine, Saint
Francis, and Saint John of the Cross, or the psychology of
Jung, stands over against technique. It becomes the synthesis
of craft and content for him.

Such an explanation must not be taken to minimize the
importance of Antoninus's religious commitment. Whether
or not the reader understands why he needs to contain his
poems within the frameworks established by the Forewords
to his books, there can be no doubt that the poet's need for
form, in this larger sense, is so genuine that we could not
have the poetry without it. And if a number of poems seem
deeply flawed because of the framework, others owe their
great success to it.

Quite aside from the influence of a religious vocation
on the development of his charismatic side, his need for
framework would help explain Brother Antoninus's attraction-
repulsion for the institutional life. The institution links a
solitary person to others; it provides a conventionalized life-
style which balances the undisciplined life of the charismatic;
it develops the intellectual and rational faculties to keep pace

with the intuition, emotion, and sensation; finally, it is, in his terms, the active life, as over against the contemplative life of the artist.

Especially as the institutional life requires that the individual submit his inspirations to the judgment of the collective, represented both by the tradition and the superior, it also provides such a counterweight to the charismatic that when Brother Antoninus speaks of the "creative tension between the point of view of the superior and the point of view of the subject," he says "That tension is the crucifixion." The point of union for the creative artist in the religious life is a cross, he says elsewhere.

In The Hazards of Holiness (1962), the steam of poetry which had been choked out in the early years of his religious vocation flows again, for he has taken as theme the spiritual aridity which shut off poetry. Once again the reader is introduced to the poetry through a Foreword which explains it in theological and personal terms. This time the poems are also framed by Jungian psychology.

The Foreword is in two senses an apology for the poetry. Antoninus justifies it as "objectification of inner experience" which he calls "the most efficacious of all acts of relief, except prayer," and he appeals to W. B. Yeats for support: "We gaze not at a work of art, but the re-creation of the man through that art...." From T. S. Eliot he takes the image of the poet as one who writes to exorcise his demons, not to communicate with others. Brother Antoninus offers poems which seek to objectify, concretize, or memorialize his inner experience. His poems represent a victory over himself, and he argues for judging them on that basis.

The second apology seeks to explain away the material from which the poetry comes, for fear that it will seem offensive or blasphemous, especially coming from a Dominican brother. Here he resorts to two explanations, the first an invocation of "that famous Dark Night of the Soul," the second the dream world of depth psychology.

"Against the grain, compounded of the hallucinatory and the obscene, no less than of the transcendental and the sublime, the imagery seeks back against the primordial anguishes, encounters the mute demon and the vocal ghost...."[13]

Once again he fights his inner war as a battle to dis-

cover a form for his poetry, but once again the form is theo-
logical rather than literary. The paired opposites occur
again, this time with much greater debt to Jung's psychology,
so the tension also exists, but over everything there is the
reassurance, cum permissu Superiorum.

The Hazards of Holiness has three sections, titled
"Friendship and Enmity," "The Dark Face of God," and
"Love and Violence." Seven of the poems are introduced by
dreams which generated them. A number of others have
epigraphs or explanations which link them to the same kind
of nonrational source. The dreams are about traveling--on
caravan, on pilgrimage, returning for the poet's mother's
funeral--and about death. Journeys, darkness, graves and
coffins, erotic images and impulses, being swallowed up,
dominate the imagery of the dreams.

The relation of freedom and guilt is the theme of
both his dream-life and his poetry. "Jacob and the Angel"
sets the tone for the entire book. In his dream, the poet
is on caravan to the Holy Land but also returning home from
exile. He and his guides make camp beside a river, intend-
ing to cross over in the morning. He has a dream-within-
a-dream that he has come home to his father's house but
finds it "deathly vacant"; he wakes to find the caravan gone
and the way across the river barred by a tall defender with
a rifle. Because he has been used by his guides, who are
thieves, the poet is indistinguishable from them and the ser-
vant shoots him. As the bullet flies across the distance,
"like a meteor from outer space," the poet feels within him-
self "the whole destiny of the human race in its struggle
toward realization, ... incredibly concretized within my one
tormented life-span, and actualized in my very flesh...."
As he sinks into the water, the poet tries to communicate
to the faithful servant "a gesture of desperate truth" to es-
tablish "the authentic character of what is real." He does
not know whether he has succeeded, but his final affirmation
is that the energies within him have been purged and trans-
formed so that the water can have no final power over this
"core of absolute existence."

The poem describes the interconnectedness of libera-
tion and guilt in the Jacob story. Jacob the supplanter is
driven into exile because of his mother's fondness, but there
he sees "the laddered angels in their intercourse with earth,"
the liberating sign which frees him "from the mother's death-
hug." But then his mother's brother, who tricks him into

marrying Leah instead of Rachel, becomes a symbol of guilt.
"Deep down the offended father/ Lived on symbolic in the
maid's evasive sire." Through service to the father-substi-
tute he gains strength to gain the next liberation, receiving
another sign of angels that he has become "father-freed."
Now he can turn toward home to offer restitution to his
brother. Now he meets the angel, whom he mistakes for
Esau, and struggles with his twin. This must be both his
ultimate restitution and his ultimate liberation; he must both
win and lose the battle, for this twin identity is both an angel
and Esau's champion.

The poem is very different from the dream. What
they have in common is the imagery associated with strug-
gling to cross the stream to confront the defender. The ob-
scure guilt-feelings of the dream, hinted at in images of ex-
ile and the vacant family home, ramify in the Jacob myth to
include both the poet's parent-child conflict and the theme of
fraternal conflict which dominates Genesis. The relationship
between dream and poem is such, however, that the latter
becomes a Jungian homily on the bible story rather than a
re-creation of its meaning.

One queasy crime--and the score-long exiled years!
How many mockeries of the inscrutable archetypes
Must we endure to meet our integration?
Is it fate or merely malice that has made
Us overreach our brother in the burdened womb?

The struggle with the angel becomes a symbol of po-
litical development and the integration of the personality as
aspects of one another. As "the night-wombed nations mur-
mur into birth" while the wrestling match goes on, Jacob's
wives, "twin aspects of his dark divided life" huddle in the
dark and pray for the outcome. He wins his final liberation,
a blessing from the angel, "who seized/ In the heart's black
hole the angel of intellection," and receives his new name,
"Israel, striver with God." Now he can go to his reconcilia-
tion with his brother, who recognizes his new nature.

As always, Brother Antoninus is at his best when
handling violent language and physical sensation and at his
weakest when he makes his fable serve a doctrine. That the
doctrine in this case is about the integration of personality
makes no difference; it is intrusive on the fable and awkward
when poeticized. Nothing in the events in the poem prepares
us for the explanation of the struggle with the angels as the
calling up of intellection from the unconscious, represented

by the "heart's black hole. " The language of the poem becomes abstract and sermonic when the theme needs to be explored through physical imagery. The questions are rhetorical in the worst sense--they are neither taken seriously as requests for information nor open enough to make the answers interesting to us.

A number of the poems show the same difficulty of reconciling the discursive and nondiscursive. "Saints," for example, is built up of short, choppy lines which convey the emotion through explosives and harsh monosyllables. But the discourse is all orthodoxy.

> Not even God
> Has power to force an evil act
> But man does!

And the reader cannot respond to the emotional tension, no matter how genuine he believes it, in such a line as "God? Saints? Faith? Rapture? Vision? Dream?--/ Where?" "The Word" is an example of the most abstract discourse broken up into short lines and made into a kind of shorthand to give the impression of poetry. No physical imagery, no metaphor or simile borrowed from the senses appears in the poem; the reader has nothing to draw him into the poem except the argument, which is as obscure as it is abstract. The poem begins:

> One deepness,
> That mammoth inchoation,
> Nothingness freighted on its term of void,
> Oblivion abandoned to its selflessness,
> Aching for a clue.

Once more we recognize the energy in the verbals, but they do not take us anywhere. The Word was made flesh and dwelt among us precisely so it need not be so abstract and unavailable to human understanding and perception. Here the senses are utterly starved. What the poem says of the Word would baffle the most severe Platonist. Where he has a metaphor by which he can develop the inner struggle with God, Brother Antoninus can make his craft work for him. "In the Breach," for example, speaks of God as both the killer and the midwife. The reluctance of the child to leave the womb and its compulsion to do so, for the sake of life, work together in his elaboration of the images of birth.

In "A Frost Lay While on California," a dream of

finding a raped dead woman and realizing that he had committed the crime stimulates a poem in which the poet engages in a colloquy with God throughout the frozen night. The figures of the woman and the dog, which appear in the dream, become images by which God describes His relationship to the poet. Stanzas alternate in which God speaks and the poet reflects on his inner state and links it to the cold darkness around him, but the power of the poem comes through the poet's reflections, for the begging of God seems diffuse and elaborate--to much what we might imagine ourselves giving Him to say in a dialogue we wrote. "I am your image."

> Close your eyes now and be what I am.
> Which is--yourself!
> The you who am I!

Operating underneath this inner dialogue, however, is something akin to Coleridge's "silent ministry" of frost. The rain which has been threatening all through the hours of the poet's vigil, comes with the dawn, "a slow spilth of deliverance," breaking up the frost; "... it was falling, I knew, out of the terrifying helplessness of God." The poem works because it relies ultimately on natural imagery and the feel of human experience to convey what is happening spiritually, rather than giving us arguments for, or opinions about, the mercy of God.

Brother Antoninus wishes to use his poetry to gain victories over himself, but the best poems, and perhaps the surest victories, are those like "In All These Acts" and "God Germed in Raw Granite," where he focuses his attention on describing the goings-on of nature with all the precise detail he can achieve. Here he might be said to follow the example of Gerard Manley Hopkins, whose finest nature poems grow out of the discovery, in the scene, that the Holy Ghost works through it, and whose finest poems about people grow from his discovery that Christ is in each of them. "In All These Acts" chronicles with horrified fascination a wind storm in the forest which tosses logs in "staggering gyrations of splintered kindling." A elk, caught between two crashing logs, is torn open and dies in spasms of agony:

> Arched belly-up and died, the snapped spine
> Half torn out of his peeled back, his hind legs
> Jerking that gasped convulsion, the kick of spasmed life,
> Paunch plowed open, purple entrails
> Disgorged from the basketwork ribs

Erupting out, splashed sideways, wrapping him
Gouted in blood, flecked with the brittle sliver of bone.

Vigorous verbs and verbal adjectives, explosive mono-
syllables, tight linking of words through alliteration and inner
rhyme, bring the scene before us in overpowering fashion.
But the scene does not stand alone: it parallels the river's
violent "frenzy of capitulation" as it destroys itself in "the
mother sea." And in a counter movement, the poet describes
the salmon leaving the sea about to make their way to the
place they were born, to "beat that barbarous beauty out"
in their urge to spawn. The elk's death-throes, the river's
self-destruction to feed the sea, the salmon's immolation-
propagation become symbols of

> ... the wakeful, vengeful beauty,
> Devolving itself of its whole constraint,
> Erupting as it goes.

The poet sees the ambiguities suggested by wakeful,
vengeful beauty, implied by the constellation of violence and
sex, and he affirms them, seeing Christ in them, "the modes
of His forth-showing,/ His serene agonization." This is as
theologically orthodox as any poem Brother Antoninus has
written, but here we believe the insight to have come from
the poem itself. Christ does not stand over against this
violence; He is not escape from the world of nature or com-
pensation for it. "In all these acts/ Christ crouches and
seethes." He is the way things are; and fascination with the
barbarous beauty expended for the continuation of the race
finally turns to affirmation of Him.

What makes the poem effective is suggested by the
phrase "These are the modes of His forth-showing." The
poet argues his poem in the images, and their larger signif-
icance arises from this unsentimental look at what they are.
To use one of the simplest critical distinctions, the poem
has shown us, rather than telling us.

Similarly, "God Germed in Raw Granite" shows us
through images the emergence of outward shape from inner
nature. Word choice and length of line distinctively shape
a poem whose theme is shape. Freedom and constraint, ex-
pressive form, the tug of paired opposites--all these preoc-
cupations of the poet's life as artist and religious enter the
poem through his description of rock, that most fixed and
static aspect of the creation. He sees into its source, its
germ, "the tortured/ Free-flow of lava, the igneous/ Instant

of conception." The germ is feminine, "Woman within!"
and the love of man for woman partakes of the desire for
inner coherence and the desire for God.

> In the blind heart's core, when we,
> Well-wedded merge, by Him
> Twained into one and solved there,
> Are these still three? Are three
> So oned, in the full-forthing...?

Theological commitments influence it--e. g. , the doc-
trine of the trinity and the conception of marriage as a type
of Christ's love for the Church--but nothing occurs in the
poem because a doctrine exists to cover such a situation.
The wonder of sexual love generates the meditation on the
mystery that two can become simultaneously one and three;
it requires no explicit reference to liturgy or scripture, no
allegorizing of the Song of Songs. We go back to the experi-
ence which was the source of the allegory and realize afresh
why human love symbolizes the divine.

The Hazards of Holiness is a flawed but powerful book.
The flaws seem greatest where the poet cannot let experiences
--dreams, temptations, sins, insights--stand by themselves
and make their own meanings. The allegorizing spirit lets
things stand for other things too easily, especially when a
Dominican brother is publishing cum permissu.

Brother Antoninus acknowledges that the religious art-
ist also struggles with the inner censor, which may tell him
that words and attitudes are unacceptable coming from him.
Those elements in his poetry which make for the reader's
dissatisfaction even in the most vigorous, deeply felt and
sincere poems, carry the cum permissu stamp on them.
The retelling of biblical stories--even the bloody tales of
John the Baptist and Judith and Holofernes, where his war-
rant for speaking of sexual enticement is clear--the media-
tions on saints, the canticles, have been hedged round by ex-
planations from the inner censor. Perhaps the clearest ex-
ample is "The Song the Body Dreamed in the Spirit's Mad
Behest," where the title, an epigraph from the Canticle of
Canticles, and a gloss on the Imagination introduce the poem
in such a way as to neutralize any shock caused by the ex-
plicitly sexual imagery.

Speaking of prayer, Martin Buber describes the tension
between spontaneity and the subjectivized reflection which as-
sails it. "The assailant is consciousness, the overconscious-

ness of this man here that he is praying, that he is praying, that he is praying."[14] A similar overconsciousness seems to operate in Brother Antoninus's poetry: he writes to objectify inner experience and to gain release from inner torment, but he also writes to instruct, to give exempla acceptable to his readers, his superiors, but primarily to that inner assailant which tells him he is writing a poem.

Not uncommonly, the worst poems written by an able poet fail not because of a change in subject matter or a change in technique but because they miss the fragile balance between extremes which he accomplishes in his best work. The characteristic techniques and attitudes, the diction and imagery, remain, but reduced to stock response. All the tensions which have shaped Brother Antoninus's poetry stand most starkly opposed in his latest book, The Rose of Solitude (1967), but now, under the pressure of his subject or of his obligation to make something affirmatively Christian of it, his poems express the worst emotional excesses and technical gaucheries of which he is capable. He calls the book a love-poem sequence and tells us it is an interior monologue continuing from "In Savage Wastes," which concluded The Hazards of Holiness. That poem tells of a monk who returns to the world when a dream shows him that he has not escaped its temptations by fleeing to the desert. His "travail of self-enlightenment" continued in The Rose of Solitude.

Behind the poems is a love affair between a monk and a divorced woman, a dancer. When a situation which must not be, is, the suffering is intense. Two kinds of fidelity clash, for each is good and bears the stamp of the divine, yet they are inimical to one another. Breaking the vows is sin, but renouncing the human love is not virtuous; something lies deeper in this conflict which must be worked through for the sake of a more profound understanding of faithfulness.

"The man of God and the woman of the world are, from the point of view of the normative consciousness, polar opposites. But like all polar opposites they are drawn together by an ineluctable attraction and mutual fascination, verifying their distinctness each on the other's being.... When these inner realities emerge and move together, what happens is an expansion of awareness beyond the code of manners that society has established for either, and a profound crisis in the moral life of two people."[15]

As this passage indicates, two kinds of doctrines will need to find expression and resolution in the poetry, orthodox Catholic theology and Jungian psychology. The handling of dreams in The Hazards of Holiness and the interview with David Kherdian would have prepared us for the Jungian emphasis. We can expect, therefore, as the Foreword emphasizes, that the masculine-feminine dichotomy will operate on many levels and that a great deal of attention will be given to archetypal figures, images, and relationships.

These ways of ordering experience to comprehend it result in two kinds of poetry in The Rose of Solitude: long poem-sequences made up of terse stanzas which are closer to entries in a spiritual diary than they are to lyrics; and long canticles exploiting a long line and loose verse-paragraph in a fashion "half rationale and half celebration." The characteristic weaknesses of each are evident in the book.

Part One of the book, "I Nail My Life," made up of three poem-sequences, gives us the data of the relationship. This is the spiritual diary, a documentary account of a developing relationship and the poet's attempt to put it in context. The separate poems are made up of the simplest subject-verb sentences put together in the simplest parallels. While the first poems, in "The Way of Life and the Way of Death," give us the sensual accompaniments of the relationships, the woman's signatures--poinsettias, the flesh of mangoes and guaves, rum--the later ones become increasingly sparse and vacant of sensory imagery.

The canticle form calls for a rich sensual fabric, the piling up of colors, sounds and tastes and luxuriating in them for their association with the loved one. Liturgies derived from the Song of Songs celebrate Mary in the language of a lover. The form tends toward shapelessness and emotional sprawl, however, since it develops out of the loose parallelism of Hebraic poetry and has no necessary conclusion or rounding off. "The Canticle of the Rose" joins emotional sprawl to theological abstraction, asserting as doctrine about the woman he loves what we could, at best, grant only as an extravagant expression of one's personal feelings. As a consequence, we withhold our assent from both the theological and the personal assertions.

And if I call you great, and if I call you holy, and if I
    say that even your sins enforce the sheer reality
    of what you are,
Know that I speak because in you I gaze on Him,
    by you I see

Him breathe, and in your flesh
I clasp Him to my breast.

From the first poems, the speaker claims to recognize some-
thing redemptive in this relationship; he calls it both neces-
situm peccatum and felix culpa. The woman becomes a type
of Christ, a symbol of divine love, a bearer of grace to be
identified through the image of the Rose with the Mother of
God. If we are to take all this as unambiguously true, we
must then ask what the issue of the book is. Surely the
torment of breaking vows must disappear in the light of such
a revelation. If that is too simpleminded an approach to
take, are we to read the book as we would read other interior
monologues--as an account of spiritual development from con-
fusion to clarity, from self-deception to honesty? Such a
stance would demand of us a certain ironic detachment and
awareness of moral and intellectual ambiguities when the
speaker makes extravagant claims for the woman he loves.
Nothing in either the poetry or the Foreword, however,
indicates that the poet wishes us to take the book at anything
other than face value.

"My art can err only in insufficiency, my fierce ex-
cesses crack on the ineluctable reality of what you are," he
insists. To take him seriously on his own terms, therefore,
means to indict him for inflating his subject beyond credibil-
ity. The poignancy of his forbidden love for a beautiful wom-
an gets lost in the extravagance of his claims for it; she be-
comes a symbol of divine love the same way the bullfrog
became a bull. We might say of the poetry that it has the
meaning but missed the experience; events are so rapidly
turned into their significance that we lose the feel and tex-
ture of experience itself, despite Brother Antoninus's life-
long preoccupation as a poet with the blunt, harsh word, the
vigorous verb. Here every noun has its Latinate-sounding
adjective; lines and phrases are strung out to prolong a
mood of hectic excitement. Striving for the vatic, the poem
achieves only the bathetic.

I have said before:
All the destinies of the divine
In her converge.

What creates difficulties in the canticle form operates
in the simple poem-sequences as well. Clearly the poet
wants to make her a symbol of many things having to do with
the opening up of his spiritual life, but once again he runs
into difficulties because the psychological-theological form he

accepts demands that she be pure archetype.   Symbols are
built up by slow accretion--the history of the rose in Western
literature illustrates the point--not by appropriation.   The
woman the poet loves does not participate in the reality she
points to; the middle ground between tenor and vehicle of a
metaphor does not exist.

There are poems and passages from poems in The
Rose of Solitude which move us by their spiritual perception
and poetic tact; when the balance is struck, the poetry is
effective in Brother Antoninus's characteristic ways.   And
even when the reader feels obliged to find greatest fault with
the poetry, there is never any doubt of the poet's intense
sincerity or that he has suffered through everything he writes
about.   If his poetry achieves the victory over himself that
he wishes, we must be grateful for that, and wish him well.
But if we bring to our reading the expectation that form and
content support each other in such a way that poetic problems
are solved poetically and not doctrinally, we must remain
dissatisfied with much of Brother Antoninus's work.   The
inner censor, whether operating from the standpoint of Cath-
olic doctrine or Jungian psychology, closes too many ways
to Brother Antoninus; the overconsciousness that tells him
he is writing imposes too heavy a burden on his work--and
perhaps on the man as well.   Externally imposed form,
which accompanies the cum permissu stamp, wrestles with
the material of his life as the angel wrestles Jacob in his
poem, with equally unclear results.   Among the chief hazards
of holiness for him seems to be the incapacity to be free as
a poet.   His tragedy may be that there can be no final vic-
tories in his inner war except at the cost of his poetry.

Notes

1 Brother Antoninus, "The Artist and the Religious Life,"
   The American Benedictine Review XI, Nos. 3-4 (Sep-
   tember-December 1960), pp233-34.

2 Brother Antoninus, "Foreword" to The Crooked Lines of
   God (Detroit: University of Detroit Press, 1959).

3 Brother Antoninus, "Pages from an Unpublished Autobio-
   graphy," Ramparts (September 1962), p60.

4 Ibid. , p61.

5 Ibid. , p64.

6   Ibid. , p58.

7   Brother Antoninus, "The Artist and the Religious Life,"
    p226.

8   Ibid. , p224.

9   Ibid. , p225.

10 David Kherdian, Six Poets of the San Francisco Renais-
    sance (Fresno, Calif. : Giligia Press, 1966), p169.

11 Ibid. , p139.

12 Ibid. , p140.

13 Brother Antoninus, The Hazards of Holiness (Garden
    City, N. Y. : Doubleday, 1962), p6.

14 Will Herberg, ed. , The Writings of Martin Buber (New
    York: Meridian Books, 1956), p110.

15 Brother Antoninus, "Foreword" to The Rose of Solitude
    (Garden City, N. Y. : Doubleday, 1967), pp x-xi.

WILLIAM EVERSON AS PRINTER

Linnea Gentry & Joseph Blumenthal.   1975 & 1977

With the publication of his first hand-printed book, A Privacy of Speech, in 1949, Everson took his place among California printers of distinction.   His monumental Novum Psalterium Pii XII in 1955 made him famous among American devotees of the craft, but it was with the publication of Robinson Jeffers' Granite & Cypress in 1975 that he gained his greatest renown.   Linnea Gentry, in Fine Print, July 1975, assesses Everson's contribution to the craft.   This is followed by Joseph Blumenthal's estimate in his magisterial survey The Printed Book in America (Godine, 1977), where Granite & Cypress represents the culmination point in the evolution of fine printing in the United States.

> As the rest of us struggle to maintain some balance in our fast-moving technological society, Everson maintains a medieval harmony of hand, mind and spirit through his continuing dedication to the handpress and all that it implies.

"As a creative man, the richest thing I can do is write a poem and the next is to print it."

Thus William Everson began the Equinox Press in 1949.   These intervening years have wrought many changes in his life.   He has known the contemplative solitude of the monastery, lent a triumphant voice to American poetry and given the "art preservative" one of its finest accomplishments in his printing of Novum Psalterium Pii XII.   Much

can be said about him but these few words are devoted to a
renewed look at Everson as contributor to the bookmaking
craft.

As the rest of us struggle to maintain some balance
in our fast-moving technological society, Everson maintains
a medieval harmony of hand, mind and spirit through his
continuing dedication to the handpress and all that it implies.
He has written a great deal about the reasons and purposes
of that dedication: in his announcement of the Equinox Press,
in his introduction to the Psalter, and in numerous articles,
interviews and notices.   His books themselves are realiza-
tions of creative fulfillment, tributes to the ideals of perfec-
tion, where handmade paper and foundry types are the natural
choices.

I needed no better reasons to pay this man a visit.
On a drizzly March day, I wended my way down the Califor-
nia coast, through redwood forests, and down an old fire
road to a secluded cabin on the banks of a stream.   The
solitude of that little cabin reflects the solitude and repose
that Everson had once found in his cell as a Dominican lay
brother and that he recognized as so important to his print-
ing.   And though he exchanged his frock for a beaded buck-
skin jacket many years ago, an atmosphere of contemplative
repose continues to surround him.   In an article that he
wrote for the Book Club of California's Quarterly News Let-
ter in the summer of 1954 as Brother Antoninus, he stated
that, as a contemplative, the printer seeks "not perfection
for itself, the end of merely human attainment, but rather
revelation, the obscure beatitude hidden in the essence of all
God-given things. "   That rare quality of revelation is the
mark not only of great art but of great printing, and it is
for this that Everson strives, as much today as he did when
printing the Psalter of Pope Pius XII singlehandedly in the
early '50s.

Everson now divides his time among his poetry, his
numerous readings across the country, and his printing at
the University of California at Santa Cruz under the imprint
of the Lime Kiln Press.   He and his students use an Acorn
handpress given to the university by Lewis and Dorothy Allen.
He gives his students no lectures, assignments or exams,
teaching them instead by having them join in creating a book
as close to a masterpiece as his energies can produce.   He
says of his students, "I address myself to a great project,
lose myself in it, and then subsume them into that project.
As we immerse ourselves in it they catch fire by participa-

tion. " Their third and latest production is a collection of
Robinson Jeffers' poetry written during the building of the
poet's stone house on the California coast. Entitled Granite
& Cypress, the book is printed on English handmade paper
in Goudy Newstyle with Castellar initials, and is enclosed in
a remarkable slipcase fashioned of Monterey cypress with a
window of granite from Jeffers' stoneyard.

Everson does not consider himself a professional print-
er and has never had an interest in making printing his live-
lihood. He says he works by trial and error and can only
judge a piece of work when it is finished. He lacks the
foresight, the precision of planning and analysis of materials
and costs to be a successful professional; he "makes too
many mistakes. " His endeavors are essentially those of a
private press. He considers his only professional capacity
to be that of a poet on the platform. Perhaps this helps to
explain why William Everson has produced so few books,
only six since he began working with the handpress. He has
printed only the poetry that an inner instinct compelled him
to send out into the consciousness of the world. Hence, the
great deal of time and painstaking care that Everson takes
with every book hasn't hampered him as it so often has other
printers.

One of the most difficult achievements in the printed
book is the harmonious marriage of type and illustration.
Everson worked with the artist Mary Fabilli in his first
books, A Privacy of Speech and Triptych for the Living, but
as beautifully executed as these were, Everson was not fully
satisfied with their effect. He feels that the artist usually
has a totally different viewpoint and wants to superimpose
his own vision over the "angelic vision" of the printer. The
artist has the power to take the book away from the printer.
The French, recognizing this, give full emphasis to the illus-
trator. Everson feels that the Allens, who work frequently
with artists for their books, lean toward an illustrative em-
phasis. However, when the printer dominates the artist, as
Everson feels was the case in the Grabhorn Leaves of Grass
illustrated by Valenti Angelo, then the artist cannot exercise
his skill to the full. In earlier times the printer and the
artist "were succinct in a religious ideal and shared basic
assumptions, drawn together by mutual concerns of the page.
The modern artist is not prepared to give of himself without
pre-formed ideas and often wants to be rid of practices that
seem old-fashioned, not knowing why they're used. " The
most successful illustrations that Everson has seen are the

the woodblocks of Aristide Maillol in Daphnis and Chloe. At
some time he would like to get the blocks and print the book
himself.

Many other printers have produced fine editions of
William Everson's poetry. He never interferes and feels
that some of them were quite successful. However, Everson
was not satisfied with the front matter that Saul Marks print-
ed for the Psalter when Everson was unable to finish the pro-
ject. He felt that Marks didn't make the right choices. "He
should have used a Goudy type. The Centaur could not match
the spirit and strength of the Goudy Newstyle. "

William Everson is a man of wide vision, who believes
in idealism and the passionate creativity of the human spirit.
He hopes some day to print the complete poems of Robinson
Jeffers in Weiss, one of his favored types. A monumental
task, yes, but not impossible for a man who is a living link
with distant times when every book was rare and wonderful.
The words with which he closed the announcement of the
Equinox Press in 1949 are as relevant now as they were
then: "A conscious attempt ... to integrate the handwork
of the past and the temper of the present."--Linnea Gentry.

One of the most skillful and articulate practitioners
of the handpress in its current widespread reincarnation is
William Everson, formerly Brother Antoninus. From the
Lime Kiln Press, the typographic workshop at the University
of California in Santa Cruz, Everson, aided by his students,
completed a magnificent volume of Robinson Jeffers' poems
in 1975. Granite & Cypress, with a woodcut title-page decor-
ation by William Prochnow, is an oblong folio which preserves
Jeffers' long lines without turnovers, set in Goudy New Style
type and Castellar initials, printed on dampened handmade
paper, with joyous, full-bodied presswork. Pure, unadorned
typography is here enhanced by extraordinary craftsmanship.

Everson is a recognized poet with several published
books of his own verse. Printing came to him by inheritance
when his father, a wandering printer and bandmaster, settled
into the small town of Selma in California and opened a print-
ing shop. Before marriage, William's mother had set type
in a small town in Minnesota. The son's decisive association
with printing came during World War II in a conscientious
objectors' camp at Waldport, Oregon, where an official month-
ly paper was issued, called The Tide. A small radical lit-

erary group thereupon issued their own underground sheet which they called The Untide, in which Everson's poems appeared. An old, worn platen press was found nearby which the writers purchased and on which they printed.

After the war, Everson returned to the San Francisco area, acquired a huge old handpress, and in 1949 printed his first significant book--his own poems, A Privacy of Speech. Meantime, he was extremely lucky, he said, to have found a job as night janitor at the University of California Press, where he could watch and perfect his knowledge of printing. On receiving a Guggenheim Fellowship for creative writing, he gave up his janitorial assignment and moved to a Catholic Worker home where he printed Triptych for the Living (1951), another collection of his own poems. "Feeling apostolic," he then joined the Dominican order as Brother Antoninus at its House of Studies in Oakland. Here, with religious fervor and the wish to make a contribution to the Catholic church, he began a folio Psalter, the Novum Psalterium. Only seventy-two pages were completed. With sponsorship from Mrs. Estelle Doheny, who had bought the printed sheets, a title page and Everson's introduction were subsequently set and printed by Saul Marks at the Plantin Press. The completed volume is an interesting confrontation of dry machine printing and dampened handpress work, both at their superb best.

--Joseph Blumenthal.

BIRTH OF A POET

Lee Bartlett. 1977

After returning to lay life, Everson was hired as poet-in-
residence at Kresge College, University of California, Santa
Cruz. Rather than teach a traditional "creative writing work-
shop" course, the poet formulated a year-long course on the
artist's vocation and called it "Birth of a Poet." During the
1975-76 term, his lectures, his "meditations," were taped
and edited for publication. This is the introduction to that
volume.

> During the following weeks, I
> attended the poet's meditation
> sessions. The atmosphere was
> that of the poetry reading--silence
> fed by the pulse of expectation.
> Students, about two hundred of
> them, sat in a large circle, a
> mandala, around Everson, and
> save for an opening poem each
> time from one of them, the au-
> dience sat spellbound throughout
> the entire meditations as the
> poet-shaman worked his magic.

Birth of a Poet emerges from the poet-shaman's arche-
typal impulse towards orchestration of experience into mean-
ing. Everson, Antoninus, Everson. Farmer, conscientious
objector, printer, religious. Lover, monk, husband. Poet,
mystic, prophet. The persona changes, but the search con-
tinues, always turning back into the self.

This study came about by accident, although in the

world of cyclic time, the world of correspondences and constellations, nothing emerges into the objective realm until the time is right. The child chooses the hour of its birth. Still, as a practical matter, the book surfaced out of a series of events which at the time seemed to be heading somewhere else. In the winter of 1974, I set out to do a series of interviews with West Coast poets in the hope of developing a more coherent notion of the importance of place in poetry and, more importantly, the nature of the West as archetype. One afternoon I heard that William Everson would be giving a reading of his work in Sacramento, and I decided that the reading might provide a good opportunity to approach him about doing an interview. I was quite familiar with his early work as collected in The Residual Years, a little less familiar with his Catholic poetry (for eighteen years he was Brother Antoninus in the Dominican Order), and had reviewed his much-neglected and newest collection of poetry, Man-Fate. I knew that he was a Jeffers scholar, and that he was perhaps one of the most eloquent and vocal exponents of the idea of place in literature since D. H. Lawrence.

On stage that evening I saw the archetypal shaman-poet. A tall old man with long hair and a beard, dressed in buckskins, wearing a necklace of bear's claw, and carrying his books in an old leather bag. A friend commented that Everson was the first poet he had even seen, and he had known many, who actually looked like a poet should look. The mental correspondence I was drawing between this man and the good, grey Whitman was not strained; moments after Everson began speaking, I was not simply impressed, but moved. As you will see when you turn to any of these meditations, Everson talks poetry. On stage, he is a man possessed, a man caught in the swirl of cosmic energy, a man truly invested by the Spirit. Only a familiarity with his work enabled me to catch the transition from the passionate lyricism, which served as an introduction to each of his pieces, to the poems themselves. After the reading, I managed to get a few moments alone with the poet to make my case, and he consented to do an interview in January at his home in the mountains of the Santa Cruz coast.

During the interview, William Everson spoke at length of his first real excursion into university teaching. Two years after leaving the Dominicans, he had accepted an offer to become poet-in-residence at the University of California at Santa Cruz. He was given free reign to define his own course range and material, and it was out of this experience that Birth of a Poet emerged. Perhaps as a combination of

his own lack of formal university training and the eighteen
years he spent in a religious order, Everson sought to re-
define the traditional lecture in terms of that with which he
was most familiar--the poetry reading. His was not to be
a course in the writing of poetry, nor was it to be a course
in critical analysis. Rather, Everson hoped to build a series
of meditations around the theme of vocation. It would be
"an approach to ascesis as applying to the vocation of poet,"
he wrote in an early course outline.

> "While not itself a rite of passage, the course
> of study will point to that crisis of conscious-
> ness in which vocation is revealed.

> "The key activity will naturally be verse-writ-
> ing, but the emphasis will not be on how to
> write a poem but on what a poet is.

> "The focus, therefore, will be more disposi-
> tive than applicative--vocation regarded as
> response to a call rather than applied tech-
> nique or rigorously cultivated craft.

> "The aquisition of technique will be pursued,
> certainly, for vocation is only confirmed in
> competence. Nevertheless, technical mastery
> will go forward strictly in the context of a deeper
> dimension--surrender to a call.

> "Not that such a call can be elicited through a
> course--any course. Rather, for one who seeks
> to be a poet, study and practice will attempt to
> clarify what he is in fact seeking.

> "Such themes as the Archetype· of the Poet; Call
> and Surrender; The Charismatic and the Institu-
> tional; Extasis and Entasis; Rhythm Versus Pat-
> tern; the Subject Versus the Method; Beauty--the
> Increment of Form, Rhetoric--the Increment of
> Purpose; Aesthetic Faith as the Constituent of
> Transcendent Form; and many others will be ex-
> plored.

> "Encounter group atmospherics will doubtless pre-
> vail, but what is sought is not togetherness, how-
> ever excoriating. Traditionally, withdrawal, si-
> lence, and solitude have been the catalysts of vo-
> cation. Toward these the work will be directed."

He told me, however, that as it developed the attempt
to create a balance between literary discipline and contempla-

tive meditation did not materialize: "On inception, the arche-
typal channel asserted itself and a wholly meditative procedure
ensued. " At first he thought to forego any academic require-
ment, convinced that the approach should in no sense be co-
erced, but the University would not hear of it. He then
adopted the alternative of assigning a parallel course to be
followed outside the classroom, leaving the meditative atmo-
sphere within unforced. Thus, the dimension of the course
expanded beyond the role of poet alone, and many other dis-
ciplines began to participate. In time, the evaluative form
Everson prepared for his students' academic files evolved to
the following statement:

> "Birth of a Poet. A venture in charismatic voca-
> tion. It explores the interior disposition necessary
> to sustain the witness which any visionary calling
> entails.

> "For this reason its relevance is not confined to
> aspiring poets alone, but applies to every role de-
> manding an heroic consciousness.

> "Its aim is wholly interior, and, like the resolu-
> tion of a ritual or the sustaining of an ordeal,
> its degree of success cannot be measured. Al-
> most certainly its relevance will show only in
> later years.

> "The passing grade indicates the student has ful-
> filled the Course-Equivalent in the alternative
> work assigned. "

In the Course-Equivalent the student keeps a record
of his dreams, and at the end of the quarter writes an intro-
duction which traces the vocational drift as evidenced in the
evolving interior scenario, correlated to the ethos of the
course as developed in the meditations. The course is a
continuing one. The fall quarter is focused on the vocational
archetype itself; the winter quarter stresses the national con-
sciousness, what it means to be an American; and the spring
quarter emphasizes the regional element, the consciousness
of the Pacific Coast.

Everson gave me two examples of student reactions to
the course taken from the introductions to the dream journals.
The first is by a male student, a psychology major, who
entered the course somewhat skeptically:

> "The dreams in this notebook are copied down from

the rather cryptic notes I made immediately following
the dream itself. I made a practice of waking my-
self with an alarm every morning at 4:30 a.m. in
an effort to catch dreams that occur earlier in the
night. . . .

"My training is in psychology, therefore my inter-
pretations of dreams (the word drips with psychol-
ogy!) is strictly Freudian (or neo-Freudian).

"From the beginning of the course I foresaw that I
would have trouble shedding myself of this perspec-
tive, and immersing myself into the archetypes and
ideas presented in the class. I am not a Jungian.

"I began to have serious doubts about whether I
would honestly be able to interpret my dreams in
the context of the class. But, something happened
that was, in all honesty, quite startling to me.

"It happened just about the time we were starting to
discuss the 'power of place' in class, and it is re-
produced in the journal exactly as it happened. Be-
cause of it, I could relate more to the final few lec-
tures than I had ever imagined.

"In a sense, my 'sense of place' was illuminated to
me. Retrospectively, it does not surprise me; I
guess I had always known it was there--but it was
revealed with such clarity that everything just
clicked. I will relate the experience:

"I was sitting in bed, trying to remember additional
dreams from the night before, when suddenly, with
literally no warning or forethought, ten to fifteen
dreams, dreams that I had forgotten from months
before, flashed into my mind in such rapid succes-
sion that I could only jot down notes on a few.

"Every dream revolved around mountains. Every
dream. It was uncanny. It was as if someone had
taken the subject index of my dreams and had pulled
the Sierra Nevada file.

"This happening is reproduced later in the journal,
so I need not go into further detail. Suffice it to
say that it was an awakening. It gave me an en-
tirely new perspective on the idea of 'power of
place. '

"After this certain things clicked together. I have
come to realize that the writer, or rather expositor,

translator, guide, that I feel the most empathy with, yes, easily the most, is John Muir. He is, to me, the archetype of the scientific man in harmony with the natural world. He embodies the spirit of the Sierra and the keeness of the perceiving man, the artist and the man of science.

"It all fits, and is not surprising to me now. I have spent many months in the high alpine country, and I have read just about everything Muir has written. But I never related to it myself, to an internalized sense of oneness with a region.

"The calling is there too, although I had never expected it to be embodied in my dreams. I am called to that region in the same sense that Muir was--to seek, to wonder, and to explain.

"He did more to bring the common man into an understanding of wilderness than anyone else.... No one today speaks as eloquently as Muir did about those elements of the wilderness that can be absorbed by a man, and change him.

"It is, of course, presumptuous of me to think that I could, but even if I don't, I know that it will always be there calling me. The alpine Sierra is not something that can be shut up inside oneself--it must be shared. One becomes almost a missionary, as Muir did....

"Therefore, the final meditations were as if they were written for me."

However, this degree of self-realization is relatively rare; no more than one or two a year have attested to such sharp clarification. More often the full weight of the meditations registers deeply enough, but the youthful psyche itself has not yet evolved to the point of surrender. This excerpt from another dream journal speaks of the impasse between the pursuit of rigorous academic goals and the need for creative expression:

"In relation to my vocation the dreams illustrated the frustration, indecision, and soul-searching I'm experiencing in attempting to determine my 'calling.'

"Whether to remain in the intellectual abyss of 'hard' knowledge at the university, or strike out upon my own and give in to the inner desire to play music, has been an all-pervading, constant question absorbing my thoughts the entire quarter.

"This class has helped a great deal in pointing
which way to pursue, yet the insecurity surround-
ing the gate to that road is too great to overcome
now.

"I truly hoped for a "visionary" dream to present
the key to unlock it, yet it never occurred. But
thanks for the insight--when it does happen I'll
know how to understand it. "

Here, clearly, the ground has been laid, and the point
of awareness recognized. Whether or not the visionary dream
ever occurs is almost incidental.

After listening to Everson's discription of the course,
it occurred to me that if his meditations were anywhere near-
ly as compelling as his readings, they should be preserved.
I suggested the idea to him, and although he had his doubts,
as I offered to do the work he readily agreed. The only
provision was that after the first few meditations were taped,
transcribed, and edited, we would make a second decision as
to whether or not to continue the project.

During the following weeks, I attended a number of
the poet's meditation sessions. The atmosphere was that of
the poetry reading--silence fed by the pulse of expectation.
Students, about two hundred of them, sat in a large circle,
a mandala, around Everson, and save for an opening poem
each time from one of them the audience sat spellbound
throughout the entire meditations as the poet-shaman worked
his magic. And magic it was, as Everson, who never once
referred to a note, plugged into the pulse of the moment to
take the circle around him far beyond the four walls which
surrounded it. The linear dimension gave way to the
cyclic.

We had made arrangements to have all the meditations
taped from that point on, and when I returned home I eagerly
awaited the first batch of tapes which were to be forwarded
to me. After transcribing four of the meditations, I edited
them into a traditional essay format. They read well enough,
but both Everson and I were a little disappointed, as they
seemed a bit loose and rambling. The transitions which
could be indicated by modulations of the voice and by gesture,
seemed to be lost on the printed page. So we finally hit upon
a compromise--I would select the high points of each medita-
tion and would present them sequentially. The essence of
the meditation would be preserved in its spontaneity, while

the repetitive extraneous matter natural enough in oral discourse, even <u>inspired</u> oral discourse, would be stripped away.   Hence, the book was born.

EVERSON/ANTONINUS: CONTENDING WITH THE SHADOW

Albert Gelpi. 1977

With Everson's return to domestic life in 1969 after eighteen years in the monastery, the period of strong religious emphasis was brought to a close. Yet both his religious image and his religious name have outlived his life in the Order, and many believe that Everson's greatest contribution to American poetry will rest through his achievement while there. In a piece slightly adapted from an article of the same title in Sequoia, winter 1977, Albert Gelpi here presents his overview of Everson's religious witness, and ranks him among his compatriots in twentieth-century religious expression.

> I would venture the judgment that if T. S. Eliot is the most important religious poet in English in the first half of the twentieth century, Everson/Antoninus is the most important religious poet of the second half of the century.

In a review almost a decade ago, I hailed The Rose of Solitude as the most significant volume of religious poetry since Robert Lowell's Lord Weary's Castle twenty years before, and argued that Brother Antoninus' poetry was more profoundly Christian than Lowell's because it was more Incarnational, whereas Lowell's lapse from Catholicism stemmed from his difficulty in accepting the awesome, violent paradoxes of the central Christian mystery. Now Lowell seems caught in the ambiguities of agnosticism, revising and adding to his random Notebook in the same, confined fourteen-line conventions. Now, too, with Antoninus' early, pre-Catholic poetry, written as William Everson, available again in the collection The Residual Years, and with a new collection, again as Everson, since his leaving the Dominican Order, I would venture the judgment that if T. S. Eliot is the most important religious poet in English in the first half of the twentieth century, Everson/Antoninus is the most important religious poet of the second half of the century.

The extreme contrasts between those two poets point to a symptomatic tension in the religious commitment. The differences are less doctrinal than temperamental: Eliot the conservative classicist submitting the weaknesses of the individual to the reasonable authority of tradition and institutional structures in order to absolve him from the exigencies of personality; and Everson, the romantic individualist, trusting reason less than the undertow of passion and instinct to write out a life-long poem, as Whitman did a century ago, of the struggles with himself to realize himself.

Many would argue that authentic religious experience must be distinguished from intellectual commitment to an ecclesiastical structure, and that the great religious poetry of the first half of the century came not from Eliot but from such figures as Ezra Pound, D. H. Lawrence, Robinson Jeffers. Such a statement is not fair to Eliot, since the philosophical meditations of Four Quartets do derive from genuine religious experiences. However, the distinction between modes of religious sensibility postulated bluntly above is fundamental and revealing.

For what links the other three poets and Everson together, for all their admitted differences, is precisely what Eliot shrank back from as from the devil: a sourcing of self in the Dionysian unconscious rather than Apollonian consciousness; a faith in the forces--pre-rational, irrational, supra-rational, what you will--instinct in nature and emergent in the human psyche. Their poetry functions in good part to articulate the eruption into consciousness of the unconscious energies which are for them the source and secret of life. Pound recovered such primal experiences in the Greek myths and the mysteries of the occult; Lawrence, like Whitman, in the divine carnality of the sexual drive; Jeffers, in the pantheism which sees in the sea and rocks and creatures of the shore "the brute beauty of God" beyond the predatory violences of the egoistic mind and will. And in the poetry of each such psychological and spiritual exploration led to open form and free verse, as the poem discovered its definition.

By contrast, the explicitly Christian poets of the twentieth century have, by and large, tended to stress the constraining limits of a radically flawed creation through which the refractions of the Spirit penetrate at best tenuously and elusively, and they have generally insisted on working within the limitations of formal conventions as a way of testing and fixing "hints and guesses," as Eliot described our experience of the Incarnation. The means and the meaning, the norms and the measure have therefore been ruminative, guarded, Apollonian in the main. The elaborated patterning of the Quartets conveys not just the timeless moments which have transformed Eliot's life, but also the abiding disillusionment with temporal existence which qualifies and survives the moments of transcendence. Marianne Moore's intricately artful syllabics are a discipline to verify and regulate the allegorist's reading of natural experience in moral and religious terms. The virtuosity of Richard Wilbur's carefully maintained poise and symmetry epitomizes his conviction that the Incarnation calls us to attend to "things of this world" for "their difficult balance" of body and spirit. The religious pieces which conclude Allen Tate's long spiritual travail are written in Dante's terza rima in aspiration towards a faith that seems all but beyond his grasp. In Robert Lowell's Catholic poems, alternately stretched and clenched on their metrical and metaphorical designs till they threaten to wrench themselves apart, the Spirit moves to save human nature in death, which saves it from natural corruption; for him, the advent of the Incarnation spells apocalypse. John Berryman enacted his religious anxiety through the knotted syntax and studied candences of Anne Bradstreet and of Henry, and even after his late return to the Church his poems vacillate between prayers for patience and impatient anticipation of breaking free of the human tragedy.

It is the very history of religious, especially Christian, poetry in the twentieth century, with its fixation on human fallibility and its consequent insistence on necessarily prescribed forms, that makes Everson's poetry seem radical, original, transformative. Most of the Dionysians in recent poetry--Allen Ginsberg, Jack Kerouac, Lawrence Ferlinghetti, like Hart Crane in the twenties--have used alcohol or drugs for release into vision, but Ralph Waldo Emerson, who opened the way for Whitman and all the later Dionysian poet-prophets, was the first to condemn such "quasi-mechanical substitutes for the true nectar," which would end in "dissipation and deterioration." The distinctiveness of Everson's achievement springs, rather, from the Dionysian character of his Christianity. This has evolved in two complementary phases:

from the beginning, his surrendering to primal experience
until at last it yielded him the Christian mystery; and his
surrendering, then, to the Christian mystery so unreservedly
that it enflamed and illuminated, below and above structured
rational consciousness, that dark area, at once the center
and circumference of psyche, where passion and spirit reveal
themselves as personhood incarnate.

**

How did this transpire through more than sixty years
of living and forty of poetry? William Everson's life has
been punctuated again and again by interruptions, abrupt
changes and seeming reversals. What has been the continuity?
Born in 1912 in Sacramento, growing up in California's
San Joaquin Valley, his grandfather the founder of an evan-
gelical sect in Norway, his stern father an agnostic, his
mother a Christian Scientist, Everson was a dreamy, with-
drawn young man, but in 1934 he discovered the master whose
work made him a poet: Robinson Jeffers. Jeffers represent-
ed an "intellectual awakening and the first religious conver-
sion, all in one." "When Jeffers showed me God in the
cosmos, it took and I became a pantheist," and "that pantheism
was based on a kind of religious sexuality," a sense of the
universal life-force compelling all things in the sexual rhythm.
Reading Lawrence a few years later confirmed for him the
sacredness, even divinity, of natural life, but stylistically
his lines adapted the expansive free-verse of Jeffers to his
own verbal movement and timbre. Everson married Edwa
Poulson in 1938 and began cultivating his own vineyard in
the valley. "August" is characteristic of much of the early
poetry in its identification with the female earth as so deep
that masculine intellect relinquishes sovereignty and the vir-
ginal poet yields to the God of Nature:

Smoke-color; haze thinly over the hills, low hanging;
But the sky steel, the sky shiny as steel, and the
     sun shouting.
The vineyard: in August the green-deep and
     heat-loving vines
Without motion grow heavy with grapes.
And he in the shining, on the turned earth, loose-lying,
The muscles clean and the limbs golden, turns to
     the sun the lips and the eyes;
As the virgin yields, impersonally passionate,
From the bone core and the aching flesh, the offering.

He has found the power and come to the glory.
He has turned clean-hearted to the last God, the
    symbolic sun.
With earth on his hands, bearing shoulder and arm
    the light's touch, he has come.
And having seen, the mind loosens, the nerve lengthens,
All the haunting abstractions slip free and are gone;
And the peace is enormous.

That peaceful harmony was shattered by the Second
World War. Everson's pantheism made him a pacifist; death
and destruction in nature were part of the ecological cycle,
but in the human order were violational because egoistic and
malevolent. The figure of the bloody warrior from his Nor-
dic ancestry stalks the poetry of the late 30's as the shadow-
inversion of the feminine pacifist-pantheist. But when the
holocaust broke, Everson retreated to nature and spent the
years 1943 to 1946 as a forester in an Oregon camp for con-
scientious objectors. "The Raid" describes war as rape,
and "The Hare" acknowledges the shadow in himself with the
awareness, "fathered of guilt," that we are all killers. Still,
fascinated as he was and remained with assertive masculinity
(Jeffers was similarly ambivalent), he chose the C. O. camp
in the name of his feminine susceptibilities.

But only at great cost. "Chronicle of Division" re-
counts the personal crisis in the global disorder: the breakup
of his marriage and the dissolution of his previous life. In
1946 he came to San Francisco to join the pacifist-anarchist
group around Kenneth Rexroth who as writers were opposing
the established academic poets and critics in the cause of
open form and spontaneity. There he met and married the
poet-artist Mary Fabilli. The sequences The Blowing of the
Seed and The Springing of the Blade hymn their union and
move the nature mysticism of the earlier poetry more ex-
plicitly into the area of human sexuality. But she was a
lapsed Catholic undergoing a rebirth of faith, and through
her ordeal Everson found his own life unexpectedly altered
and clarified:

"It was my time with Mary Fabilli that broke both
my Jeffersian pantheism and my Lawrencian erot-
ic mysticism. She personalized this, her whole
touch was to personalize, to humanize.... Also
the intuition to which her course led me is that
my mystical needs, my religious needs, which
had not really been met in my pantheism, could
only find their solution in the more permeable

human context, and in a ritual and a rite, and in
a mythos that was established in a historical con-
tinuity. "

At a midnight mass, Christmas 1948, Everson was
overwhelmed, psychologically, almost physically, by the di-
vine presence in the tabernacle, and that mystical encounter
led directly to his conversion the next year. However, the
previous marriages of both partners and the prevailing Church
procedures at the time made it impossible for them to re-
main husband and wife. The Falling of the Grain deals with
the wrenching ironics and the overriding commitment which
underlay their decision to separate. Two years later he en-
tered the Dominicans as a lay brother and served for almost
nineteen years, during which time the poems written as
Brother Antoninus made him a figure in the San Francisco
Renaissance and the Beat Generation and a charismatic pre-
sence at readings on campuses around the country.

In fact, Everson's conversion and Antoninus' monasti-
cism did not so much "break" his pantheism and erotic mys-
ticism, as break them into a new set of circumstances and
a new psychological and spiritual dimension. Now his life
was centered on the Incarnation. Not an isolated historical
event, but a daily miracle: the ongoing infusion of Creator
into creation, supremely expressed in Jesus, the god-man.
The individual hangs on that cross, where all the contradic-
tions of the human condition take on new consequence. The
natural and the supernatural, soul and body, sexuality and
spirituality--the Incarnation means that those seeming polari-
ties, often vehemently at cross purposes, are meshed at the
point of tension.

From the human point of view the Incarnation canceled
out original sin, so that God could redeem man from the
sinfulness which was part of his freedom. Everson had seen
the killer and ravager in himself; he knew that the fallible
will needed to be curbed by ethical restraints and external
norms lest creative freedom become oppression or anarchy;
and his penitential bent sought the stricter discipline of mo-
nasticism. But from God's perspective the Incarnation is
the completion of the creative act. On the one hand, God
could be seen as driven to descend into flesh to save soul
from body: the vision of Lowell's Catholic poems. But on
the other hand God could be seen as having saved man in
his human condition: no Spirit changing into flesh but Spirit
embodied; not sinful flesh but transfigured body. The impli-
cations of this mystery were tremendous and dangerous, and

Everson was driven to search them out. For when God be-
came man, did He not submerge himself in the sexual ele-
ment? In fact, was not sexuality the manifestation of that
submersion? Had He not chosen from eternity to move in
and through the sexual polarity, so that our sexual natures
disclose their divine impulsion? Then in the heart-beat,
pulse-throb, sex-urge, the Incarnation unfolds the contingen-
cies of time and space, and subsumes them. Now Antoninus
found himself confronting these paradoxes in exactly the situ-
ation which would test them most severely: separated from
the wife who was the saint of his conversion, bound by his
own election to a vow of celibacy.

Consequently the poetry of Brother Antoninus is almost
obsessively concerned with the feminine--that is, not only
women, but his own sexuality and the feminine component in
his psyche which mediates his passional, instinctual and poetic
life. Decades before he had read Jung's psychology his po-
etry was recording his own often conflicted encounter with
the major archetypes: in the psyche of a man, the shadow,
who represents his dark, repressed, even violent aspects;
the anima, the woman within, who is his soul and leads him
into engagement with his erotic and spiritual potentialities;
and, most dimly, the self, that achieved and transcendent
personhood realized through the resolution of polarities, who
reveals himself as the God within and of whom, Jung says,
Jesus is the symbol and reality. Everson's poetry through
the war had enacted an initial rejection of the shadow; now
the anima became the primary archetypal focus in the strug-
gle toward transcendence.

In the Fictive Wish, written in 1946 before meeting
Mary Fabilli, is a marvelous evocation of what Everson was
already recognizing as "the woman within":

> Wader,
> Watcher by wave,
> Woman of water;
> Of speech unknown,
> Of nothing spoken.
>
> But waits.
>
> And he has,
> And has him,
> And are completed.
>
> So she.

But what was the monk to make of her? Often she came to him as the dark temptress, allied with his own lustful shadow and luring him on to what must now be sexual sin. Many of the poems in The Crooked Lines of God, written soon after converting and becoming a Dominican, excoriate the flesh, and the poems in the first half of The Hazards of Holiness churn in the frustration not just of lust but of his passionate nature. They recount, Everson has said, his own "dark night." "A Savagery of Love" makes Mary Magdalene, the patroness of the Dominicans, the image of the purified anima, redeemed from whoredom into "a consummate chasteness," her passion focussed on the passion of the Incarnated God.

Still, even in that transfiguring focus the anima could express her passionate nature. In "The Encounter" and several other remarkable poems towards the end of Crooked Lines Antoninus becomes the woman before God, his/her whole being called into activity by His totally mastering love. "Annul in Me My Manhood" opens with the prayer:

> Annul in me my manhood, Lord, and make
> Me woman-sexed and weak,
> If by that total transformation
> I might know Thee more.
> What is the worth of my own sex
> That the bold possessive instinct
> Should but shoulder Thee aside?

"A Canticle to the Christ in the Holy Eucharist" translates the meditation into graphic imagery: the doe seized by the buck's wounding love on the slopes of Tamalpais, the woman-shaped mountain north of San Francisco:

> In my heart you were might. And thy word was
>   the running of rain
> That rinses October. And the sweetwater spring
>   in the rock. And the brook in the crevice.
> Thy word in my heart was the start of the buck
>   that is sourced in the doe.
> Thy word was the milk that will be in her dugs,
>   the stir of new life in them.
> You gazed. I stood barren for days, lay fallow
>   for nights.
> Thy look was the movement of life, the milk in
>   the young breasts of mothers.

However, by 1954 the stresses of the monastic life

had dried up the inspiration, and it could resume again in 1957 only after a profound, shattering "breakthrough into the unconscious" the previous year, made possible by Antoninus' association with the Dominican Jungian Victor White, and by saturating himself in archetypal psychology. The result was a long narrative poem called River-Root, which is the most sustained orgasmic celebration in English, perhaps in all literature. Amongst the Antoninus poems collected into The Veritable Years, River-Root can be seen as a watershed: the turning away from the often austere asceticism of the years just after conversion back down again to primal nature, now transfigured in the mystery of the Incarnation. The narrative objectivity of the poem permitted Antoninus, while still under the vow of chastity, to render the intercourse between the husband and wife with a candor that, far from detracting from its sacramentality, climaxes in a vision of the Trinity. God's entry into flesh locates the sexual mystery, its source and activity and end, in the very Godhead.

River-Root, then, represented at once a recovery and synthesis and turning point. It opened the way back to poetry--and to the world. In The Hazards of Holiness the ascetic Antoninus struggled with and against the drift that had already begun to carry him, unaware, back to Everson. The last section of that divided volume expresses the full range of his experience of the feminine archetype: from the sexual force leading men to their death in the title poem (whether demonically, like Salome and the Baptist, or heroically, like Judith and Holofernes) to the virgin mother and spiritual wisdom of "A Canticle to the Great Mother of God."

Two crucial poems here state the paradox in personal terms. "The Song the Body Dreamed in the Spirit's Mad Behest" extends the erotic imagery of bride and bridegroom from The Canticle of Canticles to allow the plunge of God into corporeal existence in blunt sexual expression possible only after Freud and Jung in this century and possible for Antoninus only through access to the unconscious:

He is the Spirit but I am the Flesh.
Out of my body must He be reborn,
Soul from the sundered soul, Creation's gout
In the world's bourn.

Mounted between the termals of my thighs
Hawklike He hovers surging at the sun,
And feathers me a frenzy ringed around
That deep drunk tongue.

And the counterthrust of the Incarnation lifts our straining
sexuality until we too are reborn, borne at last to Godhead:

> Proving what instinct sobs of total quest
> When shapeless thunder stretches into life,
> And the Spirit, bleeding, rears to overreach
> The buttocks' strife.
>
> . . .
> Born and reborn we will be groped, be clenched
> On ecstacies that shudder toward crude birth,
> When his great Godhead peels its stripping strength
> In my red earth.

"God Germed in Raw Granite" spells out the same re-
ciprocating movement: God descending into the curves and
folds of the female landscape; thence the "woman within"
awakening the man erotically to the call of Spirit; and finally
the synthesis of masculine and feminine twinned into a trinity
by and with God:

> I am dazed,
> Is this she? Woman within!
> Can this be? Do we, His images, float
> Time-spun on that vaster drag
> His timelessness evokes?
> In the blind heart's core, when we
> Well-wedded merge, by Him
> Twained into one and solved there,
> Are these still three? Are three
> So oned, in the full-forthing
> (Heart's reft, the spirit's great
> Unreckonable grope, and God's
> Devouring splendor in the stroke) are we--
> This all, this utterness, this terrible
> Total truth--indubitably He?

Could "she" remain merely the "woman within," the anima
arousing the monk to rapturous response to God? But if he
is to find God not in some disembodied heaven but in the
crucible of the heart, must he not run the risks, trusting in
Him Whom the unconscious aches to disclose, and the pas-
sions burn to attain? "In Savage Wastes," the concluding
poem of Hazards, makes the decision to reenter the world;
the way out of agonized self-absorption, like the way out of
pantheism, was "the more permeable human context."

The Rose of Solitude tells of an encounter which moved

him to his most exalted realization of the feminine. The
highest recognition that I can give the book, the final valida-
tion of poetry which refuses to distinguish between art and
life, is the fact that it will leave the reader, too, shaken
and transformed. The plot is not remarkable: Antoninus
falls in love with a Mexican-American woman, breaks his
vow of chastity with her, is led by her to repentance and
confession; in the end they part. The remarkable quality
stems from the character of the Rose herself. The sequence
gradually reveals her and extols her as the apotheosis of the
feminine. Beyond the divisions which split body from soul,
beyond the mental abstractions which man invents to cope
ineffectually with those divisions, beyond his pity and self-
pity, his hesitations, and recriminations, she emerges--all
presence and act, all physical and spiritual beauty in one--
spontaneous yet resting in herself, drawing him not by her
will but by her being what she is. The sequence is so dense-
ly and intricately woven that it is difficult to excerpt pas-
sages, but "The Canticle of the Rose," "The Rose of Soli-
tude" and "The Raging of the Rose" are prodigious feats of
rhetoric, the poet pitching language to the extremes of ar-
ticulation (the prolonged compounding of multisyllabic philo-
sophical concepts in the "Canticle," the wild incantation and
imagery of "Solitude," the synthesizing of the two modes in
"Raging") in order to express the inexpressible fact that, in
her, sexual sin becomes felix culpa and the Incarnation is
accomplished. Accomplished in her, and, through his rea-
lization of her, in himself. "The Raging of the Rose" con-
cludes with an affirmation of selfhood sourced in the "I Am
Who Am" of Genesis:

> Rose!
> Reality unfolded!
>
> On the four wings of the Cross,
> In the ecstasy of crucifixion,
> In the blood of being,
> In the single burn of beauty
>
> BE!
>
> So that
> In you,
> The consummate
> Vision of Other:
>
> In you
> I AM!

But the relationship ends in separation: the monk returning to his cell, releasing her to her own life and to another relationship. The end of the book is muted--necessarily so, since the Rose has had to be experienced, for all her glory, as forbidden, alien finally to his chosen existence.

**

Thus, after all the years as Brother Antoninus, he still had not recovered, except in exalted moments, that unquestioned oneness which he had felt with nature in the mid-thirties. During the war his refusal of the shadow-role of warrior had cast him, reciprocally, in a shadow-relationship with the patriarchal institutions which said that he should fight. In middle age his commitment to the monastic ideal had made him similarily ambivalent about "the woman within," though she was the source of his religious experience as well as his muse.

It could be no simple duality. Everson had experienced Christianity "as a Dionysian phenomenon" at the time of his conversion and in subsequent moments of mystical transcendence; and, as he later recalled it, "this same movement took me into the monastery--to exclude everything from the ecstatic Dionysian core" in the life of Brother Antoninus. Dionysus symbolizes the anima-dominated man, whose creative energy comes from his feminine affinities. In the myth Dionysus' opponent is Pentheus, the repressive law-giver, the chaste soldier-king. Dionysus is Pentheus' shadow, but is it not true that Pentheus is Dionysus' shadow as well, driving him to furious reprisals? What, then, of Everson and Antoninus? The situation is different because Antoninus is not Pentheus any more than Everson is simply Dionysus. If Everson and Antoninus are shadows to each other, they are needed so within the single personality. Between them, even if we can distinguish twin aspects of the living person, lies no fight to the death, as with Pentheus and Dionysus, but a grappling toward accommodation, begun long before Everson became Antoninus. "The Sides of a Mind" in the late thirties is only one testimonial to how generic the struggle has been.

Thus, as psychic entity, the formative "Antoninus" had embodied a reflective, scrupulous, perfectionist dimension of character which got voiced in the earlier work mostly in his concern for revision and crafted statement. Later the monastically realized "Antoninus" brought to the work an emotional spiritual clarity and an intellectual subtlety that made for the most powerfully achieved poems. Hence "Antoninus," whether craftsman or monk, was no extraneous imposition but constituted an inherent reality. As Everson's becoming Antoninus represented an extension and integration of identity, not a denial, so his departure from the monastery would not affect the alchemy of his character.

Still, the tension persisted. He could be a Dionysian Christian, but could he remain a Dionysian monk? In the late sixties he moved toward taking final vows, even while sounding more emphatically the erotic basis of spirituality. Who Is She That Looketh Forth as the Morning redresses the previous image of Mary as Wisdom in "A Canticle to the Great Mother of God" by retrieving for her, at the moment of conception by the Spirit, the erotic and chthonic powers of a goddess like Venus. Tendril in the Mesh, Antoninus' last poem as a monk, strives to assimilate and terminate another love-relationship with a woman by subsuming its graphic sexual details in an "Epilogue" which experiences Incarnation not as idealized humanity but as animistic totem:

> Dark God of Eros, Christ of the buried brood,
> Stone-channelled beast of ecstasy and fire,
> The angelic wisdom in the serpentine desire,
> Fang hidden in the flesh's velvet hood
> Riddling with delight its visionary good.

After the first public reading of this poem in December, 1969, Brother Antoninus stripped off his religious habit and announced to his shocked audience that he was leaving the Dominican Order. Shortly thereafter he married, first outside the Church and later in the Church, Susanna Rickson, to whom Tendril is dedicated. They live near Santa Cruz, where Everson teaches at the University of California.

**

The precipitate departure indicates how much as a thunderclap it came, even to himself; and the poems of Man-Fate (1974) are the words of a man caught in a psychic crossfire: Antoninus become Everson again. During the years as Brother Antoninus, nature had remained a strong religious presence for him. The elegy for Jeffers, The Poet Is Dead, works almost completely through images of the California coast, and poems like "The South Coast," "A Canticle to the Waterbirds," and "In All These Acts" project pantheism into Christian mystery. Now Everson withdrew again to nature to validate his break with Antoninus, but with a consciousness heightened and complicated by all that Antoninus had come to realize and value, and by the monastery life that Everson found it excruciating to leave behind. In the opacities of the elemental matrix he would be healed or torn apart.

That venture into the primeval is enacted in a sequence of dreams and archetypal fantasies which comprise the climax of the volume. In "The Narrows of Birth" on Christmas night, twenty-one years after his conversion experience, he dreams of joining the clan gathered around the Great Mother of Nature. He bows before her for absolution, but instead sees her followers begin the castration of a young man, whose body is "slumped in its unmistakably erotic swoon." The dreamer finds the Great Mother betraying him to join in the castration. The dream in "The Black Hills" shows Everson fighting his way back in psychic as well as historical time to recover the Indians in all their splendid strength, and to seek the blessing of his dark, dead Father, whom he loves and whom civilization taught him to dread and kill. All but overwhelmed in the furious rush of the braves, he cannot wring a word of recognition from the chief. In the aftermath of the dream he rises briefly to conscious acquiescence in the natural round, which the red men honored and the white men violated: "All Indian at last,/ I lift up my arms and pray"; but even that moment is broken off anti-climactically.

The nightmares tell what Antoninus already knew: that one cannot give over to the shadow; abandonment to the powers of darkness without a guide will end in dissolution, chaos, death. For the man, the anima can be such a mediator. She is grounded in the shadow-area so strongly that at times she seems merely his vassal and instrument: the feminine as temptation or threat. But in coping with the shadow the man also engages her. And if trusted and loved, she can free him from enslavement to the shadow, mediating the unconscious and the passions, drawing them from blind automation into activity and actualization in masculine consciousness, and thus opening the way gradually to selfhood: the apocalypse of the polarized personality into androgynous, undivided identity. The self is the psychological equivalent of the beatific vision, glimpsed in our supreme moments, but mostly striven for through the polar rhythms of living. For in selfhood the individual attains not just what is uniquely himself, but thereby attains participation in the Godhead in which we shall all find ourselves at last.

Under the onslaught of the shadow in Man-Fate Ever-

son's response is instinctive and right: he turns to touch
his wife. She is the objective verification of the anima: a
somnolent but locating presence, waiting for his return from
lonely contention with the shadow. For after the powerful
consolidation of the anima in The Rose and the subsequent
poems, now no longer alien and suspect but tallied in his
marriage, she lies ready to wake again from drowsy abeyance
to spring him into the next thrust towards selfhood. The
last words of the book are:

> I have made a long run.
> I have swum dark waters.
>
> I have followed you through hanging traps.
> I have risked it all.
>
> O cut my thongs!
>
> At the fork of your flesh
> Our two trails come together.
>
> At your body's bench
> I take meat.

Expressed in the archetypal terms of the human psyche, the
Incarnation is God entering into, permeating and operating
through the feminine, just as the Annunciation proclaims.
The concluding image above, physical yet suggestive of the
sacramental act, constitutes, more immediately and elemen-
tally than with the Rose, the personalizing of the regenera-
tive, redemptive mystery in the witness of the wife to the
power of the anima. Mother and wife and priestess in one,
she administers him nourishment needed now for the way
ahead.

THE BOOKS OF WILLIAM EVERSON

Vicky Schrieber Dill. 1978

The publication of Everson's handpress edition Granite &
Cypress crystalized his position as one of the ablest printers
in America, eliciting such responses as in the Gentry and
Blumenthal section, "William Everson as Printer," above.
There was, however, no attempt to correlate his literary
and typographical concerns until a graduate student at Notre
Dame published in 1978 the following essay in Books at Iowa,
a journal of the University of Iowa Library at Iowa City.
Here she surveys Everson's poems as they appear in his
printed editions, illuminating his holistic vision of poetry
realized in typographic form.

> As a poet-printer whose strug-
> gle to remain whole in a highly
> specialized and helplessly frac-
> tured world has produced much
> moving poetry bound in volumes
> of consummate craftsmanship,
> Everson has continued to 'em-
> brace the book. '

"Very few perfect books have even been written, and
very few that are perfect have ever been printed. One rea-
son for that is the pressure that inheres in the book as a
symbol; it is so great that the individual ... cannot embrace
the book in its totality. "[1] Much of William Everson's life
has been spent in the elusive effort to "embrace the book"
as a symbol. As a poet-printer, he has sought to make the
book as printed artifact speak a single and unequivocal truth
--the truth that artistic wholeness is possible in a diversified
and highly fractured, assembly-line society: "My whole at-

tempt in a pluralistic age is to give the book a sacral, ho-
listic character, to recover time with it. "[2] His commitment
to this aesthetic search for wholeness has prompted a re-
markable journey as writer, printer, and prophet of the San
Francisco Renaissance poets.

A Californian of Norwegian descent, son of a printer,
Everson was born in Sacramento in 1912. Before World War
II, he was a farmer-writer in the San Joaquin Valley. His
first publication, a ten-cent pamphlet of short poetry called
These Are the Ravens, appeared in 1935. He also published
two slim volumes, San Joaquin (1939) and The Masculine
Dead (1942), in the first years of World War II. The poet's
early work is dominated by images of gentle fields, wildlife,
and strong mountain children whose hardiness embodies the
continuity of human life. All that sustains and all that links
man to his past pulses from the fertile earth, mother of po-
etic art. These early poems, says Everson in a typically
natural metaphor,

> are the ravens of my soul,
> Sloping above the lonely fields
> And cawing, cawing. [3]

The holocaust of World War II shattered that tranquil-
ity which Everson had achieved in his poetic life in the late
1930s and early 1940s. As a pacifist, he chose to enter the
Civilian Public Service Camp at Waldport, Oregon. CPS
camps, such as Waldport's Camp Angel, served as alterna-
tive military duty for pacifists prior to the outbreak of World
War II. Established in 1940 by the Quakers, Church of the
Brethren, and Mennonites, the alternative service camps
brought non-resisters of varying backgrounds together for
such projects as land reconstruction, medical research, and
hunger relief. [4] Everson engaged in such tasks daily, using
free time to organize the creative abilities of his fellow pac-
ifists. At Camp Angel, he and others established the Untide
Press. The mimeographed publications of the press aimed
to communicate the importance of the pacifist cause and to
preserve an aesthetically effective description of the lives
led by members of the camps.

The first major publications of the Untide Press now
in the University of Iowa Libraries are Everson's X War
Elegies (1943) and Poems: mcmxlii (1945). Even in these
initial efforts, Everson's concern with the book as a totality
is apparent. Although mimeographed, X War Elegies includes
line drawings by artist Kemper Nomland illustrating the poems,

and, evidently, the poet felt the finished product worthy of
the signature which he placed in the University of Iowa's
copy of that volume. These evidences of Everson's holistic
approach to art reflect his belief that poetry is no longer
singularly an aural art, but is primarily read in silence from
the printed page. This change makes the printing press im-
mensely important, for the visual impact of the words on the
page must substitute for what was once the subtleties of aural
interpretation. The printing is, therefore, an integral part
of the poem's effect:

> "From the moment a poem became primarily a
> thing, an object on a page, it began to lose the
> force of its nature.... Today the fate of a poem
> may be decided by nothing more than its appear-
> ance as it is lifted to be read....
> Both the poet and the typographer are left with
> the merest devices to indicate what is actually a
> profusion of subtle effects. In printing, I have
> tried to maintain the poem's prime aural reality. "[5]

These "merest devices" include not only the typography, but
also the artwork, the weave of the paper, the kind of ink,
and the method of binding. All contribute significantly to
the creation of an aesthetically unified object.

In April of 1944 Everson, typically expressing his con-
cern for the total effect of the book, wrote to the CPS direc-
tor about the progress of the Untide Press projects. Fully
aware of the severe shortage of funds, even for necessities
in the CPS camps, the poet felt the pacifist-artist cause, as
presented in the War Elegies, urgent enough to warrant the
best possible materials and craftsmanship available.

> "We are starting work on the Elegies and hope
> to have them done in six or eight weeks. Nomland
> came down on an exchange [of camp members] and
> designed the books. If press work can live up to
> his design, this will be a really unique book not
> only in CPS but in these United States--numerous
> line cuts in the inimitable Nomland manner, color
> work throughout, fine paper, etc. I have great
> hopes for this edition. "[6]

Although this expensive plan never materialized, sev-
eral lower-cost projects were completed by the Untide Press.
In 1944, a revised edition of X War Elegies did appear.
Printed on a handpress by Everson himself, this edition (a

copy of which is now held by the University of Iowa Libraries) and Waldport Poems (1944) continue to reflect Everson's interest in the whole book as artifact.

Everson's early work illustrates even more about his holistic approach than simply the importance of visual effect. He further insists on matching the nature and quality of the presswork to what he judges as the integrity and seriousness of the subject of the poems. Art which flowers from a cause as important to him as pacifism naturally dictates a masterful press work. He notes in "The Fine Arts at Waldport," a pamphlet designed to acquaint readers with the artistic community at Camp Angel, that "Bad ideas and excellent art are not the most compatible of bedfellows."[7]

The ideas which Everson considers important enough to be included in the Waldport poems printed by Untide Press reflect upon the way of life experienced by men living in the camps. In these slim volumes, as well as in the collected poetry of The Residual Years (1944), the poet explores the nature of the tasks performed in the camps:

> To sunder the rock--that is our day.
> In the weak light,
> Under high fractured cliffs
> We turn with our hands the raw granite,
> We break it with iron ...
>
> We perceive our place in the terrible pattern,
> And temper with pity the fierce gall,
> Hearing the sadness,
> The loss and utter desolation,
> Howl at the heart of the world.[8]

The emotions resulting from separation of husbands and wives, the effects of the war on the natural landscape, and the urgency of the pacifist cause, are fit subject matter for Untide Press:

> I, the living heir
> Of the bloodiest men of all Europe,
> And the knowledge of past tears through my flesh,
> I flinch in the guilt of what I am,
> Seeing the poised heap of this time
> Break like a wave.
> And I vow not to wantonly ever take life,...[9]

The publications of Untide Press speak for the unique position of those writers, severed from the ties of the world, who published under its name.

In fact, Everson's attempt to present a coherent work of art extends even to the act of naming the handpresses upon which he does his printing. The name of his first privately-owned press reflects an orientation to nature as the wellspring of his creative powers:

> "When I left the Untide group after the war and took up my own venture, I decided to call it The Equinox Press. Not only were the equinoxes my favorite seasons ... but the name symbolized vividly the ideal of balance.... It caught up in my mind the humanist goal I had set for myself: to live a life of equipoise and moderation in the context of pure nature. "[10]

In the fall of 1947 Everson wrote "There Will Be Harvest," a poem celebrating the founding of the Equinox Press and his move to Berkeley. It is the only poem in the poet-printer's yet published verse that makes specific reference to the art of the handpress.

There will be harvest, harvest. We freighted the hand-
press
Out of the hills. Mounted at last in the little room
It waits for the black ink of its being;
And the rich paper, drawn out of Europe, it too hand-
fashioned;
The work of the hand, all; the love of the hand in its
sure sweep
When the bar pulls over; all about it the touch of a hand
Laid on it with care....
All work of wholeness executes in the enlivened eye: a
godly issue. [11]

In Berkeley, Everson associated with the group of young artists gathered around Kenneth Rexroth, but he found that the interior equipoise he sought to render in the works printed by Equinox Press had not survived the war. The experience of isolation in the camps, as well as the ravages on the natural landscape caused by the upheaval, shattered the personal and artistic integration the poet had earlier achieved. The search for new wholeness, therefore, becomes a dominant theme in the post-war poems.

That theme is reflected in The Residual Years, a col-

lection of pre-war poems and the poems printed earlier in
the mimeographed editions from Untide Press. Published
commercially by New Directions in 1948, the later poems
in the volume show a disjunction with nature and a frustrated
search for some comprehensive context in which the passion
of the poet might be ordered. Nature is now inadequate to
that task:

> Apart on his rock
> The forester sucks his sufficient quid,
> And never hears,
> At one with the landscape,
> That crouches behind its masked firs,
> Its skeletal snags,
> Brooding upon the lost myth
> Created once in its unfathomable past
> And never regained--
> But it wants to,
> It waits, it waits,
> Its immense obsession--12

One year after the appearance of The Residual Years,
Everson published his first full volume on the new Equinox
Press, A Privacy of Speech (1949). His readiness and need
for a major philosophical change, however, made that first
effort also the last printing to be completed under the Equinox
name. In the Christmas season of 1949, Everson found a
new context for his writing and began learning to express
himself poetically from a radically different philosophical ori-
entation. That Christmas a friend of Everson's, Mary Fabil-
li, invited him to attend a midnight mass where the reenact-
ment of the nativity scene deeply stirred the sensibilities of
the young poet. He recalls in his "Autobiography" how the
scent of the fir trees and the shepherd statuettes which flanked
the crèche impressed upon him a new "reality" and a
deep sense of his own need for a new perspective on the
world around him:

> "And as I sat in that familiar estrangement of
> feeling which had never left me in the Catholic
> churches, there came to me the resinous scent of
> the fir trees. ... That scene was the only thing
> I could seize on with anything like true realization
> ..., [and] out of the greatness of my need I sensed
> in it something of a verification ... that I need not
> fear, were I to come to the Christ, that He would
> exact the dreaded renunciation of my natural world.
> On the contrary, it was of His, His own, of His

making.... It was there in the Cathedral ...
wooing me to probe back behind the façade of ap-
pearances ... to seek for the reality that lay be-
hind them all. "

As a newly-committed Catholic, Everson's greatest
challenge would be to integrate the powers of the artist and
the powers of the believer. The attempt to mediate the Bac-
chic forces of poetic inspiration and invention--first as a
convert and later as a monk--led inevitably to difficulties:

"I think that the conflict [between the artist and
conventional society] is inevitable. The artist him-
self will find himself on the cross in society ...
because in that tension between the institutional
and the charismatic, the institutional mentality is
... suspicious of any charismatic phenomenon.
If you are a mystic today, you get hauled off to
a hospital for observation...."[14]

When the responsibilities of his new faith interfered with the
desires of the artist, Everson gave first priority to his re-
ligious commitment.[15] Much of the pain of that disciplining
process as well as many of the critical problems raised by
the religious priority are clearly expressed in the writings
of the Catholic period.[16]

Everson's attempt to work out the implications of his
conversion extend not only into the subject matter of his po-
etry but, further, into his handpress work. Upon dedicating
himself to the church, he renamed his press the Seraphim
Press. Whereas the Equinox Press represented the human-
istic love for perfect balance struck in the art of printing,
the Seraphim Press was so named for its higher aspirations:

"But when I entered the Church, my values,
the whole emphasis of my mind, underwent a
rapid and profound alteration. I left behind the
vision of a purely natural balance, and struck
out for the super-natural extremity, the absolute
attainment beyond all the limited attainments of
life. I laid aside the work of my humanism upon
which I had been engaged, and took up the first
of the conversion poetry which was ready to print;
and because I wanted to dissever myself from the
psychology of my past, and to make a testament
to the great things of my new discovery, I decided
to change the name of my press. "[17]

Everson continued printing while serving at Maurin House, a Catholic worker house of hospitality in Oakland. There Seraphim Press published Triptych for the Living in 1951. It is illustrated with woodcuts by Mary Fabilli, making apparent, as the colophon indicates, Everson's continued insistence on seeking a unified effect through both the meaning and the appearance of the words:

"... and indeed the book [Triptych for the Living] in its design looks back toward the primitive church in search of a model appropriate to the apostolic character of the text."[18]

That same year Everson entered the Dominican Order as a lay brother, taking the name of Brother Antoninus. He again changed the name of his press, this time to St. Albert's Press in honor of the Dominican priest revered in the house in which Everson lived. No longer seeking to print his own work but wanting to find a handpress task which would necessitate his personal immersion into the monastic community of workers, Everson began searching for a text worthy of the serious and perfect skill of a whole community of dedicated brothers. No text seemed more appropriate for such an ambitious endeavor than the new translation of the Psalter recently completed at the direction of Pope Pius XII. Everson became convinced that God had called and equipped him to do this specific labor of devotion: "[He] had led me to the handpress, and instructed me in its craft, and brought me to the Order where I might work, and then had given me the work...."[19]

Everson and the Dominican brothers worked on the printing of the Psalter in their spare time for two or more years. The task, so intricately and thoughtfully conceived, proved more formidable than was originally thought, however, and the work was never completed. In May of 1955, to celebrate the fifth centennial of the first appearance of a separately-printed psalmody (1457), Everson published the first and only folio. It is introduced with a lengthy "Note" detailing the kind of ink, paper, and binding used in the printing. As the "Note" indicates, it was a project attempted with only the most thorough preparation and by the most highly skilled craftsmen available, for "No poetry of earth has ever surpassed the Psalter in nobility of utterance, nor dealt with such intensity of man's exaltation in God's fulfillment, nor the deep abjection of his Fall."[20]

Everson found that the challenge of the Psalter project

did provide a deep immersion into the contemplative community and aided him in the many adjustments he faced as an artist there. It did not, however, engross all his concentrated life. In spite of institutional pressures and the enormous effort demanded by the Psalter, he published a significant body of poetry during those years.

Everson's first Catholic work, "At the Edge" (printed, 1952; published, 1958), is an exploration of the poet-seeker's encounter with the vast unknown of the subconscious. The poem urges the reader to move from the darkness of that realm into the exposing light of God:

> There is a mark, made on the soul in its first wrongdoing,
>   and that is a taint;
> And the mark of that taint, it must either widen or wane--
> As the soul decrees in its inclination so will it be. [21]

The radiance of God's presence is similarly the subject of two other brief poems written in Everson's early years as a Catholic poet, "A Fragment for the Birth of God" and "An Age Insurgent: Poems by Brother Antoninus." The "Fragment" is a seven-line poem celebrating the significance of the Christ-child's "little cry" and the triumph of the Holy Mother. "An Age Insurgent" like "At the Edge" is an attempt to stir the reader to be on the offensive for his Christian commitment. [22]

These short religious poems preceded Everson's first lengthy volume published commercially as a brother, The Crooked Lines of God (1960). That volume, Everson has explained, is arranged in three parts, "each corresponding to a particular phase of spiritual development, and each dominated, more or less, by the psychology of a particular saint." [23] The three saints, Augustine, Francis, and Dominic, represent both a chronological and a spiritual journey; the poet moves from the spirit of Augustinian repentance and renewal in "Out of the Depths" to the Franciscan ethic of work in "In the Crucible." There, Everson recalls, "already the cramp was setting in...." [24] The problems of attuning his naturally spontaneous and individualistic personality to the form of his new religious priorities and convictions had not been solved. The poet's creative drives were at war with his religious aspirations, and the devotee quieted the poet within. The tension which resulted from this inner war is sustained in The Crooked Lines until it is synthesized in the third and final section of the book, "Out of the Ash," by the contemplative Dominican spirit which, Everson notes,

moved him toward "Not peace, certainly, rather a new cru-
cifixion.... By 1954 the poems, which had thinned to a
mere trickle, choked out altogether, stopped."[25] The physical
rigors of the monastic life and the discipline of attempting
to "keep the lines straight" brought the volume to a close
earlier than the poet originally expected.

Everson continued, however, to pursue integration of
the creative and the religious selves throughout the early
1960s, as is apparent in his second major Catholic work,
The Hazards of Holiness (1962). In that volume the poet
seeks integration of the many areas of his life through the
writing of poems in a Jungian context, a structure which,
Everson notes, reveals "the struggle to make myself com-
prehensible to myself...."[26] He prefaces many of the poems
with a dream recollection, a passage of Scripture, or both.

The Hazards of Holiness is divided into three sections
which further reflect Everson's understanding of that interior
struggle. "Friendship and Enmith" traces the seeker's path
from darkness to the light of God. But this path leads to
an even more desperate striving--a wrestling with the inner
demon who is so deceitful that he is often mistaken for God
Himself. That wrestling is the subject of many of the poems
in the second section, "The Dark Face of God." The poems
in "Love and Violence," the third and closing section, speak
of the triumph of love through the violent struggle of the
seeker determined to cling to his God:

> Where the kites are shrieking
> There reeks the carcass.
> Where the treasure is sunk
> There cowers the heart.
> Having done such things in the green wood
> What will I do in the dry?
>
> ...
>
> Have pity on me, have pity on me,
> At least you my friends,
> For God hath touched me. [27]

Everson's dedication to his faith was continuing to pose dif-
ficulties for him poetically; the landscape with which he was
once so familiar no longer met his poetic needs. In The
Crooked Lines and The Hazards of Holiness he sought for
institutionally acceptable metaphors which would at once ad-
mit his spontaneous images and also communicate the reli-
gious intent of the poem. Such difficulties do not plague

Everson in the privately-printed volumes of this period, The
Blowing of the Seed (1966) and In the Fictive Wish (1967).
Written in 1946, but not published until just after The Haz-
ards of Holiness, these poems contrast sharply in their use
of metaphor with that in the religious poetry. Drawn from
the physical landscape, the earlier metaphors more naturally
express the content of the poems. Unlike the two major vol-
umes of Catholic poetry, these poems do not strain to re-
make the passion with which they are concerned into poetry
readily accepted by the religious community. That passion
which is the subject of The Blowing of the Seed and In the
Fictive Wish is the passion for wholeness found in the sexual
encounter.

The Blowing of the Seed details the meeting of a Nor-
dic man and a Mediterranean woman; the "cold encrusted
man" is associated with the wintry seasons while the woman
is from the "deep equatorial zone" and represents the warmth
of the earth. In the same way that the harshness of late win-
ter is tempered by the suggestion of warming spring winds,
so also the man, a remnant of the glacial age, is tempered
and softened by the loving fervor of the southern woman.
The use of the nature metaphor greatly increases the sensu-
ality of the passage:

I move to meet you now in a greening time.
I come with wind and with wet
In a soft season.
I bring you my hand.
I bring you the flesh of those fallow fallen years
And my manifest reasons. [28]

Everson's skill in appropriating the natural landscape
as metaphorical background for poetry dealing candidly with
sexual encounter is most evident in this early verse. It is
a much more difficult task, however, to transform the erotic
passion poetically into holy desire, as Everson does in this
passage from The Crooked Lines, written some 16 years
later:

My Lord came to me
In the deep of night;
The sullen dark was wounded with His name.
I was as woman made before His eyes;
My nakedness was as a secret shame.
I was a thing of flesh for His despise;
I was a nakedness before His sight. [29]

Everson's religious poetry of the late 1960s accordingly tries with increasing concentration to explore the potential of the religious metaphor. That potential is developed in The Rose of Solitude, published in 1967 by Doubleday. In this poem a monk, the man of God, encounters Rose, the woman of the world. The narrative asserts that, though these two people could have acceded to archetypal sin, they manage through the strength they gained in avoiding evil not only to remain sinless but to achieve a kind of deliverance and wholeness greater than either possessed previously as individuals. 30 Like The Crooked Lines, The Rose of Solitude attempts to deal with erotic statement clothed in an institutionally-acceptable religious language:

In the stigmata of His gaze her love coils like the flesh
  on its iron, the love-ache of the opening.
When she utters the Holy Name you would never
  doubt God died for the love of men. 31

By contrast, the early work published alongside The Rose of Solitude can deal with the erotic expression directly:

Water-woman,
Near water or of it,
The sea-drenched hair;
Of gray gaze and level
Mostly he knows her;
Of such bosom as face would fade in;
Of such thigh as would fold;
Of huge need come to;... 32

This particular poem, In the Fictive Wish, also marks Everson's return to privately handprinted work after nearly a decade of commercial publishing. The slender volume carefully observes Everson's holistic theories of art: the short lines of the poem are placed carefully within wide margins and great solicitude is taken to secure unity of typeset and paper weave. Finally, the poem is illustrated with an unusually delicate woodcut.

The Last Crusade (1969), a handprinted folio volume from this late Catholic period, a copy of which is now held by the University of Iowa Libraries, was designed and printed by Graham Mackintosh. The skillful presswork and handmade paper contribute to the total effect of the volume--that of communicating an ultimate kind of religious experience through poetry. The Last Crusade is less concerned with achieving a perfect union of subject and metaphorical vehicle, the hope of publications such as those released by the Untide and Equinox presses, than with capturing the nature of that religious experience in the book. Everson described the writing of this poem as an act which, in itself, changed and healed him, and he replied to the critical attacks on his handling of the imagery in The Last Crusade with the almost apologetic remark, "I cannot claim that a spiritual or therapeutic success guarantees a corresponding aesthetic one."[33] The religious influences so pervasive in Everson's life during this time persuaded him that the passion for balance, lifted to idolatry, can kill the poet; this is the theme of The Last Crusade. In the poem, a holy man is killed for lapsing into mere self-gratification. Since, by implication, the poem can become a form of self-gratification to the poet, it too may have to be sacrificed in order that he may attain a higher spiritual goal. That sacrifice does not, however, require the lowering of presswork or artistic standards in the crafting of the book itself. Indeed an experience as raw and devastating as that which was endured by the knight in The Last Crusade, as well as one as transcendent and liberating as that enjoyed by the poet who escaped the knight's doom, deserves the finest in skilled handprinting.

That vision of spiritual purity and devotion which Everson had so relentlessly pursued led him, perhaps more to his surprise than to others', away from the monastic life and back into the world. Tendril in the Mesh, handprinted in 1973, details the poet's psychological withdrawal from the contemplative life and his entrance back into secular life. One year later Everson commercially published Man-Fate: The Swan Song of Brother Antoninus (1974), the longest poem of which is "Tendril in the Mesh." Everson wrote of that poem, "[It] is a love poem sequence, a cycle of renewal, but it also concerns the monastic life, from the point of view of one who has renounced it."[34] The long struggle to remain within the boundaries of what is ecclesiastically acceptable writing dissolves in Man-Fate, and Everson no longer is compelled to couch passion in religious images. He speaks of his decision to leave the solitary life as a kind of return to his poetic home, to a context into which he more naturally fits. And, just as the lovers in A Rose of Solitude achieved a kind of spiritual deliverance by remaining true to their original loves, so the poet is delivered from damnation as he returns to his spiritual home:

> Whoever forsakes his element
> Is ludicrous, and in his perverse
> Exacerbation, damns his own eyes. [35]

Everson wrote "Tendril in the Mesh" while still a member of the religious order.   He read the sequence for the first time on the afternoon of December 7, 1969, at the University of California, Davis.   Having completed the reading, he publicly stripped off his religious habit, fled the stage, and returned to private life.[36]   Since this event and his marriage in the following year, the poet-printer has continued to write prolifically and to supervise work on the handpress.

Much of his recent writing has involved the preparation of various introductions and explanations for texts of Robinson Jeffers' work, including introductions for Cawdor, Medea, and Californians.   Perhaps the most extraordinary of Everson's lifelong attempts to create the unified or "sacral" book, in fact, involves the printing of Jeffers' Granite & Cypress: Rubbings from the Rock.   Every aspect of the poetic content, the landscape against which the poems were written, and the nature of the poet himself has been taken into account in the designing of this artifact.

Everson has based his conception of Granite & Cypress on the assertion that the true purpose which Jeffers found in life following the extreme disillusionment the poet suffered as a result of World War I was effected by his handling of stone--"the direct physical labor involved in building Tor House and the fabled Hawk Tower."[37]   The book is a collection of all the poems which Jeffers wrote "under the impact of stone."   The design conceived by Everson calls for the lengthy Jeffers line to be extended in the text exactly as the poet intended.   And, to avoid boredom on the blank versos, a special process was developed whereby each is printed with a reverse imprint of the recto, forming a kind of shadow used to enliven the left page.   The paper for the Jeffers volume was handmade in England, and the type was specifically chosen to support the subject matter--"stark, glyptic, truly abrasive, recalled the feeling of perceptive readers that ... to experience his language is to suffer his awful accessibility to the elements."[38]   The binding of Granite & Cypress is laced with deerskin rawhide from the California coast, and a slipcase "fashioned of Monterey Cypress, with a window of granite from Jeffers' stoneyard (rock drawn by the poet's own hands from the sea) ... brings together the book's archetypal duality: the permanence of granite wrapped in the enduring presence of cypress."[39]

Everson's edition of Granite & Cypress speaks eloquently to his desire to write and print books of poems that are,

as physical objects, works of art. As a poet, he seeks sub-
stantially to integrate the implications of his beliefs into his
works, regardless of the vicissitudes of the critical climate
into which they come. He continues to sculpture his poetic
language to meet the needs of his philosophical poetry; he
believes that the message his poetry communicates is as
important as the sound of the lines, the appearance of the
text, the appropriateness of the image. He insists on inte-
grity between the poem and the poet's life in the world as
well as between the poem and the printer's concerns. As
a poet-printer whose struggle to remain whole in a highly
specialized and helplessly fractured world has produced much
moving poetry bound in volumes of consummate craftsman-
ship, Everson has continued to "embrace the book."

Notes

1 William Everson, "The Poem as Icon--Reflections on
      Printing as a Fine Art," Soundings (8 December 1976),
      p7.

2 Ibid. , p21.

3 William Everson, These Are the Ravens (San Leandro,
      Calif. : Greater West Pub. Co. , 1935), p3.

4 For more information on the Civilian Public Service
      Camps, see Floyd E. Mallott, Studies in Brethren
      History (Elgin, Ill. : House of the Church of the
      Brethren, 1954), pp237-244.

5 William Everson, "A Note on the Psalter of Pope Pius
      XII," Novum Psalterium Pii XII: An Unfinished Folio
      Edition of Brother Antoninus, O. P. (Los Angeles:
      Countess Estelle Doheny, 1955), p xxiii.   Hereafter,
      "A Note on the Psalter."

6 William Everson, April 13, 1944. Letter to Harold Row,
      Director of CPS, General Board of the Church of the
      Brethren. Microfilm copy at the Church of the Breth-
      ren General Office Archives, Elgin, Ill.

7 William Everson, The Fine Arts at Waldport (Evanston,
      Ill. : Brethren Service Center, 1943), p2.

8 William Everson, X War Elegies (Waldport, Ore. : Untide
      Press, 1943), p[22], numbering from recto of first leaf.

9 Ibid., p[8].

10 William Everson, "Printer as Contemplative," Quarterly Newsletter [of the Book Club of California] (1954), p52. Hereafter, "Printer as Contemplative."

11 William Everson, There Will Be Harvest (Berkeley, Calif.: Kenneth J. Carpenter, 1960). See colophon.

12 William Everson, The Residual Years (New York: New Directions, 1948), pp15-16.

13 William Everson, Foreword to "Pages from an Unpublished Autobiography," Ramparts 1, no. 2 (1962-3), p60.

14 William Everson, "The Artist and Religious Life: Brother Antoninus, O. P.," The American Benedictine Review, XI (September-December, 1960), p225.

15 Paul Lacey, The Inner War: Forms and Themes in Recent American Poetry (Philadelphia: Fortress Press, 1972), p87.

16 The critical problems facing Everson can be further conceptualized along a Dionysius-Apollo dichotomy. The early poems use nature metaphors candidly to explore areas of interest to the poet, particularly the ramifications of sexual encounter. Many areas of interest could not be so candidly explored, however, when the poet's intent was religious. New metaphors were needed. The early period, can, therefore, be characterized as a period of Dionysian influence in which the unharnessed use of the natural landscape prevailed in the poems until the time of Everson's conversion. The radically disciplined monastic life then adopted by Everson required new priorities, new symbols, and self-control of the Apollonian influence--a force which remained ascendant in Everson's writings until approximately 1969. Since Everson's reemergence into secular life, the Dionysian influence is again evident, especially in "Tendril in the Mesh" (1973), where the erotic imagery is but slightly tempered from its former, pre-Catholic character.

17 "Printer as Contemplative," p52.

18 William Everson, Triptych for the Living (Oakland, Calif.: Seraphim Press, 1951). See colophon.

19 "A Note on the Psalter," p xv.

20 Ibid. , p xiii.

21 William Everson, At the Edge (Oakland, Calif. : Albertus Magnus Press, 1958), ℓℓ. 1-3.

22 William Everson, An Age Insurgent: Poems by Brother Antoninus, O. P. (San Francisco: Blackfriars Publications, 1959). See letter accompanying the volume.

23 William Everson, The Crooked Lines of God (Detroit: University of Detroit Press, 1962), "Foreword," p[2]. Hereafter, The Crooked Lines.

24 Ibid.

25 Ibid.

26 William Everson, The Hazards of Holiness (New York: Doubleday, 1958), p7.

27 Ibid. , p88, ℓℓ. 12-17, 21-23.

28 William Everson, The Blowing of the Seed (New Haven, Conn. : Henry W. Wenning, 1966), Part vi, ℓℓ. 1-6.

29 The Crooked Lines, p60, ℓℓ. 1-7.

30 William Everson, The Rose of Solitude (Garden City, N. Y. : Doubleday, 1967), "Foreword," pp x-xi.

31 Ibid. , ℓℓ. 16-19.

32 William Everson, In the Fictive Wish (Berkeley, Calif. : Oyez Press, 1967), p9, ℓℓ. 35-42.

33 William Everson, The Last Crusade (Berkeley, Calif. : Oyez Press, 1969), "Foreword," p23.

34 William Everson, Man-Fate: The Swan Song of Brother Antoninus (New York: New Directions, 1974), p vii.

35 Ibid. , p40, ℓℓ. 24-26.

36 William Everson, Tendril in the Mesh (Aromas, Calif. : Cayucos Books, 1973). Broadside.

37 Robinson Jeffers, Granite & Cypress: Rubbings from the Rock (Santa Cruz, Calif. : Lime Kiln Press, n. d.). Broadside by William Everson, p1.

38 Ibid. , p2.

39 Ibid.

TAPROOT OF INSTINCT:
THE WESTERN REGIONAL ARCHETYPE

David Carpenter. 1978

The publication in 1976 of an expanded edition of Everson's
prose study Archetype West: The Pacific Coast as a Literary
Region refocussed attention on his role as an exponent of
"the spirit of place." David Carpenter, in a paper written
for a graduate seminar at the University of Oregon, and in-
cluded in William Hotchkiss and David Carpenter, William
Everson: Poet from the San Joaquin (Blue Oak Press, 1978),
weighs Everson's early practice against his latterday theory.

> Everson sets out, or rather in,
> to discover his own heritage;
> rather than the poet's discover-
> ing the Western archetype, it
> discovers him and takes its am-
> bience from his regional identity.

"I have said it once and I say it again: whoever
uproots his instincts uproots his strength--for
with time, satiety, and discipline this dark mat-
ter may turn to spirit. "   --N. Kazantzakis.

For myself, 1976 brought in its wake not only William
Everson's essay "The Regional Incentive," as well as his
occasionally diffuse but otherwise vitally important and timely
book Archetype West: The Pacific Coast as a Literary Re-
gion, but also, through the retrospection afforded me by the
reading of those two works and by my encounter with the
poet's theories as applied to American literature and, more
specifically, West Coast literature, a clarification of an em-
phasis on California's regional power, uniqueness and numi-

212

nosity. More importantly, having been greatly impressed by
his earlier book of poems, The Residual Years, it struck
me that in Archetype West the man seemed to be putting forth
in theory what he, as a young poet in the San Joaquin valley,
had struggled with and had put forth in practice through the
medium of his art. In other words, here was a California
poet who, in his pre-Catholic poetry, had written from a
passionate impulse about the land he had grown up knowing
and, from a desire to give utterance to the regional ethos
that had been his spiritual inheritance, had chosen a voca-
tion that demanded of him an introspection that is all too
rare in our world today; then, by the dilution of the passions
and octopuslike receptiveness of youth that become, in time,
life willing, wisdom, he was able to conceptualize intellec-
tually what he, thirty almost forty years earlier, had espoused
poetically and, therefore, passionately and violently: the re-
sult is Archetype West, a key not only to the difficult realm
of regional bifurcation (sacred at the one extreme and sexual
at the other) and the potential equipoise between the Apollo-
nian and Dionysian elements found therein, but also a key to
the underpinnings of some of the richest and most inherently
American poetry that has been turned out in this century--
namely, the pre-Catholic poetry of William Everson.

In order to understand fully what is meant by "region-
al archetype," as applied to Everson's pre-Catholic poetry,
a considerable portion of this essay must be given over to
the elucidation of some basic tenets of regionalism--and
where possible examples of these tenets should be drawn from
the poet's early verse. Accomplishing this, we will then
launch out to uncover those forces which enable the poet's
region to manifest itself in extreme clarity as an archetype
through the medium of his art: we'll pursue this counter to
the original emergence, from lateral roots upward to the
central and vital taproot.

In his essay "The Regional Incentive," Everson ex-
plains man's innate need for tapping into the power of his
own region:

> "One of the deepest needs of the human soul is
> for centeredness, a focus of coherence and sig-
> nification which confers meaning on the shapeless-
> ness of temporal existence. Of the many possi-
> bilities perhaps the most basic, after man's aware-
> ness of family, is the apprehension of his imme-
> diate locale. For the surrounding landscape rep-
> resents something markedly other--indeed the

eternal presence of Otherness--and as such it
carries the vibration of divinity.... Close at
hand and yet aloofly apart, it stands as the
mandala of his unconscious associations, one
of the ineradicable patterns of psychic life.
As such, the recourse to landscape in the need
for coherence has from time immemorial ele-
vated man to his most profound religious intu-
itions. "[1]

In an attempt to comprehend the significance of regionalism,
recent writers have tended to divide into two approaches:
the phenomenological and the symbolic. Of the former, Paul
Shepard, in his book Man in the Landscape, reasons from
the territorial and biological responses:

"In man territoriality is an intricate association
of tenderness and antipathy, in which both are
closely related to the terrain. In him too the
territorial instinct varies greatly according to
circumstances. It is the household, property
in land, the tribal range. Perhaps even the
city, state, and nation are meta-territories.
The attention which the individual gives to the
territory is related to his age and perhaps the
season. Alaskan wolves do not seem to recog-
nize territorial bounds or even the context of
territorialism, until they reach breeding age,
whereupon they mate for life, learn the terri-
torial bounds, and join in to defend it. In some
primitive human groups ties between puberty and
the right to hunt hint at a similar relation be-
tween age and perception of the landscape; indeed,
the major role of the territory is perpetuation of
a reproductive unit. Territorial establishment
and maintenance is closely related to sexuality
and to other socializing processes. For love of
another is linked to love of place. "[2]

An excellent example of this territorial/biological approach
to regionalism is Everson's poem "The Homestead," wherein
the emphasis is placed on the autochthonous "perpetuation of
a reproductive unit":

Father and son, and father and son
Have given their sweat to the plough
And the torn earth leaving the share.
It is enough to say the field was turned

a thousand times
And the land still young.
It is enough to say four men have broken themselves
Unendingly treading these sun-bleached ruts.
There is nothing so timeless as struggle.
After the centuries have spent themselves,
And the sky-hungry civilizations have sprouted
    beside the seas
And rotted into earth,
There will be bent men breaking the ground and
    scattering seeds.
After the world convulses,
Heaving the hills and grey-green water,
There will be men warring against the wind,
And toiling lean-limbed beneath the slow span
    of the years.

Though this poem is relatively impersonal and non-introspec-
tive, as compared with the major portion of Everson's verse,
and resists the placement of any emphasis on the poet's sex-
uality or sexual awakening, it does describe clearly the na-
tive's timeless struggle with his region.

Of the symbolic approach to regionalism, Mircea
Eliade, an historian of religion, addresses himself to the
break in plane inherent within space itself. "For religious
man," he writes at the beginning of The Sacred and the Pro-
fane, "space is not homogenous ... some parts of space are
qualitatively different from others. " Further, he adds:

"It must be said at once that the religious experi-
ence of the nonhomogeneity of space is a primor-
dial experience, [equivalent] to a founding of the
world. It is not a matter of theoretical specula-
tion, but a primary religious experience that pre-
cedes all reflection on the world. For it is the
break effected in space that allows the world to
be constituted, because it reveals the fixed point,
the central axis for all future orientation. When
the sacred manifests itself in any hierophany,
there is not only a break in the homogeneity of
space; there is also revelation of an absolute
reality, opposed to the nonreality of the vast
surrounding expanse, the manifestation of the
sacred ontologically founds the world. In homo-
genous and infinite expanse, in which no point of
reference is possible and hence no orientation
can be established, the hierophany reveals an ab-
solute fixed point, a center. "3

In a lovely poem, "These Are the Ravens," Everson evokes
the sense of centeredness; and we see how in symbolic terms
the "fixed point" manifests itself beyond the poet's region,
after the "break in space":

> These are the ravens of my soul,
> Sloping above the lonely fields
> And cawing, cawing.
> I have released them now,
> And sent them down the sky,
> Learning the slow witchery of the wind,
> And crying on the farthest fences of the world.

In Everson's pre-Catholic poetry, the "religious ex-
perience" or awakening which Eliade writes about is essen-
tially pantheistic: it equates God with the forces and laws
of the universe. Everson himself writes that "Naturalism
itself is simply a child of pantheism"; he continues:

> "The glorification of brute nature and the celebra-
> tion of an inexorable Fate which are typical ingre-
> dients of Naturalism derive directly from the in-
> tuition that the cosmos has displaced a personal
> God as the clue to divinity. "[4]

And in the poem "Circumstance," written when Everson
was in his early twenties and approximately forty years before he
espoused the above-quoted theory, we hear the poet in his
attempt to come to terms with "an inexorable Fate," or the
"brood of those ages of chance"; but his conclusion is that
though we pray from our intuition of a divinity, we needn't
expect an answer to our prayers:

> He is a god who smiles blindly,
> And hears nothing, and squats faun-mouthed on
>   the wheeling world,
> Touching right and left with infinite
>   lightning-like gestures.
> He is the one to pray to, but he hears not,
>   nor sees....

Nevertheless, in light of Shepard's emphasis on the biological
and Eliade's emphasis on the symbolic, it should be clear
that such powerful emotional and intuitional forces in region-
alism manifest between them regionalism's force in collective
and individual motivation. Everson writes that, given region-
alism's inherent forces,

"it is no wonder that powerful semi-Modernists
like Yeats and Lorca, and stubbornly anti-Mod-
ernist ones like Frost and Jeffers, continued
all through the height of the Modernist period
to draw on regionalism's evocative appeal des-
pite the hostility of the urbanized critics, for
the numen inherent in its sovereignty cannot be
dispelled by mere theorizing.... It is within
the context of regionalism as both a sexual and
a sacred phenomenon that its power is manifest."[5]

From the beginning of his career, Everson has po-
sitioned himself against modernism or "the aesthetic hegemony
prevailing across the first half of the century."[6] For mod-
ernism, as an aesthetic movement, had defined itself over
and against romanticism; and, as William Stafford points out,
Everson "is a passionate romantic"[7]: a romantic who rea-
lizes that modern man has been twisting too long in the neo-
classical, Apollonian straitjacket of urbane aesthetics. As
Everson sees it, "Crucified in the alienation of his urbanized
hell, revolted by the dehumanization of his art, [modern man]
cries out for identification and participation. It is in such
a crisis of the spirit that the presence of region arises like
the phoenix to its ancient office."[8] And it is participation
which is the subsistent voice of the Western regional arche-
type. Man of the western United States has had to confront
nature and wrestle with it on its own terms--something about
which Europeans and eastern Americans know very little.
In Archetype West, Everson elaborates on this point:

"The East Coast provinces ... did not begin as
democracies; they began as colonies of European
derivation, and to this day manifest a residual
hierarchial disposition, however diffused by its
American transplantation. But after the estab-
lishment of our independent constitutional democ-
racy the shift westward proceeded without such
underlying suppositions, so that the Westerner
emerges, in this regard at least, a cut above
his East Coast counterpart. Not only so but
this unconscious attitude put him more in line
with the perspectives of the American Indian
and hence closer to the roots of the land."[9]

He also notices that, in the past, the Westerner's participa-
tion with nature has been violent and, to the disdain of East-
ern critics, has extended into the art of the Western region:

"Violence compels, because the Western arch-
type decrees it, but its psychological conse-
quences are denied through the imposition of
aesthetic distance and the cultivation of a mar-
moreal style". [10]

Since Everson was born in Sacramento, and raised in
the San Joaquin valley, he is what Kenneth Rexroth calls an
"autochthon":

"He cultivated and irrigated and tied up vines
and went home in the sunset and ate dinner and
made love and wrote about how he felt doing it
and about the turning of the year, the intimate
rites of passage, and the rites of the season of
a man and a woman." [11]

Well yes, Everson participated in the rituals of his region:
but Rexroth is discussing more than Everson's autochthonous
existence; he is pointing out that which made the San Joaquin
valley the "fixed center" of the "ineradicable patterns" of the
poet's psychic life. Everson describes it beautifully for us
in "Walls," wherein he also alludes to "the eternal presence
of Otherness," which was earlier mentioned:

East, the shut sky: those walls of the mountains
Hold old sunrise and wind under their backs.
If you tread all day vineyard or orchard,
Or move in the weather on the brimming ditch,
Or throw grain, or scythe it down in the early heat,
Taken by flatness, your eye loving the long
    stretch and the good level,
You cannot shake it, the feeling of mountains,
    deep in the haze and over the cities,
The mass, the piled strength and tumultuous
    thunder of the peaks.
They are beyond us forever, in fog or storm
    or the flood of the sun, quiet and sure,
Back of this valley like an ancient dream in
    a man's mind,
 That he cannot forget, nor hardly remember,
But it sleeps at the roots of his sight.

Though this poem is consistent in its tone of reverence, it
lacks the sexual element which, joined with the sacred, makes
up the regional archetype; also, this particular poem's style
can be only narrowly distinguished from the "marmoreal"
style which Everson denigrated earlier. The grace with which

the young poet's primitive roots of identity are described is superb, but the weakness of this poem, with regards to the archetype itself, is that nature's raw power is only alluded to ("the piled strength and tumultuous thunder of the peaks"); the poet stands outside participation, and in this respect the regional archetype has failed to manifest itself in clarity-- because, once again, participation is its subsistent voice. The participation that is needed, even demanded, for the archetype to manifest itself through Everson's poetry derives out of the inner violence and the psychological implosions that the poet experiences while confronting the raw violence of a "faun-mouthed" God. For instance, let us compare another of Everson's early poems, "August," to the previously quoted "Walls"; notice, if you will, the Dionysian celebratory tone and how it is fused with the young poet's sexual awakening:

> Smoke-color; haze thinly over the hills,
>   low hanging;
> But the sky steel, the sky shiny as steel,
>   and the sun shouting.
> The vineyard: in August the green-deep and
>   heat-loving vines
> Without motion grow heavy with grapes.
> And he in the shining, on the turned earth,
>   loose-lying,
> The muscles clean and the limbs golden, turns
>   to the sun the lips and the eyes;
> As the virgin yields, impersonally passionate,
> From the bone core and the aching flesh,
>   the offering.
>
> He has found the power and come to the glory.
> He has turned clean-hearted to the last God,
>   the symbolic sun.
> With earth on his hand, bearing shoulder and
>   arm the light's touch, he has come.
> And having seen, the mind loosens, the nerve
>   lengthens,
> All the haunting abstractions dip free and
>   are gone;
> And the peace is enormous.

Still, even in this poem the emotional/psychological intensity has not yet reached the point of violent implosion--the force that, beyond participation, enables regionalism to transcend and through apotheosis to emerge as the Western regional archetype.

Everson has written that for him "the regional awareness had indeed been one of the indelible memories of childhood"; and he goes on to explain:

"but it became conscious only in my dual awakening, my identity as poet, confirmed in post-adolescence by my encounter with woman. Woman and region fused together in an ineluctable synthesis that constituted what I can only call an entirely new identity, an unprecedented sense of my own self-awareness. Not only did I see myself in human terms as the native of the San Joaquin, but in religious terms I saw myself as the predestined voice of that region. "12

It was at the point of his new self-awareness as "the predestined voice" of his region, that Everson began to internalize the "brute" violence, the emotional and intuitional forces inherent in his region. But before we go any farther in pursuit of the violent aspects of Everson's poetry, we should look at a poem, "Feast Day," wherein the "ineluctable synthesis" of woman and region is described:

Peace was the promise: this house in the vineyard,
Under the height of the great tree
Loosing its leaves on the autumn air.
East lie the mountains;
Level and smooth lie the fields of vines.
Now on this day in the slope of the year,
Over the wine and the sheaf of grain,
We shape our hands to the sign, the symbol,
Aware of the room, the sun in the sky,
The earnest immaculate rhythm of our blood,
As two will face in the running light,
Ritual born of the heavy season,
And see suddenly on all sides of reality,
Vivid again through the crust of indifference,
Waken under the eye.
East lie the mountains,
Around us the level length of the earth;
And this house in the vines,
Our best year,
Golden grain and golden wine,
In autumn, the good year falling south.

Here the erotic and the religious conjoin to complete the "regional mandala" that is the soul's orientation point in reality. This particular poem was written on Thanksgiving Day

in 1939, just after the opening of World War II in Europe.
In the poem the sense of erotic identification and regional
equipoise is manifest, but within three years that same war
was to wrench Everson, his woman, and his region apart;
but, nevertheless, he has remained a regionalist in a broader
sense: he identified with the San Francisco Bay Area in the
late forties and fifties, and has recently put down roots in
Santa Cruz.

Like Jeffers, Everson's own writing style was born
out of the ruggedness and violence of the Western region; an
excellent example of this may be taken from "Trifles":

> The man laughing on the steep hill tripped
>   on a stone,
> Fell among boulders, suffered his life out
>   under the noon sun.
> The young wife, when the tire blew on the
>   Trimmer road,
> Took that long crash screaming into the rocks.
> By sand slipping, by the shoe splitting
>   the narrow street,
> By the parting of atoms,
> By the shaping of all those enormous trifles
>   we plunge to that border,
> Writhing under the long dark in the agony
>   of destruction,
> The great sky and the flaming west riding
>   our eyes,
> Gathering in from the heavy hills, and the
>   tides of the sea. . . .

In this poem, as compared to "Walls," the onslaught of in-
tensity has taken the place of a relatively formal structure
as a consciously practiced artistic value; of course this is
not to say that structure is lacking in the poem, but the dif-
ference here is that the content and/or subject-matter and
natural violence dictate the poem's form--that is, the long,
flowing and seemingly racked-out lines emphasize the savage
sweep of the impersonal ordering of circumstances. The
seemingly unstructured appearance of the poem on the page
is a denial of the uses of restriction; but it is a positive ef-
fort to subsume the contour of structure that underlies a
given phenomenon: after all, the regional archetype is of
necessity rooted in space and time in the phenomenal world.

In _Archetype West_, Everson quotes Josephine Miles
who, in her book _Eras and Modes in English Poetry_, express-

es how, of the three universal styles of poetry (the low or colloquial, the middle or observational and meditational, and the high or ceremonial), it is the high style that has been most unfashionable in modern times:

> "The high style has been ignored, or at best,
> since Pope's Peri Bathous, has had an unfa-
> vorable press. Yet if we think of the high style
> also as deep, not only as empyrean but as sub-
> terranean and submarine, we may recognize its
> serious function for the present day. To clear
> and polished surfaces it adds depth, however
> murky; to the objectivities of thought, action,
> and the thing in itself, it adds the subjectivity of
> inward feeling tumultuously expressed. Like the
> word altus in Latin, which means both high and
> deep, it relates the gods of the solar system to
> the gods of the solar plexus."[13]

And Everson then asks, what "idiom could more truly express the native pantheism than one which 'relates the gods of the solar system to the gods of the solar plexus?...'" Then he goes on to quote Miss Miles' definition of this "high style" in American poetry:

> "The American poetry of praise has a long, free
> cadenced line, full of silences, symbols, and im-
> plications. It has a cumulative structure, build-
> ing up to a height of force and feeling, whether
> by imprecation or rhapsody. It has a phraseology
> of resounding sound and of warm responsive sense,
> suggestive of height and depths beyond the reach
> of form or reason. At its worst it can be dan-
> gerously loose, semi-conscious, and irresponsi-
> ble; at its best it can be powerfully aware of
> moving forces and meanings...."[14]

"The American," wrote the late Perry Miller, "or at least the American artist, cherishes in his inmost being the impulse to reject completely the gospel of civilization, in order to guard with resolution the savagery of his heart."[15] This savagery of the heart is what Miles suggests will be better expressed by the "high" and "deep" style of poetry; again, this style adds depth to polished surfaces, and it adds the "tumultuously expressed" inward feeling to "the objectivi-ties of thought, action, and the thing in itself." So in one of Everson's most important transitional, pre-Catholic, and regional poems, "The Springing of the Blade," we witness an enactment of Miles' formula of the high style; notice in this passage the "cumulative structure"--intensified by alliterative, consonantal and assonantal patterns:

> And the earth bears. Back of the house
> The blackberry riots the fence, swarms the tree,
> Hiding the fruited runner under the thorn.
> The apple, loosened, launches the long way downward,
> Marked in its passage by the leaf's whicker.
> All through the hovering deadness of the night
> They give, go down. We heard the pears
> So fall in the Valley. In the Hood River country
> Where the thick Columbia thrusts its flattened
>   weight to the sea,
> We heard that sound. And in the orchards of Sonoma,
> All night, the round fruit spun out its brief duration,
> Limb to loam. And heard now, once more, like a
>   pure pronouncement
> Out of the past; in the mind seized, fixed in its fall,
> Made absolute in the dark descent; as the round
>   earth itself,
> In any instant of its wide reel, may be so caught,
> And all its godly creatures struck in their
>   perilous stance--
> So the apple, falling. Come morning find them
>   cold, dew-glistened,
> Spiked with straw, the mute wind fallen members.

Here nature's violence turns the poet's passion into exaltation; and, as Everson has written, "the glorification of nature that pantheism encourages is but a step to the glorification of the masses, who are the most elemental class and hence closest to nature."[16] And in the stanza directly following the passage cited above, from "The Springing of the Blade," we witness the Western regional archetype manifested in extreme clarity:

> There will be harvest. For the look of love;
> For the hope cried out of the great love held,
> Cried out for the child to fill, fulfill, bless
>   the body's being.
> For the light that lies on the full of the arm,
>   the roundness,
> A slowness gathering under the knees,
> The easeful tread of a woman, walking, waiting
>   for bearance.
> These make their prophecy. I make my prayer
> That the shut-back seed may be restored, and

the restoration
Blaze with the spring, brood with the summer,
Break forth with the fulgent fall,
Fill the last lack of life, the hymn be heard.

This is the glorification of the masses, conjoined with the glorification of region; the charismatic aspect, or magic, of the region is charged with its mixture of the ecstasy of the flesh and the rapture of the spirit: the poem itself becomes what Everson has called the "crucible of apotheosis," from which the Western regional archetype emerges as the authentification of life. Furthermore, as Everson has pointed out, in true apotheosis "a sense of discovery as well as consummation suffuses the texture of utterance, transmuting the formative thesis into electric consequentiality. "[17]

So, as Eliade has written, "the manifestation of the sacred ontologically founds the world." The sacred, however, teems with an inexorable and unexplainable violent force which must be infused into the art of the Western artist, if the Western regional archetype is to be manifested out of art. Everson reduces nature's raw violence by subjectivizing it, centroverting its cruciality through travail (this becomes predominant in his later Catholic poetry); and the psychological implosions caused by the subjectivization of this raw violence are expressed best when the expressions epitomize not only the unmanaged impulses of the poet's heart but also the "savagery" of the people's heart: only then does art lay bare the spine of an ancient and an indescribable affinity between man and nature, which is the soul's rescue. Everson addresses himself to the use of violence in art:

"Conventional morality decries the presence of violence in art because it is unable to grasp it in its quality of contemplative fitness. It is seen solely as a stimulus to action. The artist, however, knows that firmly situated in the domain of the aesthetic, violence elevates fragmentation from chaos into transcendence, subsumes the rupture of material forms into a superior wholeness. "[18]

Often Everson not only infuses violence into his poems but also shock, in order to shake the reader out of his complacency and to make him sense or see, if only for a moment, that he too is part of the "superior wholeness." In "San Joaquin," Everson says of "city-folk" that "who would touch them must stun them;/ The nerve that is dying needs thunder to rouse it. " We would be mistaken if we felt com-

fort that he addresses these lines to "city-folk," because he
is speaking to anyone who has willingly accepted alienation
from his native source, the land. "The Outlaw" is an excel-
lent example of how Everson can shock his readers into an
unexpected awareness of their own "faun-mouthed" gods:

> I call to mind that violent man who waded the north.
> He imagined a slight,
> Killed for it;
> Made outlaw, lay in the echoing waste;
> Fled to far cities;
> Knew dangerous about him the subtle strands of
>   communication
> Ticking his doom.
> Cornered at last he knelt in the night
> And drew like magnet the metal loosed in the
>   acrid air.
>
> And so went down.
> Nor ever knew that what brought him such bounty
> Was only the wearing out of a way--
> He and the wolves and the dazed tribes
> Numb in their dissolution.
> Blind in their past,
> The past betrayed them;
> The trees of tradition screened from their sight
> The enormous forest of the waiting world--
> As we, we also, bound in our patterns,
> Sense but see not the vestigial usages grooving
>   our lives.
> Like some latter-day outlaw we crouch in our rooms,
> Facing the door and the massed future,
> And draw doom down on our heads.

The excruciating tension between the civilized head and the
primitive heart is not Everson's alone. It is the American
heritage.

We have seen how the poet's sense of centeredness
stemmed from his region, and how, with his sexual awaken-
ing, the sexual and the sacred joined together to generate the
magic of the regional archetype. Just as the poet reaches
out from his regional reality to discover the world, so the
regional archetype reaches out of the poet's art to embrace
humanity. The thrill of discovery ran through the bones of
Americans with the trek into the Western frontier; and when
a lone traveler turned and cried back to his hesitant follow-
ers, "It is here and it is ours!," Americans from the West

to the East reveled in the accomplishment: this same spirit is embodied in the Western regional archetype--indeed, it emanates from it. So, Everson sets out, or rather in, to discover his own heritage; rather than the poet's discovering the Western archetype, it discovers him and takes its ambience from his regional identity: "Only as I have encountered the past/ Can I measure the margins of what I am." The Western regional archetype is manifested through the poem, and it speaks out from the heart-felt depths of Everson's soul.

> Suddenly the dark descends,
> As on the tule ponds at home the wintering
>   blackbirds,
> Flock upon flock, the thousand-membered,
> In for the night from the outlying ploughlands,
> Sweep over the willows,
> Whirled like a net on the shadowy reeds,
> All wings open.
> It is late.   And any boy who lingers on to watch
>   them come in
> Will go hungry to bed.
> But the leaf-sunken years,
> And the casual dusk, over the roofs in a
>   clear October,
> Will verify the nameless impulse that kept him out
> When the roosting birds and the ringing dark
> Dropped down together.

Finally, the taproot of instinct is not only formed by and nurtured on the given regional mandala, it is that essence and strength become wisdom which has once again, eight years since he left the Catholic order, brought William Everson home and verified the nameless impulse by which he has always been driven--to dig down to and then bring forth into light the clutched-for and grasped dark matter of instinct that becomes spirit: unlike any roosting bird, it is cawing, cawing above the farthest fences of the world.

Notes

1   William Everson, "The Regional Incentive," San Jose State Studies II:3 (November 1976), p1.

2   Paul Shepard, Man in the Landscape (New York, 1967), p33.

3 Mircea Eliade, The Sacred and the Profane: The Nature of Religion (New York, 1950), p20.

4 Everson, "Regional Incentive," p7.

5 Ibid.

6 Ibid. , p1.

7 William Stafford, The Achievement of Brother Antoninus (Glenview, Ill. : Scott, Foresman, 1967), p5.

8 Everson, "Regional Incentive," p5.

9 Everson, Archetype West (Berkeley, Calif. : Oyez, 1976), p8.

10 Ibid. , p18.

11 Kenneth Rexroth, "Introduction" to William Everson, The Residual Years (New York: New Directions, 1968), p xvi.

12 Everson, "Regional Incentive," pp7-8.

13 Josephine Miles, Eras and Modes in English Poetry, 2nd ed. , (Berkeley: University of California Press, 1964), p224.

14 Ibid. , p225.

15 Perry Miller, Errand into the Wilderness (Cambridge, Mass. : Belknap Press of Harvard University Press, 1956), p261.

16 Everson, Archetype West, p47.

17 Ibid. , p85.

18 Ibid. , p13.

THE ROOTS OF RECOVERY: TEN MEDITATIONS

Bill Hotchkiss. 1978

Just as Everson's emergence after the difficult Depression
and war period was crowned by The Residual Years at the
close of the forties, so was his emergence as Brother An-
toninus crowned by The Rose of Solitude at the close of the
sixties.   But once again his abrupt change of direction indi-
cates that his ordeal of emergence must be undergone anew.
That he has, however, sources sustaining him in this ordeal,
is indicated by Bill Hotchkiss in his overview of Everson's
achievement.   From William Hotchkiss and David Carpenter,
William Everson: Poet from the San Joaquin (Blue Oak Press,
1978).

> The dignity of pain, the violence
> of fire and flood, the serpent,
> the vulture and the coyote, the
> dry earth, the awaited rains, the
> violence at the heart of the arche-
> type, the procreative force also
> at the heart of the archetype,
> the strange, terrible, unbelievably
> beautiful, half-heard music of
> Pan, the great god of all weath-
> ers--to worship the earth and
> the force which creates and end-
> lessly alters the earth is to wor-
> ship all aspects of the manifesta-
> tion and the promise.

FIRST MEDITATION:

A cool evening at the end of the drought year summer,

and thin streams of high mist are running over the Santa
Cruz Mountains. The long heat seems to have broken, and
there's a promise of rain within the week--something about
the texture of the night, the taste of the air, the slow breath-
ing of the firs and redwoods and alders and bays. Big Creek
is low, perhaps the lowest it has ever been; but from where
we sit, the sound of water running among granite rocks is
quite distinct.

We are gathered about an open fire, its flames licking
up at the darkness and diffusing a pleasant warmth. The two
huge, twisted redwoods reach over us, creating an atmosphere
of closeness, an island in time. As we finish eating, the
two dogs, one black and one white, engage in a sudden dis-
pute over a scrap of meat. They lunge at each other and
fall sideways into the fire. We pull them out quickly, swat
at the fringes of burning hair, and the crisis is over. They
are not hurt--may even have learned a lesson.

Those present: Allan Campo, David Carpenter, Lynn
Gooding, Stan Hager, Debbie Gates, Mark Maynard, my wife
Judith Shears, our daughters Anne and Jennifer, myself, and
Susanna and Bill Everson and their son Jude. The place is
the poet's home, Kingfisher Flat on Big Creek, a meadow by
the stream, and three buildings constructed years back as a
fire station. One is a storage shed. One is the poet's print-
shop and study. The other is the house, its lighted windows
visible under the curtain of redwood branches.

We have been speaking of the California terrain, the
coast, the valley, the Sierra, the effects of the drought, the
burning earlier this summer of the Ventana Wilderness, an
area that was sacred to Robinson Jeffers, and of those who
first came over the mountains a century and a quarter ago--
Jed Smith, Kit Carson, Caleb Greenwood, Joseph Walker,
Jim Beckwourth, the Donners. Bill Everson sits back away
from the fire, in the half shadows, perfectly blended with
the setting. His handsome, bearded face is touched at by
the firelight. We drink wine. We are waiting for Everson
to read his new poems, poems of the drought, its effect on
the land and the wild things, its effect on the humans who
await the hoped-for rains of autumn.

It is September 10, 1977. On this day the poet is
sixty-five years old. He reaches over for the manuscript,
opens to the beginning, leans forward, and begins to read.
Somewhere up the canyon an owl calls and then is silent. We,
too, lean forward.

SECOND MEDITATION:

Among the critics, no doubt, there are those who reg-
istered both shock and dismay on the night of December 7,
1969--or whenever the word got to them--for on that night
Brother Antoninus, at the conclusion of a reading at the cam-
pus of the University of California, Davis, pulled off his
Dominican robes and reassumed his identity as William Ever-
son. Ultimately he would marry a young woman named Su-
sanna Rickson, with whom he had fallen in love. The Do-
minicans had lost their premiere poet, but the separation
had been in the making for some while. Such volumes of
the Catholic period (no doubt a misnomer, for Everson re-
mains Catholic) as The Crooked Lines of God, The Hazards
of Holiness, and The Rose of Solitude, in the afterlight of
the breakaway, reveal at work the very forces which pre-
cipitated that rupture.

The culprits, I submit, were Eros and Pan, two en-
tities which subsume themselves into the figure of Dionysus--
the force of love regenerate through the earth itself, the Life
Force, mysterious, terrible, beautiful. These lines from
"The Tendril in the Mesh":

> Oh splendor of storm and breathing! O woman!
>   O voice of desire!
> Tall power of terminal heights where the
>   rain-whitened peaks glisten wet!

In the conjunction of Eros and Pan, the figure of
Dionysus is re-emergent. Restrained Eros breaks loose.
The logic of Pentheus is no match for the ebullient life force
of the wild domains of Dionysus. Mythologies fuse, and the
elemental nature of man asserts itself:

> Kore! Daughter of dawn! Persephone! Maiden
>   of twilight!
> Sucked down into Pluto's unsearchable night for
>   your husband.
> I see you depart, bearing the pomegranate seed
>   in your groin.
> In the node of your flesh you drip my flake
>   of bestowal.

And the poem concludes in an epilogue in which the
Christ figure is equated with Eros:

> Dark God of Eros, Christ of the buried blood,

Stone-channeled beast of ecstasy and fire,
. . .
Call to me Christ, sound in my twittering blood. . . .

The recent publication of Everson's River-Root--a
poem written in 1957 but not issued during the poet's Cath-
olic period, no doubt because of the work's graphically ex-
plicit sexual content in a context seemingly unrelated to any
kind of church doctrine (though the lovers are properly mar-
ried in the church so that they can "raise the kids Catholic")
--may now be seen to have signalled a return to the temporal
human realm, even as it denotes intensely the call of both
Eros and Pan. The central metaphor is that of the big river,
the continent-drainer, the Missouri-Mississippi--its source,
its extent, its flow, its resolution, its process and its time-
lessness:

River-root: as even under high drifts, those fierce
        and wind-grappled cuts of the Rockies,
One listening will hear, far down below, the softest
        seepage, a new melt, a faint draining,
And know for certain that this is the tip, this,
        though the leastest trace,
Is indeed the uttermost inch of the River.
. . .
And now over all the rock-walls the River sweeps,
        he stoops and plunges.
He has found his scope and is on his way.
Let slopes drop slides, let ponderosas topple
        athwart him--
Log jams of winter, storm-sundered roots and the
        breakage of forests
Clog up canyons--for him these are nothing.
. . .
Out of the fields and forests, out of the cornland
        and cottonland,
Out of the gut, the taut belly and smouldering
        lava-filled loins of the continent,
The male god draws, serpentine giant, phallic
        thrust and vengeance,
The sex-enduring, life-bestowing, father of
        waters: the River.

River-Root is an astounding poem, a great poem, a
celebration of Pan-Eros such as has never before been at-
tempted in the poetry of the English language. Its theme,
that of spiritual purification by means of intense sexual ex-
perience (indeed, the lovers are transformed into something

beyond themselves, into titanic inscapes of the sexual and procreative energies of the earth itself), is dealt with, significantly, in terms of the land, the vastness of the American continent and of the unifying force of its greatest river system:

> For the strong long River
> Leaps to the Gulf, earth-lover, broacher, dredger
> of female silt and engorger, sperm-thruster.

River-Root is a major work, too long, too complex, too rich and varied in its levels of awareness for me to do justice to it here. But it is a crucial, a central work--and it was written in 1957. It represents the quintessential expression of those energies which drove the poet through the years of his early work, the panoply of voices from which the poet turned when he moved within the hegemony of the Catholic Church--voices, however, which would not be stilled and which, latent for eight years, burst forth in the magnificent flood of River-Root.

Yet William Everson would remain Brother Antoninus for another twelve years.

In the light of River-Root, the question would seem not to be, "Why did Antoninus leave the Dominicans?" but rather, "Why did Everson join them?" For the earth-continuity of Everson's poetry is not actually broken at all by the Catholic interlude, even though theological themes dominate his work during this period; and, indeed, through these years the Church possessed one who is her most significant poet in this century. Even in dealing with the most holy of themes, however, it is evident to me that Everson/Antoninus is about the business of re-structuring Catholic thinking, underscoring the significance of Eros and Pan and producing thereby something of a Dionysian interpretation of the Christian mysteries and restoring the earth-closeness and vitality which seem to have characterized early Christianity--so that the norms of dogma are ruptured, the cosmic egg is cracked, and Divinity shines from the burst wholeness:

> You will go forth, Magdalene, into the dust-
>   driven world,
> Bearing everywhere about you
> The stamp of a consummate chasteness....

This same poem, "A Savagery of Love," draws focus on the cross itself, the cross of death and life, as creating during those few hours a tangible link between earth and heaven, a phallic cross that produces a terrible and vital conjunction between the energies of earth and air, of body and spirit:

Your rebeginning,
Of what had been begun on the day of the Death,
The day the eagles paired over Juda,
And the Cross tore a hole in the sky.

Even here, in dealing with the most holy of themes, the imagery of the terrain of Western America, the great thunderheads above the Sierra Nevada, east of Everson's native San Joaquin (the mountains a disturbing ever-presence in the early poems) most surely makes its presence felt:

And beautiful as the mate-flight of eagles,
When from their wind-shuttled eyrie
They then cast forth;
And on wakening wings
Take sky;
And over the thrusted
Welter and maze of wide sierra
Climb the pouring up-shaft of air;
And high where the thunderheads mushroom and coil
Turn to; and in the gyre and sweep
That is a tremendous strength of wings,
Clutch claw to claw and the beaks clash....

"A Savagery of Love" was written in 1952, about a year after Everson's entry into the Dominican Order. During the following year, the poet was at work on "A Canticle to the Christ in the Holy Eucharist." The poems were not coming easily, and Everson/Antoninus turned again to the earth and to the life forces of the earth as a source of inspiration--as though there were some inherent magic in the mere presence and awareness of the California landscape, a feral and rejuvenating force sufficient to draw forth once more the long lines of celebration, to urge into voice one who had "the many days and the many nights ... lay as one barren...." The poem is, in effect, a pilgrimage to the springs of Divinity, and that Divinity is both manifest and attainable from and of the earth itself. The poet is likened to a barren doe that finds its mate on Tamalpais:

In my heart you were might. And thy word was the
  running of rain
That rinses October. And the sweetwater spring in

the rock.   And the brook in the crevice.
Thy word in my heart was the start of the buck that
    is sourced in the doe.
Thy word was the milk that will be in her dugs, the
    stir of new life in them.
You gazed.   I stood barren for days, lay fallow
    for nights.
Thy look was the movement of life, the milk in the
    young breasts of mothers.

The music we hear is that of the syrinx of Pan; and
what is perceived is the arcane, animal enactment of the
sexual and procreative mystery.   The anima of the poet is
impregnated by the animus force of the buck, the wild in-
scape of the Divine, of the Christ that more nearly resembles
the Dionysus force, pulsing through nature, perpetually re-
generating itself.   But the time of the year is October and
the Green God, its force momentarily expended through the
masculine image of the buck, will draw back once more into
the earth, to await the resurrection of spring.   The doe--
and by analog the poet--will contain and nurture the seed:

Thou art gone.   I will keep thy wound till you
    show.   I will wait in the laurel.
I know as the knowledge is of the doe where she
    lies on Tamalpais.
In the deep madrone.   In the oak.   In the tall
    grove of the redwoods.
Where she lies in laurel and proves the wound
    on the slope of Mt. Tamalpais.

In the underworld, the laurel is sacred to Dionysus,
even as it is sacred to Apollo in the world above.   Christ,
then, is revealed as the seethe and the fuse of things, the
life force, the mysterious solicitude and unquenchable urge
toward living substance, its potential contained within the
grains of the soil.

THIRD MEDITATION:

One of the best-known of the poems of Everson/An-
toninus is the extremely beautiful and moving "A Canticle to
the Waterbirds," a composition of seventy-four lines of free
verse, a poem which the poet most commonly presents as
the introductory work in his readings.   The "Canticle" was
written in 1950, well after his conversion to Catholicism but
before his entry into the Dominican Order.   The poet was at

that time working at the Catholic Worker House of Hospitality which had recently been opened in Oakland, California; the first draft of the "Canticle" is dated August 5.

As the poet notes in "Writing the Waterbirds," his preface to the Eizo edition of 1968, "It was not ... composed for the Feast of St. Francis, as the by-line under the title reads in the Poem's original appearance. ... No celebration of a saint, therefore, gave the poem birth, but something of deeper travail. It was an impulse only the birds could release." And the poet continues:

"In many ways I do not understand it. The paucity of the early drafts indicates the thing had pretty well worked itself out in the unconscious before pencil ever touched paper, and, contrary to prevailing opinion, when this happens it is a sign that you are in the presence not of already known but of a living mystery. The poem, granted, is perfectly comprehensible; what is difficult to grasp is how it works. A simple meditation of the mutual relation between birds and God and man, it develops, extends itself, finds its point of culmination, and closes."

"A Canticle to the Waterbirds" moves forward with a vast tameless energy; it sings like the sea itself and the cries of the birds of the coast. Its locus is California, whence it reaches out, both north and south, to encompass, draw together--the violence, the inexorable certainty of the life process, the equally inexorable and (from a human point of view) utterly careless process of death, the delicacy and magic of the coastal birds and the birds of the valleys inland, sheer spirals of flight drenched in sunlight and fog, the bays and river mouths and headlands of the long Pacific shore. All of this, an immense, moving, living, dying image, is presented as a proof of the existence of the Divinity. No--the Divinity needs no proof; and in the voices of the birds, we hear a song which gives "a praise up to the Lord."

The poem is not easily comprehensible at all, and it produces a magically troubled effect upon the minds of many of those who hear it or read it for the first time. The beauty of nature is replete with violence and death, and violence and death, therefore, are to be both reverenced and honored, even as the joyous, explosive force of life is to be both reverenced and honored.

Clack your beaks you cormorants and kittiwakes,
North on those rock-croppings finger-jutted into
    the rough Pacific surge;
You migratory terns and pipers who leave but the
    temporal clawtrack written on sandbars
    there of your presence;
Grebes and pelicans; you comber-picking scoters
    and you shorelong gulls;
All you keepers of the coastline north of here to
    the Mendocino beaches....

    This is not traditional Catholic thought; and, were it
not written by one who is specifically identified as a Catholic
poet, would not be supposed to be Catholic at all. It is not
merely that the poem celebrates the creation in a non-human
way, but that it draws focus on the overall process of life-
death alternations in such a way as is utterly beyond the hu-
man orientation of the Hebraic-Christian tradition. At the
same time, the poem is an impassioned attempt to extend that
Hebraic-Christian tradition so as to include the whole of the
animal kingdom within the hegemony of a God whose way is
violence and who is neither benign nor malign--who simply
is, incomprehensibly.

    The birds are unconscious worshippers of the great
being. They accept, for they cannot do otherwise, and they
live out their lives within a closed system of the alternations
of what might be called providence and dissolution:

But mostly it is your way you bear existence wholly
    within the context of His utter will and
    are untroubled.
Day upon day you do not reckon, nor scrutinize
    tomorrow, nor multiply the nightfalls with
    a rash concern....

    What the birds do not do, the human creatures do:
"scrutinize tomorrow" and "multiply the nightfalls with a rash
concern...." The birds are "of another order of being, and
wholly it compels."

    Everson, as is well known to all students of his work,
was--and is--a disciple of Robinson Jeffers. Jeffers' Inhu-
manist vision--a vision which denies man his assumed cen-
trality in the great scheme of things and, indeed, which often
views mankind as the disrupter and corrupter of that scheme
of things--is founded solidly on the ancient doctrine of Pan-
theism, with the Divinity revealed to mankind through the

beauty of creation, the "trans-human magnificence." Everson, on the other hand, has sought a more personal Divinity, a Divinity toward whom mankind may turn for succor. "A Canticle to the Waterbirds" is a calling out to that human-concerned Divinity--but, significantly, the calling is uttered through the cries of the birds. If it is in one place, it must certainly also be in the other. Or the "other" is of a different order of being; and the birds, therefore, must have been given "the imponderable grace to be His verification,/ Outside the mulled incertitude of our forensic choices...."

FOURTH MEDITATION:

"A Canticle to the Waterbirds" draws the poet's thinking to a point of possible resolution--"balance or reconciliation of opposite or discordant qualities," to use Coleridge's phrase. Life and death together are to be reverenced and honored, for each alike is under the direct influence of the great will of a benignant and concerned, multilaterally personal God, known to be personal through agency of the Vice-Gerent, Christ. Everson's earlier pantheism is simply to be subsumed within the greater circle of God the Father, but at the same time it is to remain intact. Two truths cannot contradict each other; if they are truths, they will invariably be found to be compatible--even synonymous.

A passage from the preface to the 1948 edition of The Residual Years may serve us here:

"The development, if it is related to mankind, may be seen in the gradual realization of man as a conscious being, who learns to perceive a sequence in the episodic welter of his past, drawing as it lengthens a continuity at once purposive and obscure, the disparity between expectation and fulfillment forever yielding the impact of joy and anguish which, for me, establishes so profoundly the meaning of life as revelation.
"In that sense, then, the work of a life is a chronology, drawn from event to event. The years reveal, reveal and recede into the dark residuum that is the totality of our experience, that keeps and preserves the forward-flowing line of growth, the progression of our lives."

A year later Everson was converted to Catholicism.

One may reasonably ask, then, what was he converted from?
What was he leaving behind? We have Everson's own an-
swers, in the form of his still-unpublished spiritual auto-
biography, Prodigious Thrust. I have studied this volume
both carefully and with great interest: it reveals a hugely
complex psyche and a profound intelligence at war with itself,
in crisis, in despair, in exultation, in agony, endlessly re-
searching its motives, goals, desires. As a critic, however,
I see the pages from the outside--since I have not been
obliged to live it, feel it, be it.

   The analyst would go back into the early family situa-
tion to determine the child's relation to mother and father,
to siblings, to the forming of life habits, to traumas, to ad-
justments to peers and to the opposite sex. Such, however,
is beyond both my own capacity and the scope of this paper.

   What I do see is the image of a young man, married
happily, tending a vineyard in the San Joaquin Valley, a young
man who is already an immensely accomplished poet, one
who has been profoundly influenced (in the positive sense) by
the figures of Robinson Jeffers (the Pan-force) and by D. H.
Lawrence (the Eros-force). I see this image from "Feast
Day":

       East lie the mountains,
       Around us the level length of the earth;
       And this house in the vines,
       Our best year,
       Golden grain and golden wine,
       In autumn, the good year falling south.

Or these lines, from "Walls":

       The mass, the piled strength and tumultuous
          thunder of the peaks.
       They are beyond us forever, in fog or storm or
          the flood of the sun,
       Back of this valley like an ancient dream in
          a man's mind,
       That he cannot forget, nor hardly remember,
       But it sleeps at the roots of his sight.

Or this, from "San Joaquin":

       This valley after the storms can be beautiful
          beyond the telling,

Though our city-folk scorn it, cursing heat in the
    summer and drabness in winter,
And flee it--Yosemite and the sea.
They seek splendor, who would touch them must
    stun them;
The nerve that is dying needs thunder to rouse it.

But events beyond California, and beyond America,
make their presence felt, intrude, as the world drifts toward
the bloodbath and the horror of World War Two. In "The
Illusion" the poet cautions himself:

Think of the torn mouths begging release down the
    groove of the years;
Sit in your peace, drinking your ease in a quiet room,
Soft in your dreams--and the men falling.

Then it is autumn, 1940, and a moment of decision
has come. Everson realizes that he cannot participate in
the coming war, as he tells us in "The Vow":

I, the living heir of the bloodiest men of all Europe;
And the knowledge of past tears through my flesh;
I flinch in the guilt of what I am,
Seeing the poised heap of this time
Break like a wave.

And I vow not to wantonly ever take life....

This decision leads to a labor camp for conscientious
objectors, to Waldport, Oregon. A severance is made with
the res publicas, America, with the San Joaquin, his personal
territory and the source of his poetry, the realm of the Pan-
force, where, as he says in "The Rain on That Morning,"

The rain on that morning came like a woman with love,
And touched us gently, and the earth gently, and closed
    down delicately in the morning,
So that all around were the subtle and intricate touchings.
The earth took them, the vines and the winter weeds....

Further, as a result of the forced separation, Ever-
son's wife drifted away from him--a severance from Eros,
a severance from the archetype of the feminine. The time
of tending the vines of Dionysus was over. Significantly, at
the war's conclusion and the release of the conscientious ob-
jectors, Everson did not return to his native San Joaquin,
the area for which he had come long since to think of him-

self as the "appointed voice." He went instead to San Francisco and the Bay Area, resumed his life, and fell in love with a young woman who was immensely talented, divorced, Catholic, and neurotically guilt-ridden.

The solution seemed to lie in a withdrawal to the inward life, to the life of the psyche and the soul, to the one principle that was constant: and the woman had taken him to the Church. He embraced it, and then set about to change its thinking. And the result may well have been the most significant body of Christian poetry written in this century.

FIFTH MEDITATION:

If both Pan and Eros had been denied, however, in the conscious turning away from the home territory and from the allegiance to (or dependency upon) the feminine, nevertheless the Dionysian conjunction of these two forces continued to exert a central power over the poet's mind. Everson/Antoninus sympathized deeply with the energies which lay at the roots of the Beat Movement, the San Francisco Renaissance, with which he has ever since been associated.

In "Writing the Waterbirds," cited earlier, the poet himself remarks that the poem "is indeed in the Beat fashion --may even be the archetypal Beat poem, since it preceded Ginsberg's Howl by five years, but it is probably not violational enough to claim that honor." And, indeed, it was precisely for the Dionysian energies which Everson/Antoninus perceived behind the smoke-screen and city-centered furor of the Beat Movement that caused him to sympathize and identify with the purposes of that movement. Dionysus had come to the city, and within a very short time the Theban converts would be moving out into what remains of rural California to take up their alternative lifestyles and otherwise to pay homage to the god. The energies would shift to the Mendocino and Humboldt coasts, to the San Juan Ridge and other areas of the Gold Country, to Bolinas and Big Sur, to small, out-of-the-way towns all over Western America.

In 1957 the poet would write River-Root, a work that would go unpublished until 1976, then to be presented as a Bicentennial offering:

"In preparing this manuscript for publication, its specifically American character became more keenly impressed upon me than I had earlier felt it.

And I realized that in issuing it during this 200th anniversary of our founding I am, in effect, offering it as a poet's gift to the Nation; and so dedicate it, as Whitman might have, to the Bicentennial of these States."

With the revision and consequent publication of River-Root, a poetic drought which had plagued Everson in the period following his breakaway from the Dominicans was ended. The repressed Eros-force had earlier exploded (had never actually stopped exploding), and the poet had found himself passionately in love with Susanna Rickson, and he had left the solitude of the monastery to enter once more into the temporal life, so that William Everson, the man, had re-emerged after a self-imposed exile of twenty years. The lovers married and moved ultimately to Kingfisher Flat, in the mountains north of Santa Cruz, and Everson became poet in residence at Kresge College at the University of California, Santa Cruz.

But with the publication of River-Root, the poet made his separate peace with America as well, and the Pan-force could emerge fully in a series of poems of astounding intensity and power and characterized by a ripened philosophic calm and acceptance, even in dealing with the most volatile subjects. These poems, of which I will attempt a critical overview, are conceived of as central to a volume to be entitled The Integral Years, the third volume of the poet's life trilogy, along with The Residual Years and the soon-to-be-published The Veritable Years.

First, however, we must return to 1958, the year following the composition of River-Root, for the poet was at work on a masterpiece which was to become one of the best-known of his works--"In All These Acts," a poem whose title is given a subscript from The Gospel According to Thomas: "Cleave the wood and thou shalt find Me,/ lift the rock and I am there!"

In dealing with "In All These Acts," it is well not to overlook the fragment from Thomas. "Cleave the wood and thou shalt find Me...." One thinks of Thoreau, reaching down into the shallow stream to lay hold of God--the seminally generative force behind the surface of things, ever-present, ever alive. For the transcendental pantheist, it is not the surface of things which is God, but what creates that surface, what lies behind and within it. This line from Jeffers: "This is the infinite energy, the power of God, forever working--

toward what purpose?" And these:

> I have heard the summer dust crying to be born
> As much as ever flesh cried to be quiet.

The God is ever-present and creates the "trans-human magnificence," but how is one to deal with the violence at its core? This is the identical problem that Everson/Antoninus dealt with in "A Canticle to the Waterbirds," but now he approaches the problematic issue directly, explicitly, though once more in a non-human context. An elk is broken under falling trees torn over by a sudden, violent surge of wind:

> But the great elk, caught midway between two
>   scissoring logs,
> Arched belly-up and died, the snapped spine
> Half torn out of his peeled back, his hind legs
> Jerking that gasped convulsion, the kick of
>   spasmed life,
> Paunch plowed open, purple entrails
> Disgorged from the basketwork ribs
> Erupting out, splashed sideways, wrapping him,
> Gouted in blood, flecked with the brittle sliver
>   of bone.
> Frenzied, the terrible head
> Thrashed off its antlered fuzz in that rubble
> And then fell still, the great tongue
> That had bugled in rut, calling the cow-elk up
>   from the glades,
> Thrust agonized out, the maimed member
> Bloodily stiff in the stone-smashed teeth ...

The avalance goes down into the river canyon, the river surges to the sea, "Destroying itself in the mother sea," but already the salmon are there to begin their upstream pilgrimage to reproduction and death. "Too few the grave witnesses," the poet says; but nevertheless,

> In all these acts
> Christ crouches and seethes, pitched forward
> On the crucifying stroke, juvescent, that will
>   spring Him
> Out of the germ, out of the belly of the dying buck,
> Out of the father-phallus and the torn-up root.

The incredible and seemingly purposeless violence that is somehow a oneness with generation is faced, brutally, directly, and "In all these acts/ Christ crouches and seethes...."

The apocryphal Gospel has insisted: "lift the rock and I am there!" In Jeffers' "The Bloody Sire," the second stanza runs:

What but the wolf's tooth whittled so fine
The fleet limbs of the antelope?
What but fear winged the birds, and hunger
Jeweled with such eyes the great goshawk's head?
Violence has been the sire of all the world's values.

Again and again, throughout his work both "profane and sacred," Everson/Antoninus has confronted this force, approaching it now from one angle, now from another. It is, somehow, precisely this with which he must make his peace. The recognition of violence in his own nature, deep in his own inherited genes, drew him to "The Vow" and the consequent disruption and dislocation of his life. He had earlier faced it in "Circumstance," a poem published in the San Joaquin volume of 1939:

He is a god who smiles blindly,
And hears nothing, and squats faun-mouthed on
the wheeling world,
Touching right and left with infinite lightning-like
gestures.
. . .
He is the god to pray to; he sits with his faun's mouth
and touches the world with hovering hands.
He is the god--but he sees not, nor hears.

This is the same force that is now interpreted, in 1958, as the "Christ [that] crouches and seethes, pitched forward/ On the crucifying stroke, juvescent...." In "A Canticle to the Waterbirds," this Great God Pan would take on the guise of Yaveh-Haya and would receive the praise of the "Wave-haunters, shore-keepers, rockhead-holders, all cape-top vigilantes," who are implored to:

Send up the strict articulation of your throats,
And say His name.

SIXTH MEDITATION:

January 20th, 1962, marked the death of Robinson Jeffers--a death that was to have a profound influence upon Everson/Antoninus. The year following saw the beginning of critical work on Jeffers that was to culminate in the 1968 publication of Everson's full-length scholarly study, Robinson Jeffers: Fragments of an Older Fury (Oyez), one of the very finest works ever devoted to the great California poet--as well as to later introductions to reissues of Jeffers' Cawdor/ Medea, Californians, and The Double Axe, as well as to compilations of previously unpublished work by Jeffers, The Alpine Christ and Brides of the South Wind, complete with critical commentaries, and to the publication (at Lime Kiln Press, University of California, Santa Cruz) of a collection of Jeffers' poems which Everson entitled Granite & Cypress, a hand-printed masterwork.

And that year saw as well the first appearance of the 176-line classic elegy, "The Poet Is Dead," a memorial piece in tribute to Jeffers, "to be read with a full stop between the strophes, as in a dirge."

Everson once publicly noted that "Robinson Jeffers was my father," and then went on to explain his meaning, for he is the disciple who never actually met his master, respecting the elder poet's privacy too much to intrude. In any case, a little more than a year after the publication of Fragments of an Older Fury, Brother Antoninus would re-emerge as William Everson. This may be rather more co-incidental than otherwise, and yet it was partly as a means of seeking a more personal Divinity than that afforded by the Inhumanist vision of Jeffers which drew Everson into the Catholic Church in the first place.

The death of this spiritual father elicited a sustained stream of critical work on Jeffers, work that has about it an intensely personal and sometimes even confessional tone. Tribute is paid to the spiritual father--as the vision of the disciple is defined and clarified against that of the mentor. And yet, even as the process of definition and clarification proceeds, the Everson/Antoninus vision is encompassing and re-embracing, struggling back to terms with, the Inhumanist credo.

From the mid-thirties onward, Jeffers had become ever more an exile in his own country, just as had Everson/Antoninus. They are two kindred spirits who nonetheless moved in seemingly opposite directions; the common roots which Everson shares with Jeffers are revealed in Everson's criticism, a criticism which has been germinal to the present upswing of the Jeffers reputation.

"The Poet Is Dead" is, in my judgment, the most

beautiful and most carefully and yet passionately wrought tribute ever offered by one poet to another.   F. I.   Carpenter, perhaps the ranking Jeffers scholar, noted at a Jeffers conference at Southern Oregon College that "The Poet Is Dead" is "as good as the best of Jeffers."   Indeed, many of the rhythms and images, even phrases, are drawn from Jeffers' own work, but crafted into a compelling and even "gut-wrenching" whole:

> For the poet is dead.   The gaunt wolf
> Crawled out to the edge and died snapping.
> He said he would.   The wolf
> Who lost his mate.   He said he would carry
>   the wound,
> The blood-wound of life, to the broken edge
> And die grinning.
> . . .
> The great tongue
> Dries in the mouth.   I told you.
> The voiceless throat
> Cools silence.   And the sea-granite eyes.
> Washed in the sibilant waters
> The stretched lips kiss peace.

Even in the presence of Thanatos, the force of generation, momentarily hidden, makes its presence felt:

> But in the gorged rivermouth
> Already the steelhead fight for entry.
> They feel fresh water
> Sting through the sieves of their salt-
>   coarsened gills.
> They shudder and thrust.

But the cold tide, Thanatos, is dominant:

> In the shoal-champed breakers
> One wing of the gull
> Tilts like a fin through the ribbon of spume
> And knifes under.

The imagery is intense, even as the language is restrained, even as the enforced praise in "A Canticle to the Waterbirds" is now hushed in a severe and yet heroic, melancholy silence.   The immensity of the entire Pacific littoral, the meditation of which was able to spring Everson/Antoninus forward a dozen years earlier, is now characterized by its Nordic harshness and inevitability, even as its totality was

"Grasped in the visionary mind and established--/ But is sunken under the dark ordainment.... "

Jeffers was dead. And so, perhaps, was the compelling need to <u>resist</u> the full implications of the mentor's vision.

SEVENTH MEDITATION:

Thanatos and Eros.

Though one should be wary of <u>post hoc</u>, <u>ergo propter hoc</u> reasoning, a confrontation with death may often be observed to be followed by a vital resurgence of the life force, as by means of the agency of Eros. If such is the pattern in the present case, and I believe it is, then perhaps the significance of Antoninus' writing and publishing during the period following "The Poet Is Dead" is more than simply apparent.

The Rose of Solitude is issued in 1964, followed by The Blowing of the Seed in 1966, Single Source in 1966, The Vision of Felicity in 1966, the full edition of The Rose of Solitude in 1967--the latter containing in part "The Rose of Solitude," "The Canticle of the Rose," and "The Afterglow of the Rose," poems depicting an intense physical and spiritual, male-female, relationship. The Blowing of the Seed was written during 1946 and, as the poet notes on the colophon, "belongs to the period of The Residual Years. For several reasons it was not included in that book and is here and now published for the first time." The poems concern the poet's relationship with Mary Fabilli, his second wife. And Single Source goes back to the period of 1934-1940, also containing poems not included in The Residual Years.

Also in 1967 came In The Fictive Wish (containing a woodcut by Mary Fabilli); a separate edition of A Canticle to the Waterbirds was published in 1968, Fragments of an Older Fury in 1968, The Springing of the Blade in 1968 (written in 1947), a new edition of The Residual Years in 1968, The City Does Not Die in 1969, and also in 1969 The Last Crusade (the theme, erotic and violational, written in 1958).

In the preface to the 1974 Man-Fate volume, the poet tells us:

"These are the poems of a man undergoing a major break fairly late in his years. It is a love poem sequence, a cycle of renewal, but it also concerns the monastic life, from the point of view of one who has renounced it. The love of woman and the love of solitude have contested together, and solitude has lost."

"Tendril in the Mesh," the first poem in the volume, is dedicated to Susanna and was written, at the poet's own word, between 1966 and 1968, while he was at Kentfield Priory in Marin County, at a time when "the author was still in vows," and when "the author had no intention of leaving his Order." It is a poem in which, as noted earlier, the Christ figure is equated with Eros.

Speaking of himself in the third person, Everson tells us:

"All the rest of the poetry is aftermath. At Stinson Beach, a small oceanside community north of San Francisco, he took up residence with his young wife Susanna, and her infant son. There he began to work out the implications of his break, composing across the years 1970 and 1971 the troubled verse that completes this volume."

The poems are indeed troubled, but they are joyous and humanly alive as well, as with these lines from "Dark Waters":

> Weasel-woman:
> Drive devils out of my blood.
> Scare off fear.
>
> I have made a long run.
> I have swum dark waters.

Or these, from "The Gash":

> I sense the mushrooms in the night,
> Tearing their way up through loose soil,
> Brutal as all birth.
>
> And I bend my head,
> And cup my mouth on the gash of everything
>   I craved,
> And am ravaged with joy.

The temporal and domestic implications of the worship of Eros, however, are still to be contended with, a theme that Everson addresses humorously (while still being deadly serious) in "The Narrows of Birth," in which, in a dream, the poet witnesses the castration of a young man, his Doppelgänger, the ghost of his past. The dream was apparently occasioned by a Christmas gathering of the clan, the Feast of the Matriarch, as Everson calls it, in which the full implications of the Domestic World are realized:

> Across the fire I face the matriarch,
> My ancient ancestress, the fountainhead of
> my blood,
> Saying, "I have come back, Mother,"
> And I bow my head as a penitent. . . .

With the mutilation of the young man, the protagonist awakens to find himself in bed with his wife:

> I touch her again, the flank of woman,
> Modulant with the subsumed
> Rapture of life. And everything I have come for
> Clutches my throat,
> Warring in the narrows of this birth.

A far more significant poem, however, is "The Black Hills." A separate peace has been made with Eros, but the figure of Pan--that is, a specific sense of re-identification, reverential and profound as it was in the early poems--has remained illusive. If Pan had earlier been subsumed by Yaveh-Haya through the agency of Christ, the figure of Dionysus had inevitably emerged; even as Pentheus, in The Bacchae, had attempted to surround, imprison, Dionysus, only to discover that the god had easily slipped out of the chains and had seemed to shake the palace to its foundations in the process, ultimately seducing Pentheus out into the wilds and to death at the hands of the crazed women, so Everson finds himself faced with the same potential fate. However, the Divinity depicted in "The Black Hills" is not a wily, Odysseus-like Dionysus. It is not even Pan, for its context and its awareness are thoroughly American, native American--and its hatred issued down upon the poet-speaker in bursts of wind:

> I gather into focus the incredible emanation,
> The torrent of hatred pouring into me.
> It is as archaic and irreducible as weightless stone,
> A kind of psychic lava,

Pouring across the narrow space
And the cavity of the years.

And it is male.
The savage violence.
The primal pride.

For this I have come.

In dream, the poet rides to where the exhausted Sioux
endured ambush,

Riddled under the skirl of lead
From the snout carbines. Scalped, mutilated,
The sex of the women hacked out with bowie knives,
Jabbed over saddlehorns, to be worn
Swaggering back to the stockade saloons,
Derisive pubic scalps, obscene trophies
Of a decimated people, a scalped land.

We think back to "The Vow," and the line: "I, the
living heir of the bloodiest men of all Europe." For in "The
Black Hills" the speaker comes, bearing the cumulative guilt
of his race, he, personally, is somehow guilty of the genocide
practiced against the Indians. In some way, this American
Spirit of the Earth must be appeased. The speaker immerses
himself in a series of images from the imagination of boy-
hood: "Roman Nose, Black Kettle,/ Red Cloud, Crazy Horse,
Gall, Sitting Bull...."

"Father," I cry, "Come back to us!
Return to our lives!"
My words ring through the dusk,
And a wind springs up, rattling the leaves.
"I have come to close the wound,
Heal the gash that cuts us from you,
And hence from the earth!"

But the force is unrelenting, and the speaker shouts the one
thing left:

The old, hopeless human attestation:
"I love you!"

Nevertheless, the wave of hatred is merely increased;
actual wind roars down the canyon, flings gravel: "And sud-
denly the rain begins." The speaker attempts once more to
summon up the Indian images out of boyhood, and then even
these fade:

A sudden
Spasm of hysteria doubles me up.
I relapse into uncontrollable sobbing.
"I love you," I scream. "Can't you hear me?
God damn it, I love you!"

The dream ends, and the poet awakens, though vestigal
fragments of the dream blend with reality. He walks outside,
through the darkened house, hears the breaking of waves on
the beach:

But opening the door
The drench of moonlight embraces me,
A sudden inundation of suffused radiance.
It is the beautiful, unsullied present,
Eternally renewed, eternally reborn.

This moment of oneness, allowed under the influence
of the feminine symbol of the moon, is "too heartbreakingly
much," and the poet-speaker passes back within the house,
aware that the past is forever beyond him and that only the
illusion of embracing the past is possible. The speaker then
stumbles and cuts his heel on a plastic toy, "The dropped
plaything of my wife's infant child," the present enforcing its
claims in a most absurd and inconsequential way--and yet:

... reaching down I feel blood on my thumb,
Where the bones of all the buffalo
Gashed my heel.

Resolution with Pan has been approached but, I think,
not ultimately accomplished--even though the token wound
from the present might be construed as sufficient to allow
for a kind of ritual wrist-cutting and blood-mingling, the act
in recognition of blood brotherhood. However, the force of
malediction, in the very nature of its intensity and hatred,
would seem still to have about it elements of God the Father,
the Yaveh-Haya into which the poet had long before attempted
to subsume the Pan-force that "squats faun-mouthed on the
wheeling world...."

EIGHTH MEDITATION:

The recovery, the acceptance itself, would lie across
a period of some five years of poetic drought following the
completion of the Mate-Flight volume, though hardly a drought

in terms of other writing, as noted earlier and as substantiated by a glance at the recently published <u>William Everson:</u>
<u>A Descriptive Bibliography, 1934-1976</u> (Scarecrow Press,
1977). But a poetic drought it was, a drought broken at the
height of the great California drought of 1976-1977, even as,
to the south, the Ventana Wilderness was exploding with fire.

Two things seem to have led up to the re-emergence
of the poetic voice. First was the revision and ultimately
the publication of <u>River-Root</u>, this poem from 1957, as already noted, drawing together the forces of Eros and Pan,
underscoring their mutual dependency and their inherent oneness. Second was the completion and publication of a volume
that will ultimately be seen as a kind of declaration of independence and a statement of definition for the literature of
Western America--the prose study, <u>Archetype West</u>. Other
authors, in the years ahead, will no doubt expand upon, elaborate, concur, or argue with the aesthetic, psychological,
and critical judgments made in this volume--but the book is
there, and there first, a tentative definition of the literary
character of the West.

For the poet, to deal with this concept and to make
his judgments was also, in effect, to make once more a social fact of his own regional identity, even though he deals
in no particular way with his personal role within the archetype. Nevertheless, he is speaking for the region as a whole,
and in so doing he has accepted both the <u>res publicas</u> and all
the obligations and implications within both the terrain itself
and within those who have identified with it and written of it.
He sees and accepts and praises the violence at the core of
the archetype, even as he identifies Jeffers as its seminal
figure:

"... he assails all the American assumptions
with the massive right of his invective consciousness--American optimism, American service,
American wealth, American power. But when
they are gone it is seen that these native obsessions have been somehow attested to, evoked in
the sense that their root-obsessions in the American psyche have been given expression in the
interior violence of the poet.

. . .

"... fresh from the maternal impress in the
death of the mother, the poet seizes back on the
<u>anima</u>, the feminine principle in the deeps of the

masculine unconscious, and thrusting her forward
puts her through violation after violation until all
the dross of her conditioning is purged away and
she burns pure fire.

. . .

"Here we see the transcendentalist impulse re-
ducing the protective limitary boundaries of hu-
man convention in order to touch a trans-moral
expansiveness that is illimitable. The instru-
ment is violence. . . .

. . .

"The important thing here is that the negative
facet of the American psyche did not achieve
apotheosis until Jeffers carried it to the ulti-
mate, and opened up the pantheistic affirmation
inherent in its skepticism. Only then could the
divinity caged in the nuclear material entity, the
numen, show its true face, and the Godhead blaze
through. Whitman is the sunrise in the East, but
Jeffers is the sunset in the West. It is bloody
and violent, but it is the last light given us. We
deny it at our peril. "

What lies behind Archetype West is the concept that
the very nature of the American West--its native peoples, the
insurgent Spanish, the American explorers, trappers, fron-
tiersmen, the waves of migration westward to the Pacific,
the hugeness and wildness of the terrain, the great mountain
chains, the vast diversities of climate, the scorched, treeless
deserts, the tremendous forests of pine, fir, and redwood,
the lure and frenzy of the Mother Lode and the Comstock--
all of these forces, from the very beginning, conspired to
produce a consciousness and a vitality differing, one might
almost say, in kind, from those of the East. Western Amer-
ican thinking is somehow, indelibly, different. Westerners
are almost a separate people, a separate nation. The promise
of the West has been the original promise of America; but
here, under the pervading influence of landscape and heritage,
that sense of promise has expanded, at times, beyond all pre-
vious proportions.

"In the lateness of its development, sensing the
closing of possibility behind it as the rest of the
country matured, and longing for finality, the
West cried 'Eureka! ' thereby placing its emphasis
on the primacy of discovery, convinced that in

discovery lay apotheosis. In the judgment of the
East it achieved not apotheosis but extravagance,
an excess of sentiment articulated in a superfluity
of utterance. But this cannot be denied: even as
an extravagance it is one that is built upon the as-
pirations of the nation as a whole, extended to the
outmost margins, and projected against the possible
as a profound hope of the motives that impel us all.
Herein lies the real force behind its gigantic visions
and its resounding words. "

NINTH MEDITATION:

For the benefit of those who may read this essay at
some real remove in either time or distance, I should re-
mark briefly about the California drought of 1976 and 1977,
a drought which may continue, insofar as any of us knows,
for an indeterminate period. Rainfall during these two years
has been perhaps a third of normal. Snow in the mountains
has been light, and the sustaining snowpacks did not form.
Streams which, within living memory, have never gone dry
before are dry now. Reservoirs are empty. Two summers
ago light rains and cool weather in August prevented the in-
ferno which we all feared. This past summer brought no
such blessing, and half a million acres burned, the greatest
of the fires being one which consumed the larger portion of
the Ventana Wilderness near Big Sur and another which con-
sumed a huge portion of the area north of Mount Lassen.
At one point there were some five hundred separate fires
raging throughout the state of California.

The mother land was burning. The bare peaks of the
Sierra, devoid of snow, hung like a ragged curtain along the
east. Water supplies and country ponds dwindled to near
nothingness. Rivers were reduced to pathetic, slow-moving
creeks. Millions of trees turned brown, died. Grasslands
ranged over by cattle or sheep took on the appearance of
semi-desert. The impact was profoundly felt along the entire
length of the state.

The impact upon the consciousness of William Everson
took the form of sympathetic identification, even as he came
to construe the implications of the drought in metaphorical
and personal terms; and his own poetic drought was broken
even as the physical drought continued.

Reverence for the land has never ceased to be a cru-

cial and utterly central element in the verse, whether of
Everson or of Antoninus; and now, even as the streams of
the coastal mountains waned, the poetic stream began once
more to flow. And what emerged was different than what
had gone before--different in the sense that the poems reflect
an identity realized and established and accepted. A new col-
lection of poems emerged, The Masks of Drought, as yet in-
complete and of course unpublished, poems which incorporate
within the Everson cosmos the dissonant elements of the vision
of Robinson Jeffers--not only a reverence for, but an accep-
tance of the calm and implacable violence which is somehow
indivisible from the force of generation.

"The Summer of Fire" begins: "California is burning!"
Dry lightning walks on the hills, and:

> North of us
> Mount Diablo wrapped itself in a crimson mantle
> And claimed its name: a surging inferno.
>
> To the south
> Big Sur exploded: empacted brush,
> Flattened by heavy snowfalls of the past, lay on
> the slopes
> Fifty tons to the acre round the Ventana Cones,
> And the runaway burn tore rugged country
> Like a raging bull.
>
> This morning at dawn
> The sun rose bloodily through a pall of smoke
> From sixty miles south. At noon
> Our shadows, askew on the ground,
> Cast an amber aura.

The poet considers that, in the cyclic process of the
passing centuries, all of this has happened before and will
happen again:

> And indeed
> Out on the flat the twin giant redwoods
> Carry the scars of ancient fire from centuries
> back,
> Ennobling them, were that possible, with the
> dignity of pain.
>
> Farther up the slope the blackened hollows of
> burnt-out stumps
> Honor the primal war between them,
> Vegetation and flame.

One is life and one is death,
Yet polarity binds them. Definition is the clue.
Only out of the screaming tension, each true to
    its own,
Comes clarification.

In a "year of extremes," the poet asserts, "the great
God of All Weathers/ Grinds down the mountains...." In
the face of natural immensity, mankind is pigmy-like, and
dances between the primal forces of fire and water:

... reeling between the twin flagellations,
Shaking a puny fist at the sky, cursing and
    blaspheming,
Till old age chastens him to dignity at last.

The poet-speaker considers, however, that age has not
brought to him such proposed dignity:

To the contrary.
The pummel of suppressed exultance
Rages through me, crying,

"Burn! Burn!
All you dead grasses, fallen under the scythe,
Wild iris, leopard lily, sweep skyward in flame,
Meet fire in heaven with fire on earth!"

It is not, however, some "idiot catastrophe the heart
craves," but rather the ecstasy of identification with the un-
leashed, vast forces of nature, the timeless, ongoing forces
which perpetually create and re-create the planet with con-
stant change and constant beauty--inhuman beauty. The
speaker looks up at the towering trees, inscapes of life and
death, forever burned and forever growing, part of the whole,
destined:

And I cry:

"Burn! Burn!
O chaste ones, magnificent presences,
Scream in the ecstasy of consummation,
Torch and expire!"

At the same time, inside the house, in the human
realm which is only seemingly apart from and opposed to the
greater process of life/death alternations, the poet-speaker
remembers that

>   ... my young wife
> Fixes the supper, her lithe body
> Moving between the table and the stove,
> Sinuously alive.

The microcosm is juxtaposed to the macrocosm, and twin
claims are proposed to the mind of the poet. No choice is
enforced. The two are drawn together, each feeds on the
life of the other, and the result is acceptance, the unattain-
able beauty and the human closeness:

>   I look at the sky
> One final time. Over my head the first star
> Glitters through haze, a liquid agate.

The heart may indeed crave a oneness with the mac-
rocosm; but in the human realm, in the "reality" of the
young wife fixing supper, in the realm of specific human
fidelity, there is peace--a man and a woman, together, in
the right place.

"The Summer of Fire" marks a signal moment in the
process of the re-emergence of William Everson as poet,
but the poems had begun to flow, slowly, a year earlier.
Man-Fate was indeed, as the subtitle says, "the swan-song
of Brother Antoninus," both in the sense of a final performance
and in the sense of the swan as a phallic being, Zeus and
Leda, an erotic celebration, even as it is the fate of man
to cleave unto woman. Then the poems ceased to come.

For a poet, nothing is so fearful as an extended dry
period when the words will not come, when the images will
not manifest themselves, when the themes will not cohere.
It is a kind of death, a nullity, a time that can only be worked
through by means of moving into prose or by means of
going back to older work and, through the magic of revision,
of seducing the unconscious once more to engage itself. The
mind may be thrown into a state of near panic, and one be-
gins to look into the glass and see no image there.

In "Runoff," Everson details something of this, as
viewed at the moment of renewal:

> Four wet winters and now the dry.
> All the long season a sterile frost
> Grips the mountain, the coast like flanged metal
> Bent thwart the sea.

A rain comes, and the protagonist and his mate rise early and walk down to the stream, only to find "a river of ink," a heavy runoff of mud and leaves:

All that autumn-spun opulence
Frost drove down and ruthlessly squandered
Four moons back, to rot where it fell,
Now crawls to the sea, a liquid bile.

The woman says, "Why, the mountain is menstruating!" The protagonist agrees after a moment and senses "A deep cleansing, this rite of renewal," and he tells her:

Touching you and creek-throb in the same impulse
I am healed of frost:
Woman and water in the bloodflow.

Again, in "Kingfisher Flat":

In the long drought
Impotence clutched on the veins of passion
Encircles our bed, a serpent of stone.
I sense the dearth in you also,
The bane that is somehow mine to impose
But yours to endure....
. . .

I think of the Fisher King,
All his domain parched in a sterile fixation
    of purpose,
Clenched on the core of the burning question
Gone unasked ...

And in "Rattlesnake August," a pet dog having been bitten, the vet shakes his head and says:

"This God damned drought
Forces them down from their mountain dens
To creek water. We've known places this year
No snake's ever been seen in before,
And we're not done yet."

The death of a pet dog. The protagonist addresses his mate:

I see tears bline your eyes.
Tonight, I know, you will tear my snake-totem

Down from the wall, and burn it, bitterly,
Your lips moving, your eyes blue ice.

I do not begrudge it: your way is the best.

Everson then continues with a meditation upon the sig-
nificance of what has happened, the serpent symbolic both
of evil and of wisdom, phallic, a dark force of the earth,
the malign (from a human perspective) aspect of Pan and of
Eros as well.   And, speaking of the snake (and the principle
for which the snake metaphorically stands), the poet concludes:

> For he, too, loves life. He, too,
> Craves comfort, smells it cunningly
> Out. And when Fate accosts--
> Licks his lip and stabs back.

But perhaps the most significant as well as the best
of the poems thus far written for The Masks of Drought se-
quence is a piece entitled "Rite of Passage," a poem depict-
ing the aftermath of an out-of-season hunter's shooting of a
young buck--shot but not tracked down and taken.   The deer
dies in a meadow, fenced to enclose two red bulls:

> The following day
> A great black bird rose up when we came,
> Lurched clumsily off--the wings made for soaring
> Baffled now in this hemmed enclosure,
> This deep forest field.

By night the carcass attracts coyotes; in the morning
"the great bird was back," and a dozen others as well.   They
perch on the deer's body,

> ... angling each other out
> At the plucking, obscenely gobbling
> The riddle of gut.
>
> Our abrupt arrival
> Sent them hissing aloft....

When the speaker comes by again, the two bulls stand
beside the remnant, "Bellowing, lugubriously lowing," and
the speaker and his companion, themselves "disbelieving,"
speak to the bulls as if to console them.   Weeks pass, and
nothing remains "but a chewn shinbone and a scrap of hide"
in the pasture where the two bulls graze.   And when the
rains of the equinox come, the body-print of the deer emerges

fertilized, green where the deer had lain and been eaten and the remainder rotted and leached into the soil.

And we said:
The cycle is complete,
The episode is over.

But the silence that hung about that place was haunted,
The presence of something anciently ordained,
Where we, unconscious acolytes, with the birds
and the bulls
Enacted its rite: there in the immemorial clearing,
The great listening mountain above for witness,
The sacrificial host between the river and the woods.

The dignity of pain, the violence of fire and flood, the serpent, the vulture and the coyote, the dry earth, the awaited rains, the violence at the heart of the archetype, the procreative force also at the heart of the archetype, the strange, terrible, unbelieveably beautiful, half-heard music of Pan, the great god of all weathers--to worship the earth and the force which creates and endlessly alters the earth is to worship all aspects of the manifestation and the process.

In the Man-Fate volume, in a poem entitled "The Gash," though speaking in quite a different context, Everson has told us that: "There is nothing so humbling as acceptance."

It is no doubt a dangerous critical practice to comment upon the implications, both artistic and personal, of a collection of poems that is still involved in the twin processes of creation and revision--as is the case with The Masks of Drought. Other poems are yet to be written, and it is therefore conceivable that these might appreciably alter the significance of the whole. At the very least, it is probable that a few of the lines which I have quoted may be changed by the time they reach publication.

But the collection marks a genuine shift in the overall direction of Everson's verse--not a shift, perhaps, but rather a leap forward. It is not simply that the poet has come full circle, returning now to the specific earth-themes of the pre-Catholic poems. Rather, it seems to me, he has integrated the full implications of both The Residual Years and The Veritable Years.

He has broken the mask. He has reached through the surface and has grasped the fire.

TENTH MEDITATION:

September 11, 1977.   A thin morning fog is quickly
dispelled by the intense sunlight of the beginning of autumn.
Judith and I have slept in the print shop, in the guest room.
In the adjoining room are Bill Everson's hand press, a wood
stove, a stuffed mountain lion (purchased--rescued--some-
where in Mexico), numerous shelves of books, a table cover-
ed with more books, correspondence, and manuscripts--all
of these no doubt arranged in a manner comprehensible only
to the poet himself.   I make note of a couple of volumes I'd
like to borrow.   I think Bill has left them out to tempt me.
Yet another room houses a desk, typewriter, and more books
--among these the poet's Jeffers collection as well as a col-
lection of his own printed volumes.   Above the desk, in a
red binding, is a copy of Allan Campo's monumental study
of Everson's work, Soul and the Search, as yet unpublished.

On the floor of the main room, at this moment, are
several sleeping bags filled with people.   I step over them
and walk outside to the creek, stare down at the granite bed
and the shrunken stream.

There is smoke from the chimney of the main house,
and I think I detect the odor of coffee and sausage.   The
human inhabitants of Kingfisher Flat have stirred into life.

After breakfast, Stan Hager starts his chainsaw.   A
tangle of bay logs came down with last winter's worst storm,
and Hager goes to work on them.   Everson and I and Debbie
Gates carry the eighteen-inch sections over to a pile where
Bill will split them into firewood for the winter.   To one
side stand Allan Campo and David Carpenter, apparently
having revived some portion of the previous evening's discus-
sion.   The two dogs sit and watch, having decided against
any continuation of their discussion.

Later we all decide to walk to the falls, a mile or so
up Big Creek Canyon.   Little Jude leads the procession along
the old Jeep trail beside the creek.   At one point we stop,
and Bill points out a fifty-foot tall Douglas fir that has grown
from the top of a large redwood stump, the redwood having
been cut perhaps sixty or seventy years ago.   Midday sun-
light filters down through the lacework of alder and fir above
us.

Only a small stream of water plunges down over the
smooth rocks, and Judith tells Anne that the pool below the

falls, much lower than the last time we had seen it, is probably too cold to swim in. Annie is not convinced.

I decide to climb around the bluffs to the top of the falls. A few minutes later I am standing above, looking down. On a huge, silvered redwood log, left tilted across boulders by some flood of a few years past, everyone is seated, Bill and Sue Everson in the middle. I do not hear any voices except those of Jude and Annie, who are building something out of rocks beside the pool.

The sunlight is a rich, bright yellow; and the air is extremely clear.

SELECTED BIBLIOGRAPHY

PRIMARY SOURCES

An Age Insurgent. San Francisco: Blackfriars Publications, 1959.

Archetype West. Berkeley, Calif. : Oyez, 1976.

Birth of a Poet. Santa Barbara, Calif. : Black Sparrow Press, 1978.

Black Hills. San Francisco: Didymus Press, 1973.

The Blowing of the Seed. New Haven, Conn. : Henry W. Wenning, 1966.

Canticle to the Waterbirds. Berkeley, Calif. : Eizo, 1968.

The City Does Not Die. Berkeley, Calif. : Oyez, 1969.

The Crooked Lines of God. Detroit: University of Detroit Press, 1959.

The Hazards of Holiness. Garden City, N. Y. : Doubleday, 1962.

In the Fictive Wish. Berkeley, Calif. : Oyez, 1967.

The Last Crusade. Berkeley, Calif. : Oyez, 1969.

Man-Fate. New York: New Directions, 1974.

The Masculine Dead. Prairie City:. Press of James A. Decker, 1942.

Poems: MCMXLII. Waldport, Ore. : Untide Press, 1945.

The Poet Is Dead. San Francisco: Auerhahn Press, 1964.

The Residual Years. Waldport, Ore. : Untide Press, 1944.

The Residual Years. New York: New Directions, 1948. Expanded edition, 1968.

River-Root. Berkeley, Calif. : Oyez, 1976.

Robinson Jeffers: Fragments of an Older Fury. Berkeley,

Calif. : Oyez, 1968.

The Rose of Solitude. Garden City, N. Y. : Doubleday, 1967.

San Joaquin. Los Angeles: The Ward Ritchie Press, 1939.

Single Source. Berkeley, Calif. : Oyez, 1966.

The Springing of the Blade. Reno, Nev. : Black Rock Press, 1968.

Tendril in the Mesh. San Francisco: Cayucos Books, 1973.

These Are the Ravens. San Leandro: Greater West Pub. Co. , 1935.

Triptych for the Living. Berkeley, Calif. : Seraphim Press, 1951.

The Veritable Years. Santa Barbara, Calif. : Black Sparrow Press, 1978.

The Waldport Poems. Waldport, Ore. : Untide Press, 1944.

War Elegies. Waldport, Ore. : Untide Press, 1944.

Who Is She That Looketh Forth as the Morning. Santa Barbara, Calif. : Capricorn Press, 1972.

The Year's Declension. Berkeley: Library, University of California, 1961.

SECONDARY SOURCES

Bartlett, Lee, and Allan Campo. William Everson: A Descriptive Bibliography, 1934-1976. Metuchen, N. J. : Scarecrow Press, 1977.

Ethridge, James M. Contemporary Authors, IX-X. Detroit: Gale Research Co. , 1964.

Everson, William. Earth Poetry: Selected Essays & Interviews, edited by Lee Bartlett. Berkeley, Calif. : Oyez, 1979.

Kherdian, David. Six Poets of the San Francisco Renaissance: Portraits and Checklists. Fresno, Calif. : Giliga Press, 1967.

Meltzer, David. , ed. The San Francisco Poets. New York: Ballantine Books, 1971. (Re-issued in 1976 as Golden Gate; Berkeley, Calif. : Wingbow Press).

Murphy, Rosalie, ed. Contemporary Poets of the English Language. New York: St. Martin's Press, 1976.

Taylor, Jacqueline A. "Civilian Public Service in Waldport, Oregon, 1941-1945; The State Faces Religion, Art, and Pacifism." Thesis, Department of History, University of Oregon, 1966.

INDEX